ASCENT
CENTER FOR TECHNICAL KNOWLEDGE

AF877777

# 3DEXPERIENCE CATIA 2022x
# Introduction to Modeling
# Part 2

***Learning Guide***

***1st Edition***

# ASCENT - Center for Technical Knowledge®
## 3DEXPERIENCE CATIA 2022x
## Introduction to Modeling - Part 2

1st Edition

Prepared and produced by:

ASCENT Center for Technical Knowledge
630 Peter Jefferson Parkway, Suite 175
Charlottesville, VA 22911

866-527-2368
www.ASCENTed.com

ASCENT - Center for Technical Knowledge (a division of Rand Worldwide Inc.) is a leading developer of professional learning materials and knowledge products for engineering software applications. ASCENT specializes in designing targeted content that facilitates application-based learning with hands-on software experience. For over 25 years, ASCENT has helped users become more productive through tailored custom learning solutions.

We welcome any comments you may have regarding this guide, or any of our products. To contact us please email: feedback@ASCENTed.com.



AS-3DE22-ICM1-SG2 // RS-3DE22-ICM1-SG2

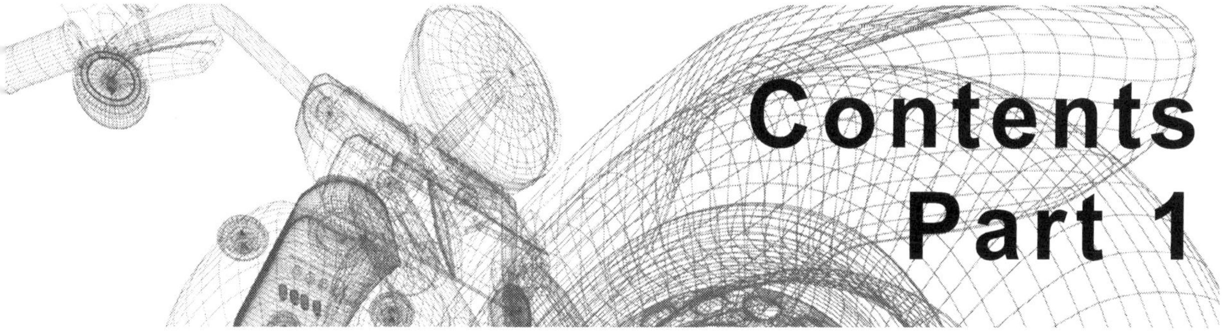

# Contents Part 1

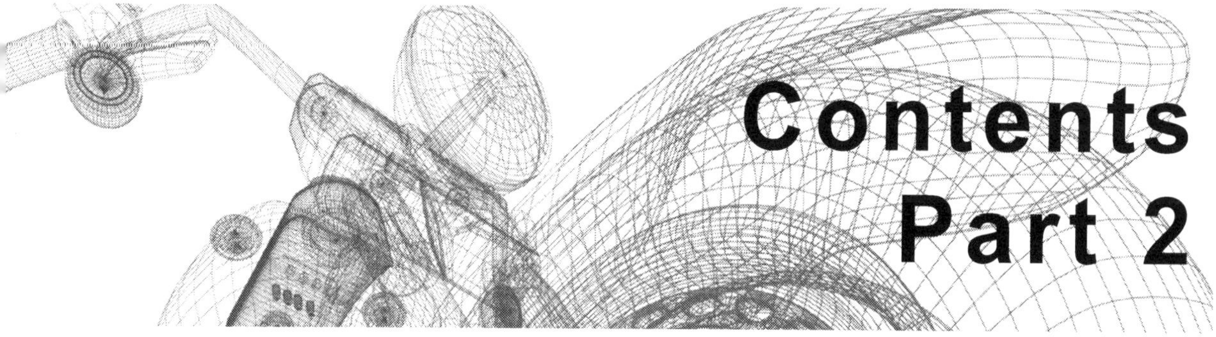

# Contents Part 2

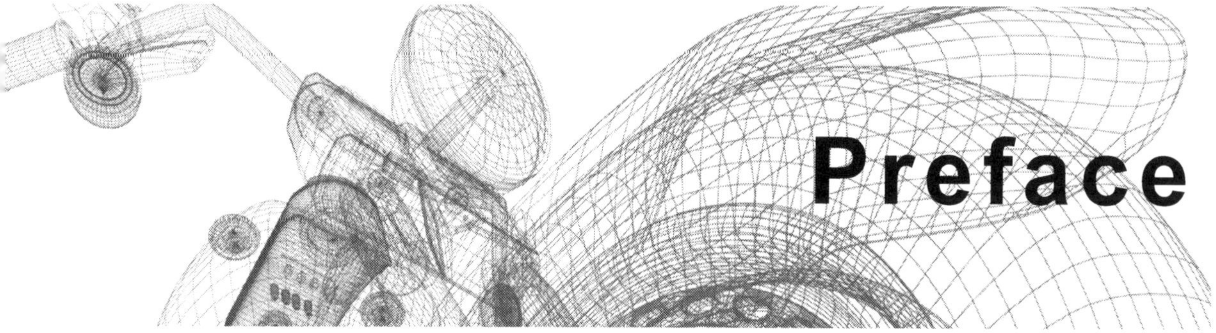

# Preface

The *3DEXPERIENCE CATIA 2022x: Introduction to Modeling* guide can help you with learning the process of designing models using the 3DEXPERIENCE platform - from conceptual sketching to solid modeling, assembly design, and drawing production. Upon completion of this guide, you will have acquired the skills to confidently work in the 3DEXPERIENCE platform and gained an understanding of the parametric design philosophy of the CATIA apps.

## Topics Covered

- 3DEXPERIENCE Platform Overview
- 3DEXPERIENCE Platform PLM Objects
- Launching the 3DEXPERIENCE Platform
- 3DEXPERIENCE Platform User Interface
- Customizing the 3DEXPERIENCE Platform
- Creating and Constraining Sketch Geometry
- Sketched Feature Techniques and Formulas
- Adding Material with Pad and Shaft Features
- Removing Material with Pocket and Groove Features
- Creating Reference Elements for construction and measurement
- Fillet, Chamfer, Hole, Draft, and Shell Dress-Up Features
- Pattern, Copy, and Mirror Duplication Features
- Thin Features, Stiffeners
- Rib and Slot Features
- Multi-sections Solid Features
- Feature Management Using the Hide/Show, Activate/Deactivate Functions
- Parent/Child Relationships and Feature Failure Resolution
- Obtaining Part Information
- Managing Object Lifecycles

- Assembly Design using Engineering Connections and Constraints
- Constraint Creation and Assembly Management
- Obtaining Assembly Information (Measure, Clash, and Bill of Materials)
- Working with Drawings in the 3DEXPERIENCE Platform
- Working with Multi-Body Models
- Effective Modeling Tips and Techniques

## Prerequisites

- Access to the 3DEXPERIENCE CATIA 2022x platform, including access to the CATIA Part Design, CATIA Assembly Design, CATIA Drafting, ENOVIA Collaborative Lifecycle, ENOVIA Product Finder, and ENOVIA Design IP Classification apps.
- Permission to import 3DXML files.

## Note on Software Setup

This guide assumes a standard installation of the 3DEXPERIENCE platform.

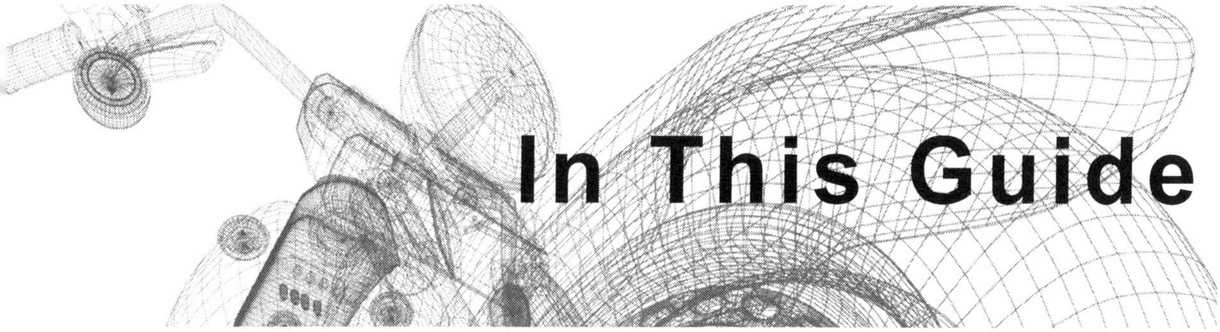

# In This Guide

The following highlights the key features of this guide.

| Feature | Description |
|---|---|
| **Practice Files** | The Practice Files page includes a link to the practice files and instructions on how to download and install them. The practice files are required to complete the practices in this guide. |
| **Chapters** | A chapter consists of the following - Learning Objectives, Instructional Content, Practices, Chapter Review Questions, and Command Summary.<br>• **Learning Objectives** define the skills you can acquire by learning the content provided in the chapter.<br>• **Instructional Content**, which begins right after Learning Objectives, refers to the descriptive and procedural information related to various topics. Each main topic introduces a product feature, discusses various aspects of that feature, and provides step-by-step procedures on how to use that feature. Where relevant, examples, figures, helpful hints, and notes are provided.<br>• **Practice** for a topic follows the instructional content. Practices enable you to use the software to perform a hands-on review of a topic. It is required that you download the practice files (using the link found on the Practice Files page) prior to starting the first practice.<br>• **Chapter Review Questions**, located close to the end of a chapter, enable you to test your knowledge of the key concepts discussed in the chapter. |

# Practice Files

To download the practice files for this guide, use the following steps:

1. Type the URL ***exactly as shown below*** into the address bar of your Internet browser to access the Course File Download page.

   *Note: If you are using the ebook, you do not have to type the URL. Instead, you can access the page simply by clicking the URL below.*

   **https://www.ascented.com/getfile/id/dactylorhizaPF**

2. On the Course File Download page, click the **DOWNLOAD NOW** button, as shown below, to download the .ZIP file that contains the practice files.

3. Once the download is complete, unzip the file and extract its contents.

   **The recommended practice files folder location is:**
   *C:\3DEXPERIENCE Introduction to CATIA Modeling Practice Files*

   *Note: It is recommended that you do not change the location of the practice files folder. Doing so may cause errors when completing the practices.*

**Stay Informed!**

To receive information about upcoming events, promotional offers, and complimentary webcasts, visit:

*www.ASCENTed.com/updates*

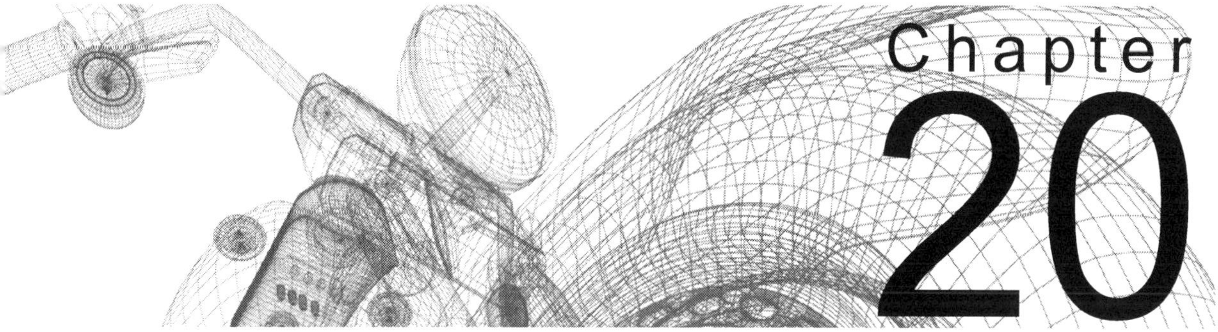

Chapter 20

# Working with Multi-Body Models

CATIA models can be built with multiple bodies. In this chapter, you examine tools to help navigate and modify parts built in this method

## Learning Objectives in This Chapter

- Learn how part bodies are organized.
- Insert additional bodies and a geometrical set.
- Understand Boolean operations for combining bodies.
- Understand the options available for feature visualization.
- Review several best practices for reviewing or modifying multi-body parts.

 

# 20.1 Body Organization

Typically, all features you create are added to the PartBody in the specification tree. This linear tree structure is acceptable for models with a low feature count or simple geometry. CATIA enables you to create multiple bodies in a single 3DPart model and to structure your model based on your design intent.

When planning the creation of a part, such as a car rim, the designer might break the model into three functional areas: base, spokes, and air chamber, as shown in Figure 20–1.

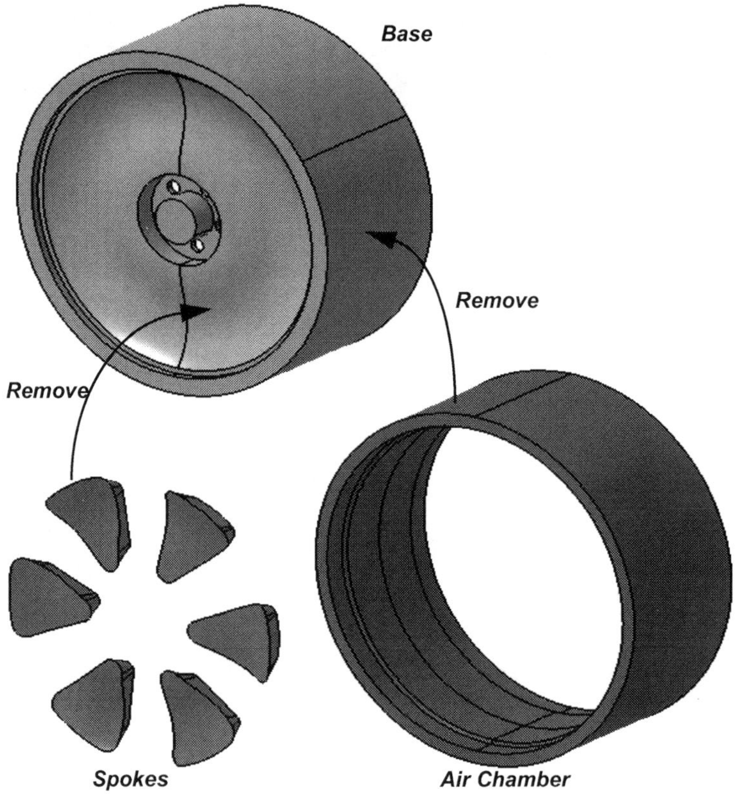


**Figure 20–1**

These bodies can then be combined using boolean operations to create the model shown in Figure 20–2.

**Figure 20–2**

Using boolean operations to create a model provides the following advantages:

- Update times are reduced, since a multi-body approach provides a more organized specification tree. For example, the six cutouts from the Spoke body are removed from the base geometry in a single step. If a standard modeling approach were used, each cutout would be developed and then removed individually, requiring extra update time.
- Features are grouped by function or area. By naming bodies after their group of features, the model structure is easier to interpret.
- Visualization tools are available which leverage the multi-body approach. For example, **Hide/Show** can be used to hide the geometry from the base and air chamber bodies. This enables the designer to simplify the model display while working on the spoke geometry. With a standard modeling approach, solid features cannot be independently hidden and must be deactivated to remove them from the display.
- The creation of the part model becomes easier when the model is divided into smaller, functional areas. A complex model becomes more manageable when the designer can focus on a smaller area of geometry to develop.
- Features such as a Shell or Fillet can be restricted to a finite area of the model. For example, if a specific area of the model requires a constant wall thickness, a Shell feature can be applied to only this area by breaking it out into a separate body.

Some disadvantages of using boolean operations include the following:

- Developing the model is time consuming, since the creation of a multi-body part requires planning of body organization and feature placement. In addition, you might need to frequently switch between bodies to position features correctly.
- Designers who are not familiar with the multi-body approach and boolean operations find interpreting and modifying these parts difficult.
- It is important to consider the complexity, feature count, and amount of possible downstream modification beforehand. Although this technique yields performance gains with big models, the development and planning required might be overkill for smaller models.

### Inserting a Body

To add a body to a part model, right-click the model name in the specification tree, select **3DShape object** and click **Body**, or click  (Body) in the *Structure* section of the Action Bar, as shown in Figure 20–3.

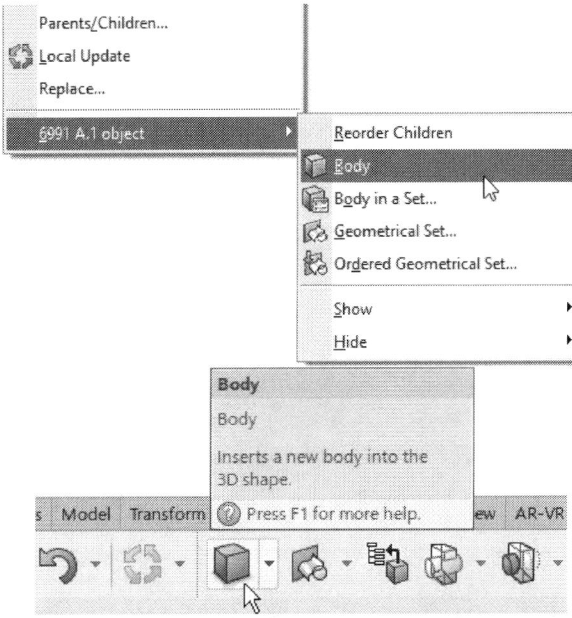


**Figure 20–3**

 

The body is added after the active body in the specification tree with the name Body.#, where # is a sequential number, as shown in Figure 20–4.

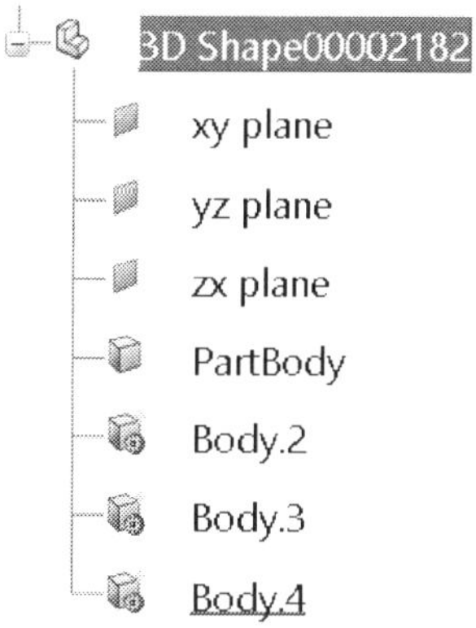


**Figure 20–4**

To activate a body, select it in the specification tree and click (Define In Work Object). The body is underlined to indicate it as the body to which new features are to be added.

## Organizing Geometrical Sets

A geometrical set is a container for any reference planes, lines, or points that have been created while developing the part geometry. To organize a multi-body part, geometrical sets are typically placed beneath the body to which they are referenced. If the geometrical set already exists, it can be placed beneath a body by right-clicking on it, selecting **Geometrical Set.# object> Change Geometrical Set**, and then selecting the body in the Change geometrical set dialog box, as shown in Figure 20–5.

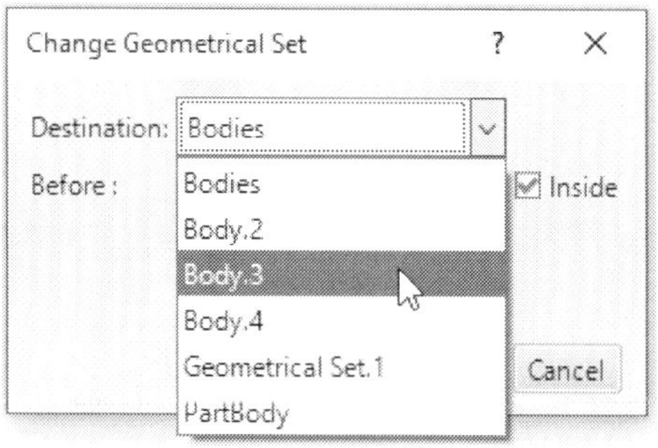


**Figure 20–5**

# 20.2 Boolean Operations

Bodies are combined using boolean operations. There are various boolean feature types that can be used in some of the complex models that you might need to review or modify in your work environment. Figure 20–6 shows the Boolean tools which are found in the *Structure* section of the Action Bar.

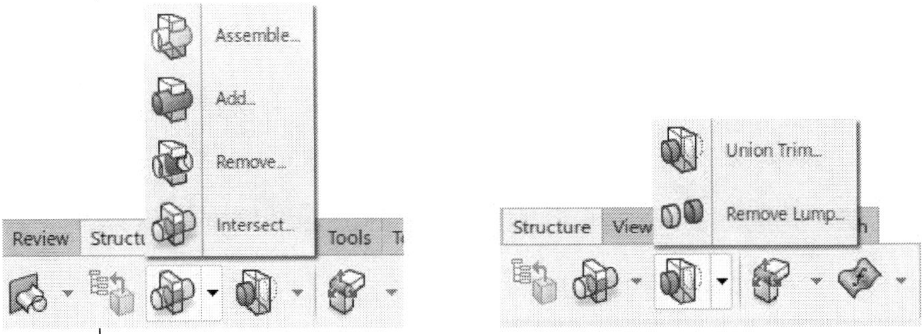


**Figure 20–6**

The boolean operation types and results are described as follows:

| Operation | Result |
|---|---|
| (Assemble) | Pocket = Pocket<br>Pad = Pad |
| (Add) | Pocket = Pad<br>Pad = Pad |
| (Remove) | Pocket = Pocket<br>Pad = Pocket |
| (Intersect) | Shared volume |
| (Union Trim) | Select faces to keep and/or remove<br>(adds part of selected body) |
| (Remove Lump) | Reshape a body by selecting faces to remove and/or faces to keep |

When a boolean operation is performed, the source body is connected to the target body through the boolean feature. For example, when a Core (source) body is removed from the Cavity (target) body, the specification tree displays as shown in Figure 20–7.

***Before boolean operation***

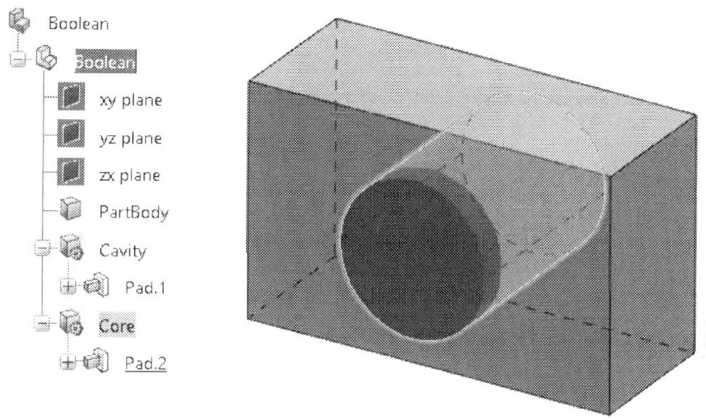


***After boolean operation***

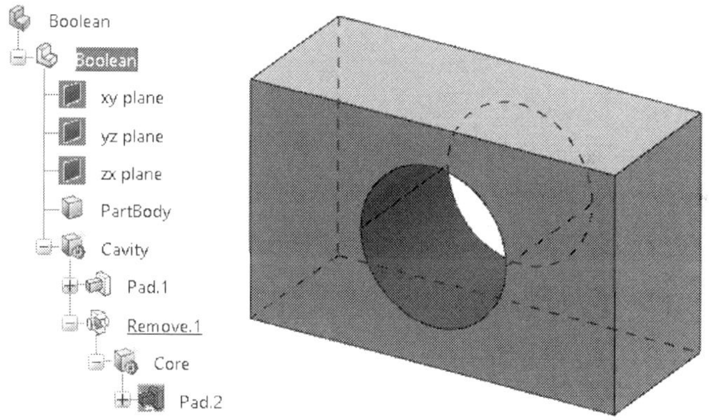


**Figure 20–7**

# 20.3 Feature Visualization

When modifying multi-body parts, it can be difficult to locate a feature due to the multi-level structure of the part. The following techniques can be used to locate a feature for modification:

- Center tree & Reframe On
- Search - show power input
- Geometry Display Options

## Center tree & Reframe On

These options are available in the shortcut menu and can be used to connect the model to the specification tree, as shown in Figure 20–8.

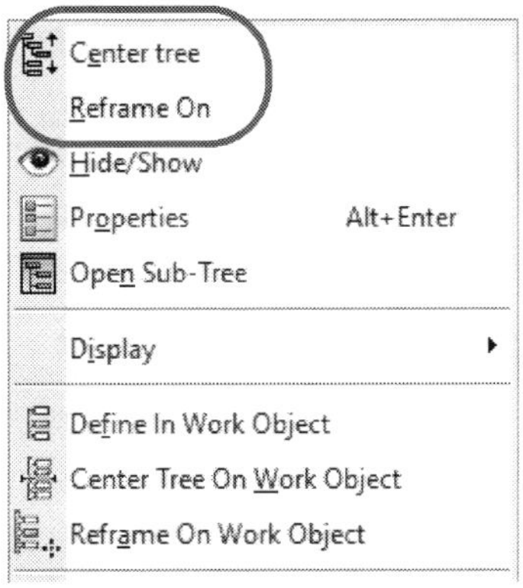


**Figure 20–8**

- To locate a feature of the model in the specification tree, right-click on the feature in the model display and select **Center tree**. The software expands the specification tree, highlights the selected feature, and places it at the vertical center of the window.
- To locate a feature from the specification tree on the model, right-click on the feature name and select **Reframe On**. The software zooms into the model to display the selected feature.

## Search

The **Search** tool can be used to locate features by name, type, or color. To enable the tool, right-click on the screen and select **Display>Status Bar** to display the *Power Input* field at the bottom right corner of the screen. The *Power Input* field can be used to search for objects.

Use the following syntax to search and select features:

| | |
|---|---|
| **Name** | n:<feature name> locates a feature by name. For example, entering **n:sketch*** selects all features whose names start with sketch. |
| **Type** | t:<feature type> locates a feature by type. For example, entering **t:point** selects all points in the model. |
| **Color** | col:<color> locates a feature by color. For example, entering **col:red** selects all features that have been assigned the color red. |
| **Visibility** | vis:<hidden/shown> locates a feature by its display status. For example, entering **vis:hidden** selects all hidden features. |

## Geometry Display Options

You can control the display of the model based on the active body or geometrical set. These tools are useful in organizing the display of a complex, multi-body part, because they enable the designer to focus on the geometry of the active body or geometrical set. These options can be accessed by opening the Preferences dialog box (select **Me**> **Preferences**). Expand **Common Preferences> Object Properties> 3D Shape> Display**, as shown in Figure 20–9.

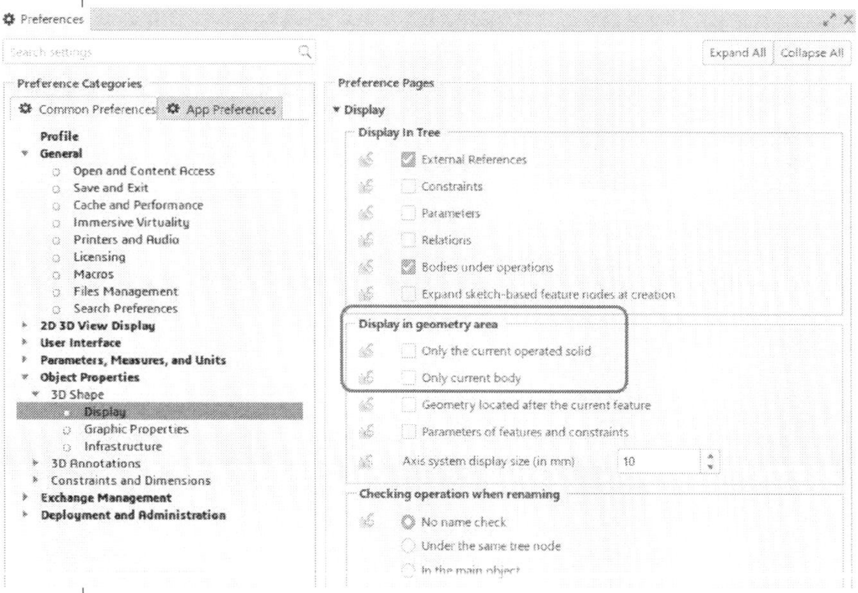


**Figure 20–9**

The options are also located in the App Options panel, as shown in Figure 20–10. To access this panel, right-click on the screen and select **Display>App Options**.

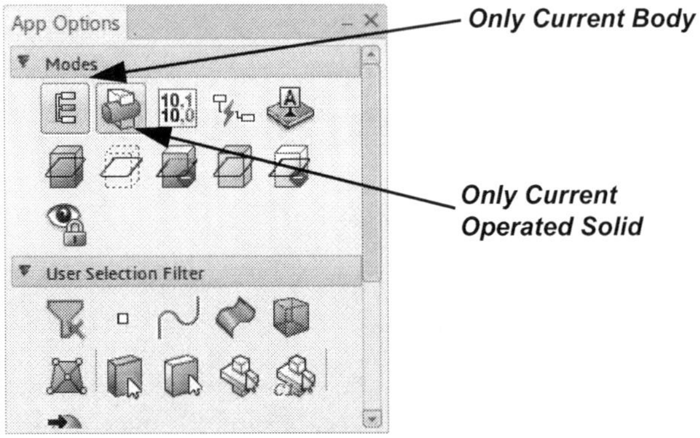


Figure 20–10

## Only Current Operated Solid

When  (Only Current Operated Solid) is selected, all bodies and geometrical sets display, except for any parent bodies. Figure 20–11 shows a scenario where **Body.3** is activated but all features in the parent **Body.2** are not displayed. However, all features of **Body.3**, **Body.4**, **Geometrical Set.1**, and **Body.5** display.

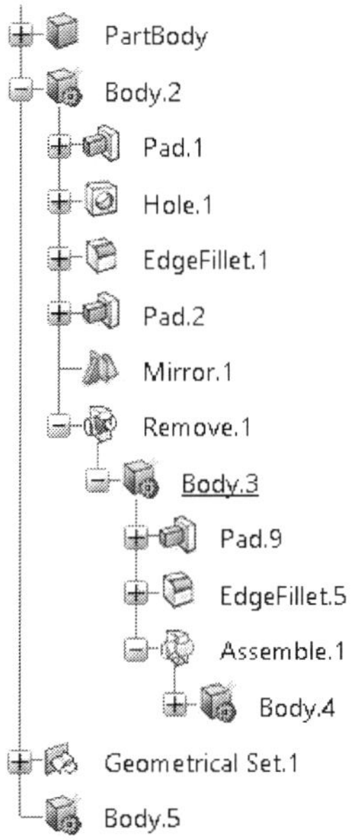


Figure 20–11

## Only Current Body

When (Only Current Body) is clicked, only the geometry of the active geometrical set or solid body displays. Bodies located beneath the active body (through a Boolean operation) are also displayed. Figure 20–11 shows a scenario where only the geometry of **Body.3** and **Body.4** display. Since **Geometrical Set.1** and **Body.5** do not belong to **Body.3**, they are hidden.

# 20.4 Tips and Techniques

Use the following tips when reviewing or modifying multi-body parts:

- Use the (Scan or Define In Work Object) tool found in the *Review* section of the Action Bar. Select the **Update** option to review the creation of the model. When working with someone else's data, it is recommended to become familiar with their design intent and model creation techniques.

- Use the **Parents/Children** tool to review the parents and children of a feature to be modified. To understand the modification process, it is recommended to investigate the children of this feature and the relationship that has been developed.

- Review any parameters and formulas that have been created. Often, designers drive frequently modified dimensions by parameters easily accessed in the specification tree. You might not need to drill deep into a model to make a common modification.

- To help you interpret the model when adding new geometry to the model, name the features as they are created. To develop a consistent model, try to match the original design intent.

- Place features in the body to which they apply, as shown in Figure 20–12. For example, Fillet features should be added to the body that contains their reference geometry. If the Fillet references an edge created by a boolean operation, the Fillet must be placed in the body that contains the boolean Add feature. This is because the lower-level body does not contain the required reference.

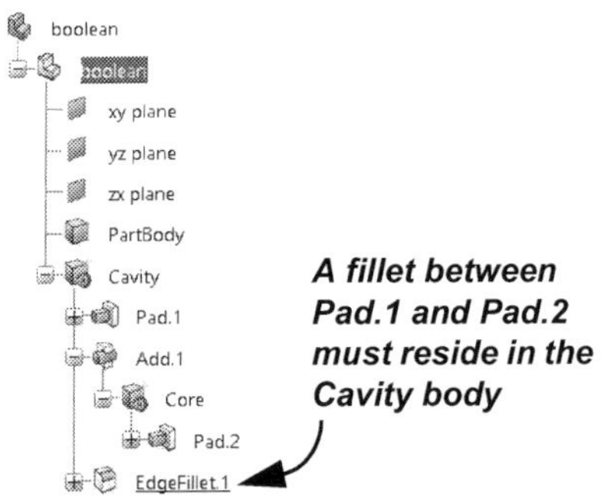


**Figure 20–12**

# Practice 20a Boolean Operations Overview

## Practice Objective

- Review the Boolean operations of a model.

In this practice, you will open a part file of a cast/machined part. The features are organized by using casting and machining operations. Boolean operations have been used to achieve the final part geometry, and inherently provide flexibility in terms of viewing different states of the model.

### Task 1 - Open the part and investigate the bodies and boolean operations.

1. Import **Cover.3dxml**.
2. Right-click **Cover** and select **Open**. The model displays as shown in Figure 20–13.

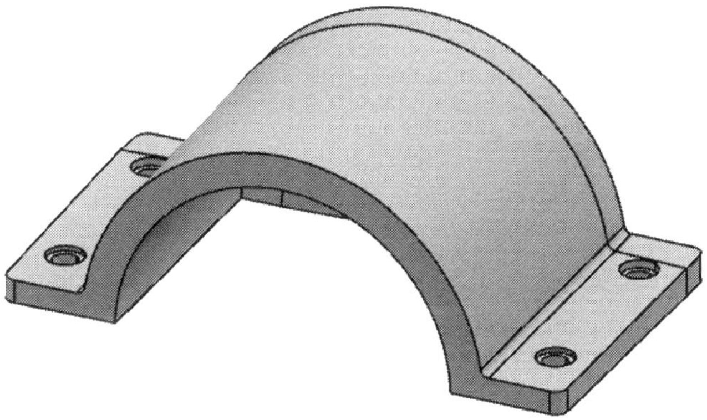

**Figure 20–13**

*When using **Boolean** operations, you must ensure that no geometry is created in the PartBody. This provides more flexibility in that the PartBody can only be used as the operand, and not the operator (i.e., a PartBody cannot be removed from an inserted body).*

3. In the specification tree, note that no geometry has been created directly in the PartBody, as shown in Figure 20–14.

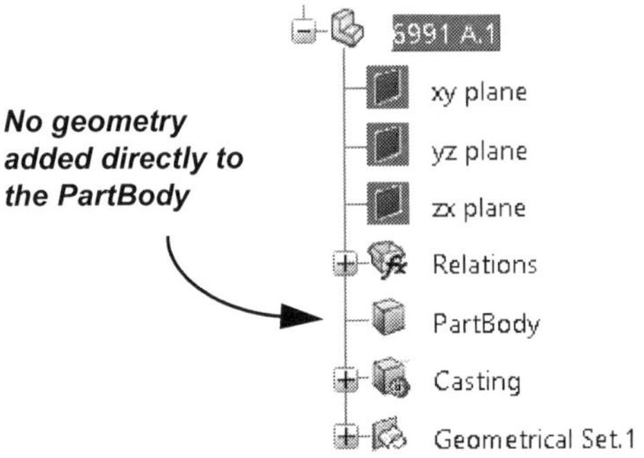


**Figure 20–14**

4. Expand the specification tree and note the features listed under the **Casting** body, as shown in Figure 20–15.

*Note that no holes, grooves, or pockets are found in the casting body.*

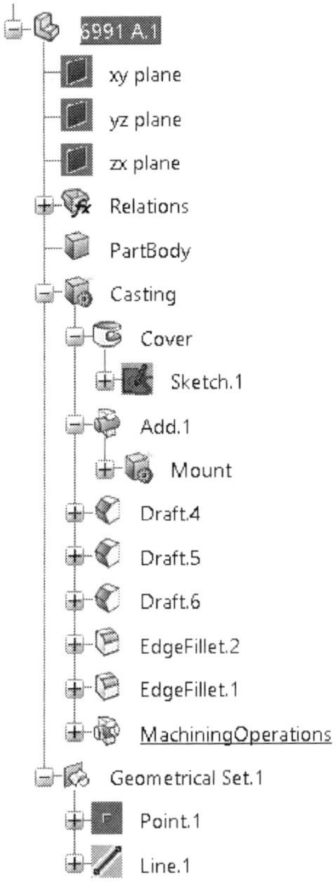


**Figure 20–15**

5. Spin the model to the approximate orientation shown in Figure 20–16.

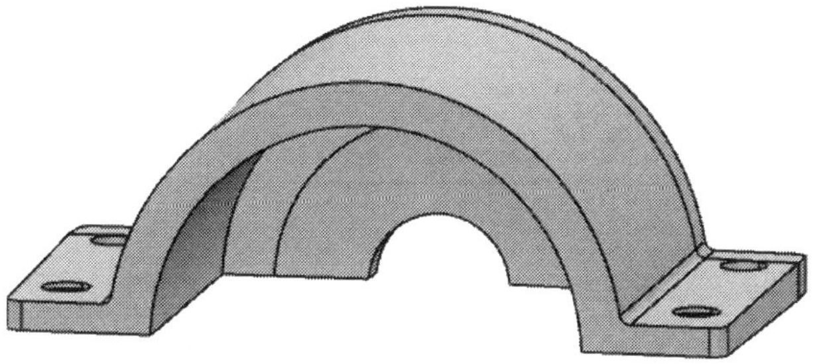

**Figure 20–16**

## Task 2 - Deactivate a body.

1. Expand the **MachiningOperations** feature and note the bodies and features listed, as shown in Figure 20–18.

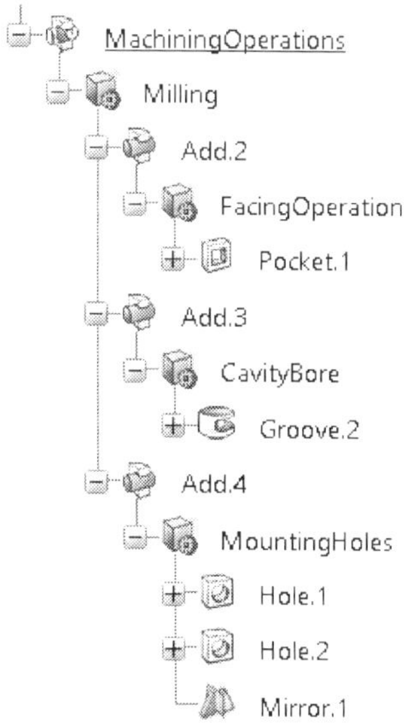


**Figure 20–17**

2. In the specification tree, select **MachiningOperations**, right-click and select **MachiningOperations object**>**Deactivate**.

3. Click **OK** in the Deactivate dialog box.

*Using bodies and boolean operations allows you to quickly and logically organize the features in your models.*

4. The model updates as shown in Figure 20–18. Note that the features to be machined into the cast part are removed.

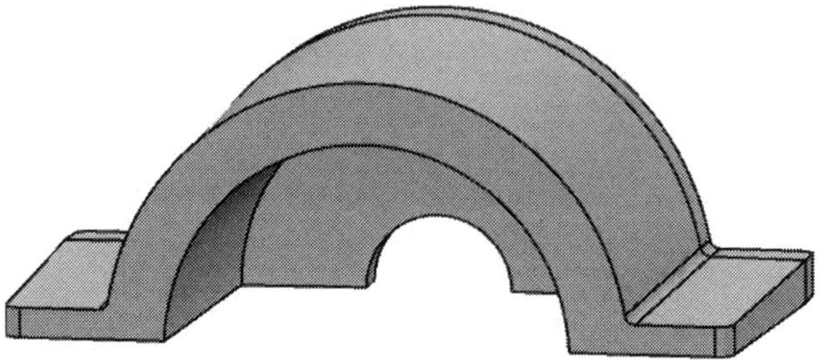

**Figure 20–18**

5. Activate the **MachiningOperations** feature.

6. Save the part and close the tab.

# Practice 20b Boolean Operations

## Practice Objective

- Model using Boolean operations.

In this practice, you will create a part file and structure the part by creating the required bodies. Geometry is created in the appropriate bodies, and **Boolean** operations are used to achieve the final configuration.

### Task 1 - Create a new part.

1. Create a new 3D Part titled **JCS31-3**. Apply the same title to the 3D Shape. Ensure that the **Enable hybrid design** option is cleared.

### Task 2 - Insert bodies.

*Note you can also select the 3D Shape in the specification tree and select (Body) from the context toolbar.*

1. In the *Structure* section of the Action Bar, click (Body) to insert a body. Repeat the operation two more times.
2. Rename the three new bodies as **Case**, **DVD**, and **Cutout**, as shown in Figure 20–19.

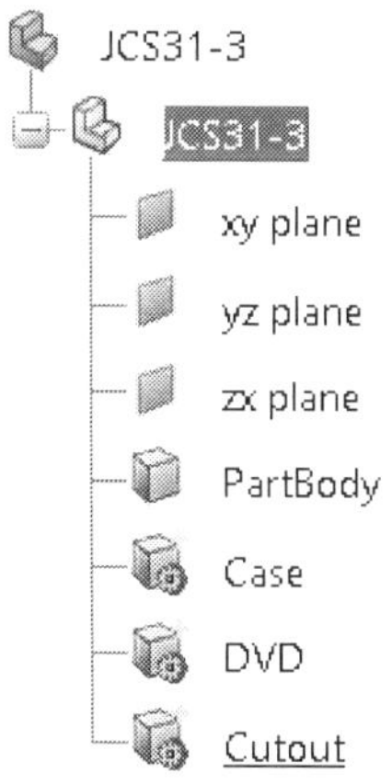


**Figure 20–19**

3. Select the **Case** body and select (Define In Work Object) from the context menu.

## Task 3 - Create a Pad feature.

1. Select the **xy plane** as the sketch support and activate the Sketcher app.

2. Sketch a 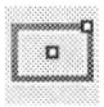 (Centered Rectangle). Create two dimensions with the values, as shown in Figure 20–20.

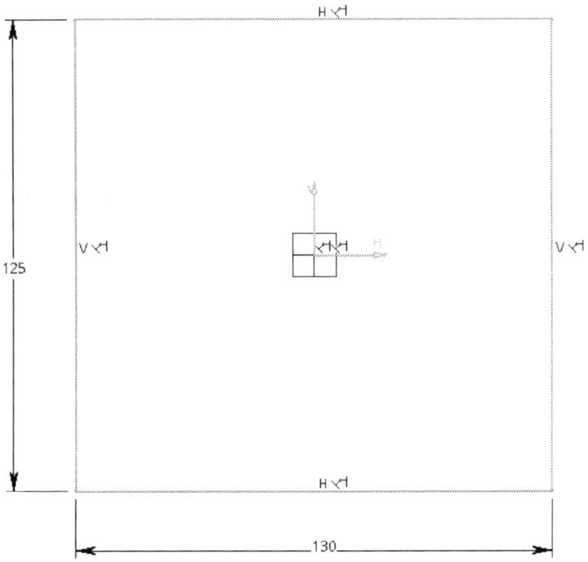


**Figure 20–20**

3. Exit Sketcher.

4. Create a Pad. In the *Length* field, enter **4**. Ensure that the directional arrow points up, as shown in Figure 20–21.

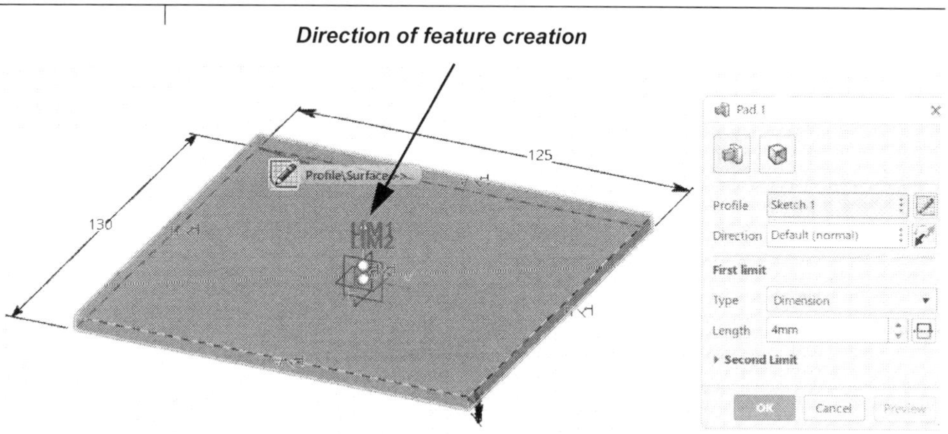


Figure 20–21

## Task 4 - Create a reference plane.

1. Create a reference plane offset from the xy plane by **2.5**. Ensure that the directional arrow points up, as shown in Figure 20–22.

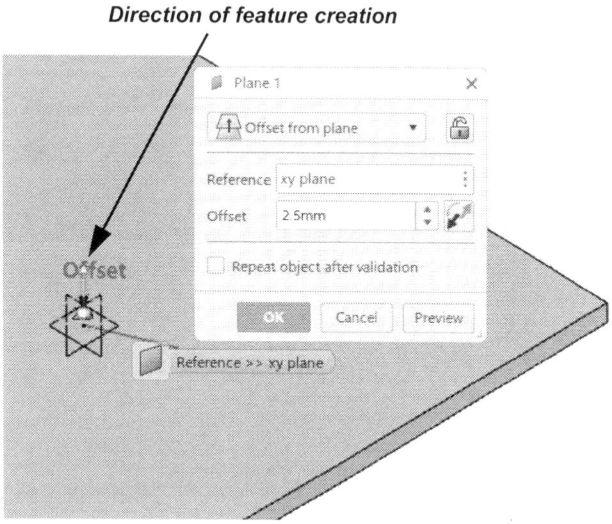


Figure 20–22

2. Rename the plane as **DVDPlane**.

3. Define the **DVD** body as the In Work Object. The specification tree displays as shown in Figure 20–23.

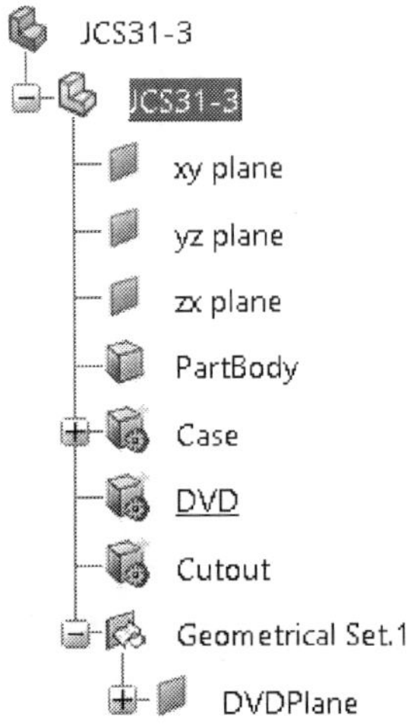


Figure 20–23

4. Hide the **Case** body.

**Task 5 - Create a sketch.**

1. Select **DVDPlane** and activate the Sketcher app.
2. Sketch and dimension the two circles shown in Figure 20–24. Create the circles such that the centers are located on the origin. The diameters are 15 and 120.

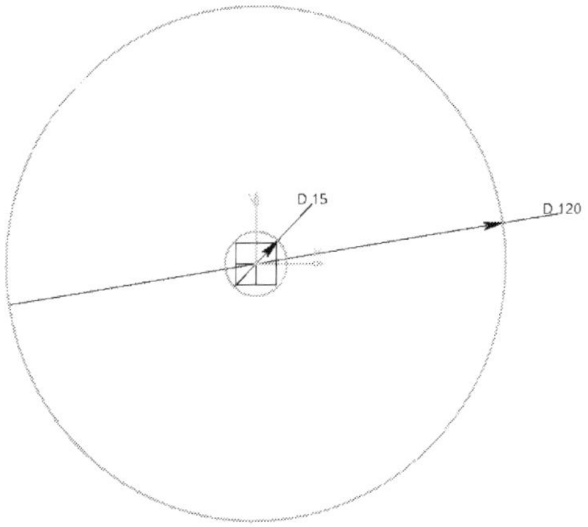


Figure 20–24

3. Exit the Sketch app.

## Task 6 - Create a Pad feature.

4. Click (Pad) and select the sketch.

5. In the *First Limit* area, in the *Length* field, enter **4**.

6. In the *Second Limit* area, in the *Length* field, enter **1.5**, as shown in Figure 20–25.

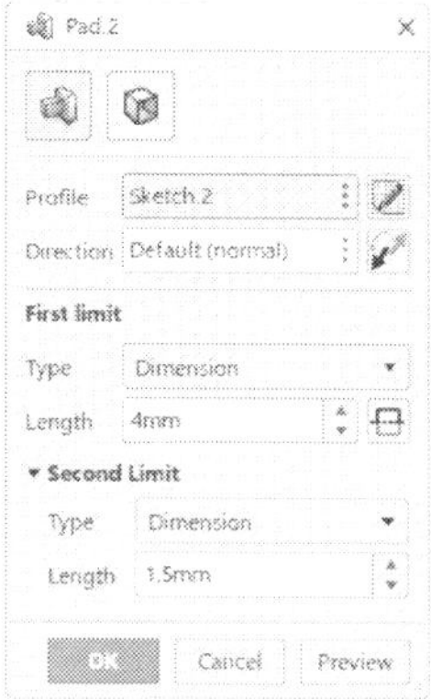


**Figure 20–25**

7. Click **OK** to complete the pad.

8. Create the sketch shown in Figure 20–26 on the bottom surface of the model. Ensure that the circle is centered on the origin.

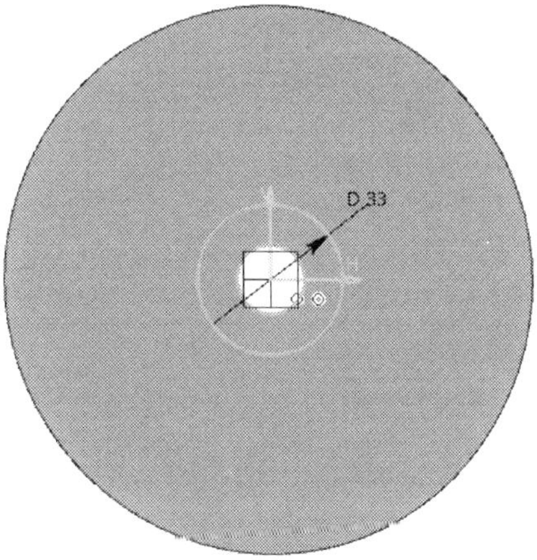

**Figure 20–26**

9. **Click** (Pocket) and select **the sketch**.

10. In the *Length* field, enter **1**.

11. Click **OK**. The Pad feature displays as shown in Figure 20–27.

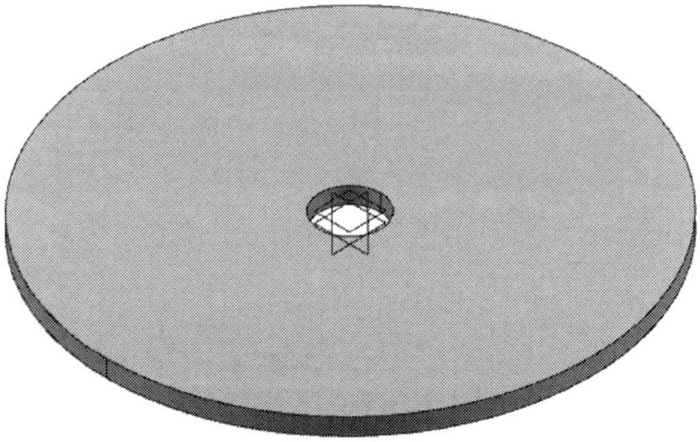

**Figure 20–27**

12. Rotate the model to view the bottom surface, as shown in Figure 20–28.

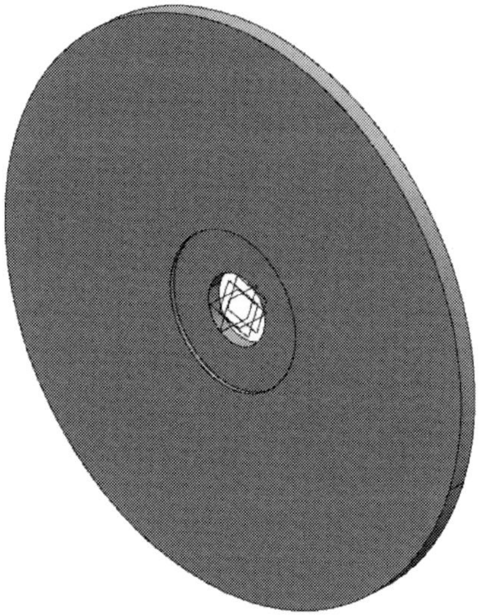

**Figure 20–28**

## Task 7 - Create an Edge Fillet.

1. Create a **0.5** Edge Fillet on the edge shown in Figure 20–29.

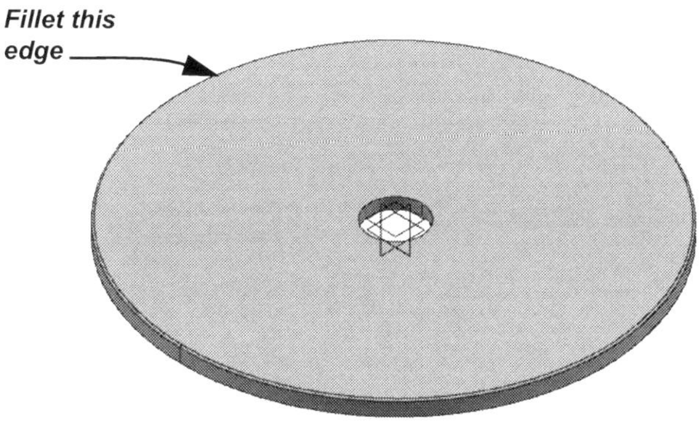


Figure 20–29

2. Define the **Case** body to be the In Work Object. The specification tree displays as shown in Figure 20–30.

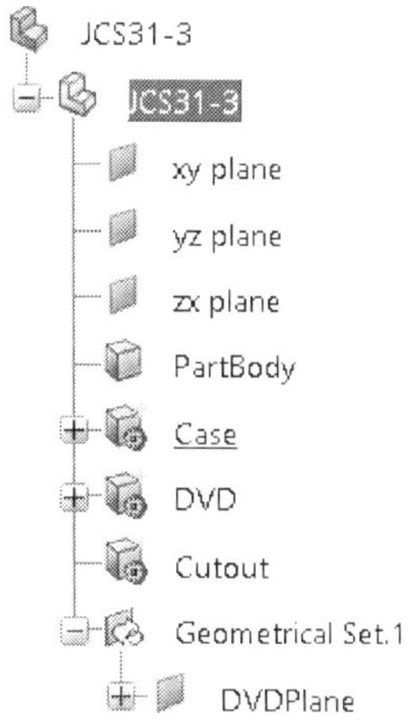


Figure 20–30

## Task 8 - Perform a Boolean operation.

*You might need to display the Boolean Operations toolbar to use the **Remove** icon.*

1. Select the background of the display to clear **Case** body.
2. In the *Structure* section of the Action Bar, click  (Remove).

3. The Remove dialog box opens as shown in Figure 20–31.

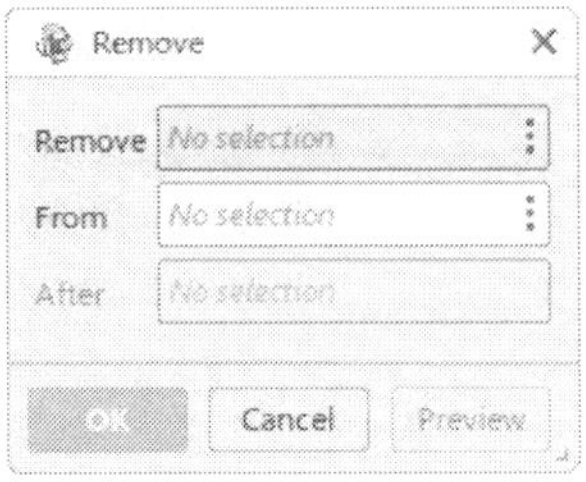


**Figure 20–31**

4. Click in the Remove field and select the **DVD** body.
5. **Case** should automatically be selected in the From field.
6. Click **OK** to complete the operation.
7. Hide the datum planes.
8. The model displays as shown in Figure 20–32.

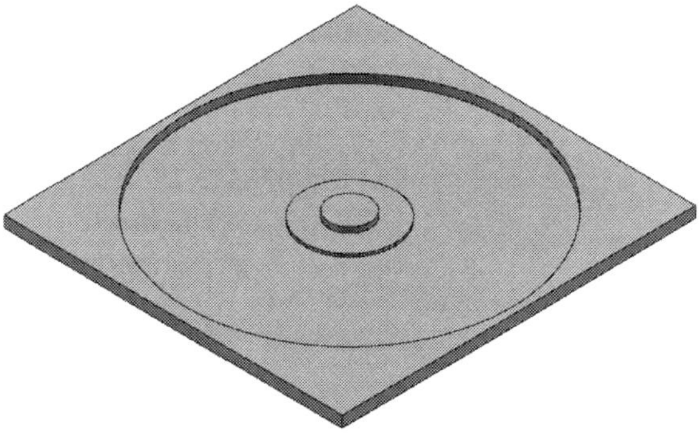

**Figure 20–32**

## Task 9 - Create cutout geometry.

1. Define **Cutout** body as the In Work Object.

 

2. Select the top surface as shown in Figure 20–33, and enter the Sketcher app.

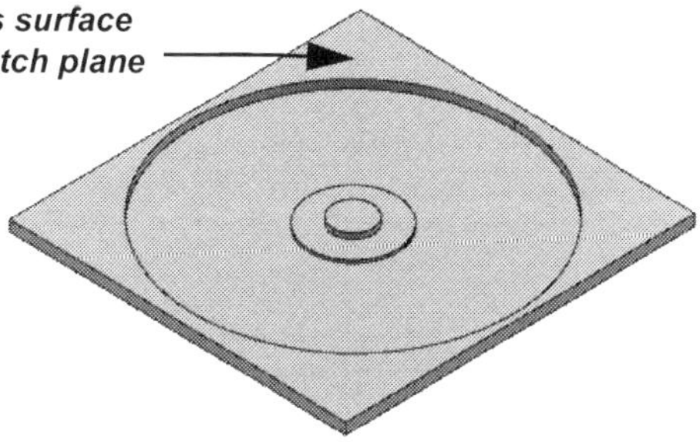


**Figure 20–33**

The sketch view displays as shown in Figure 20–34.

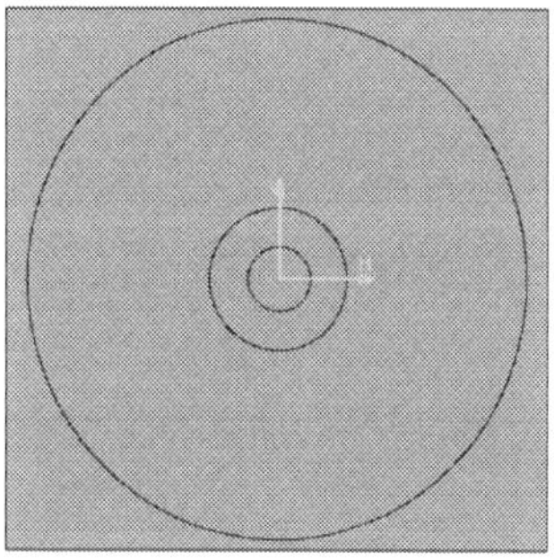

**Figure 20–34**

3. Double-click on  (Offset) and offset the three edges shown in Figure 20–35 by **1** to the inside of the geometry.

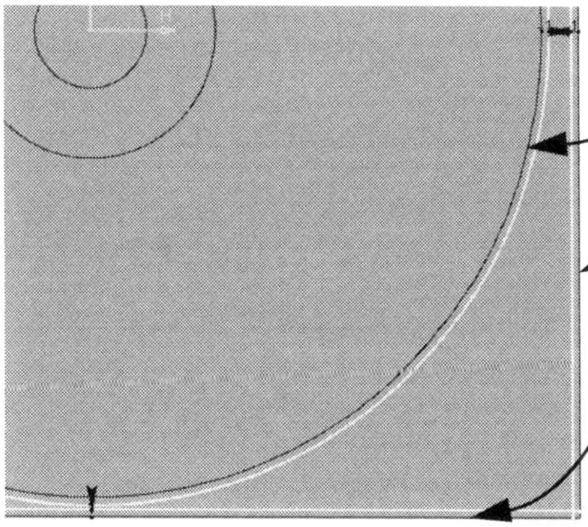


**Figure 20–35**

4. Sketch a horizontal and a vertical line. Ensure the lines snap to the previously sketched entities, and that the Horizontal and vertical constraints are applied. Add the **55** and **45** dimensions, as shown in Figure 20–36.

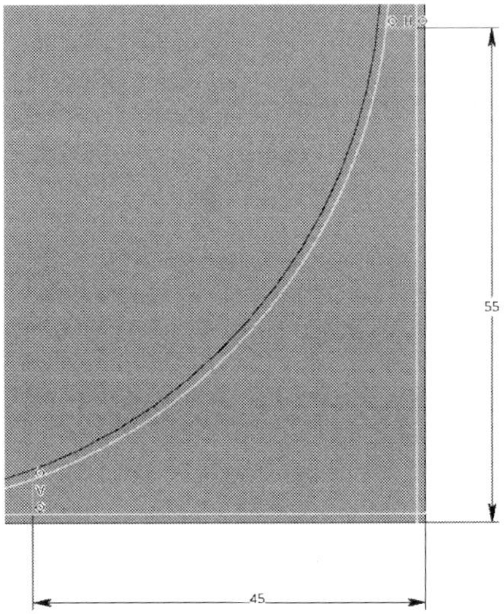


**Figure 20–36**

5. Click  (Trim) to clean up the geometry as shown in Figure 20–37.

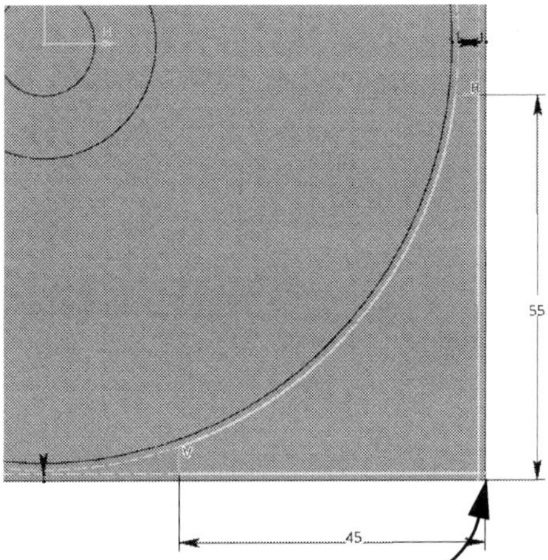


**Figure 20–37**

 

6. Select all of the sketch geometry and use (Mirror) to mirror the sketch about the horizontal axis. The sketch displays as shown in Figure 20–38.

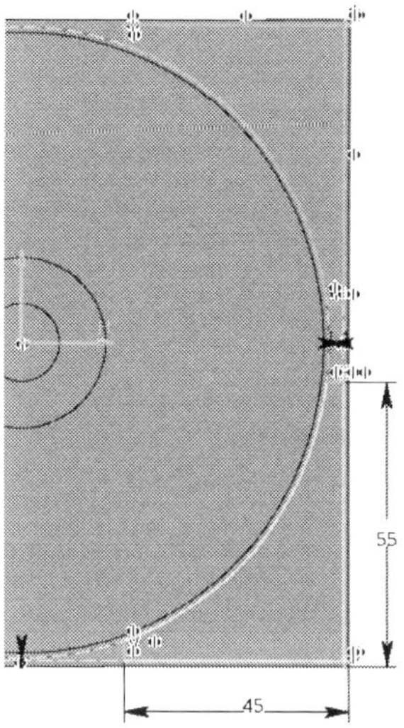


**Figure 20–38**

7. Exit the Sketcher app.

## Task 10 - Create solid geometry.

1. Create a Pad **2mm** in length in the direction toward the existing geometry, as shown in Figure 20–39.

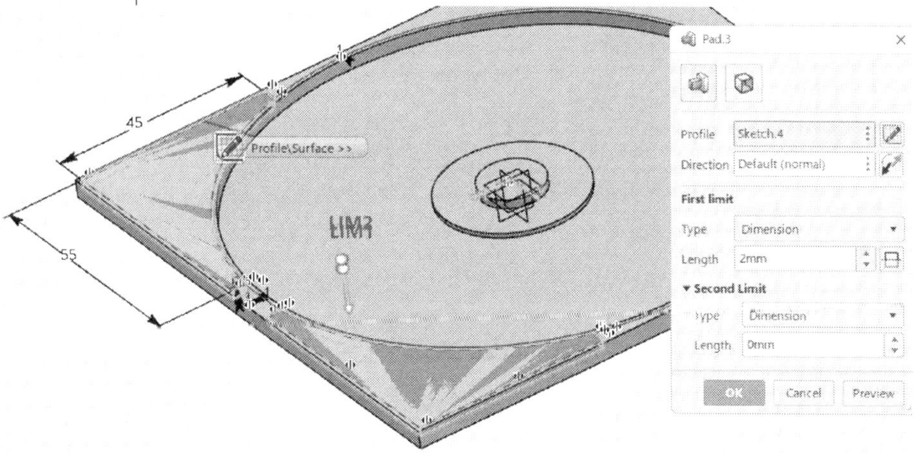


**Figure 20–39**

2. Mirror the Pad feature about the yz plane. The model and the specification tree display as shown in Figure 20–40.

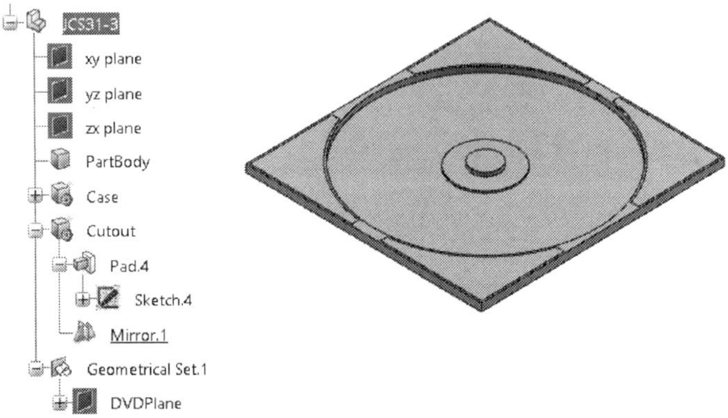


**Figure 20–40**

3. Define the **Case** body as the In Work Object, and clear the **Case** body by selecting the background of the display.

4. In the *Structure* section of the Action Bar, click  (Remove) to remove the **Cutout** body from the **Case** body. The model displays as shown in Figure 20–41.

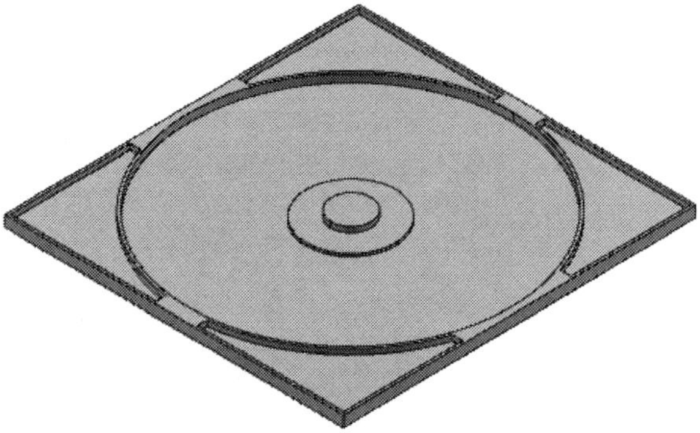

**Figure 20–41**

## Task 11 - Create a sketch.

1. Select the planar surface shown in Figure 20–42 and activate the Sketch app.

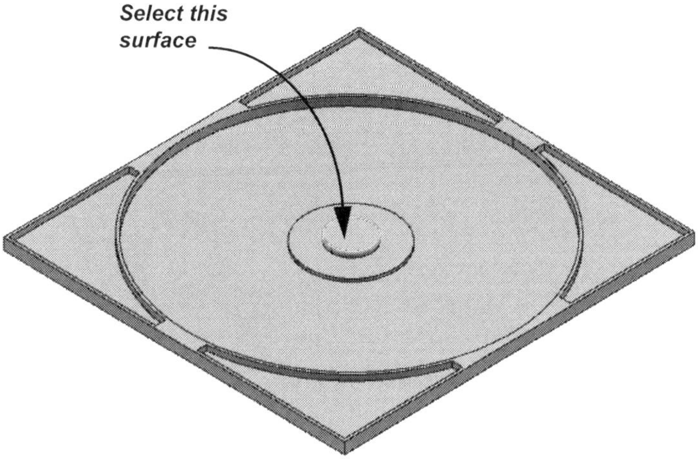


Figure 20–42

2. Use  (Offset) to offset the circular edge to the inside by **1**, as shown in Figure 20–43.

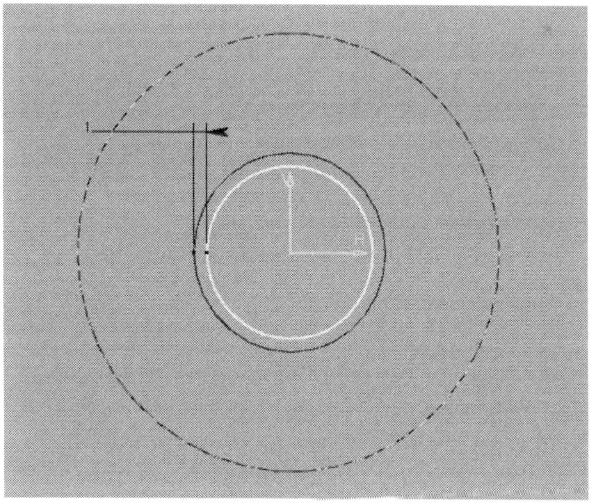

Figure 20–43

3. Create a Pocket feature **2.5** deep using the sketch you just created. The Pocket feature displays as shown in Figure 20–44.

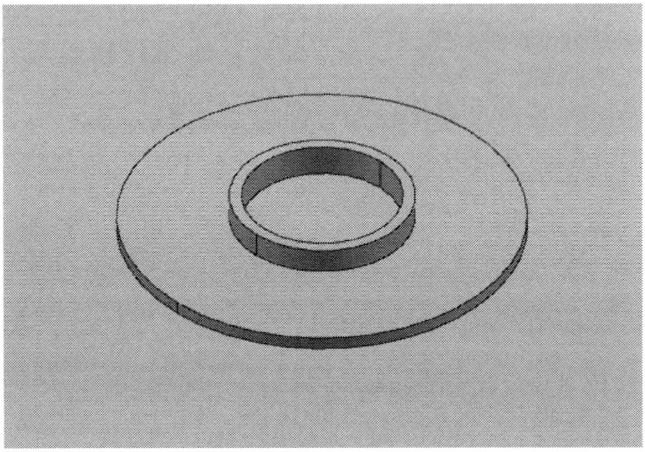

**Figure 20–44**

4. Save the model but do not close the tab.

## Task 12 - Cut and paste a body.

1. Import **CenterCutOut.3dxml**.
2. Right-click CenterCutOut and select **Open**.
3. Copy the **CenterCutOut** body as shown in Figure 20–45.

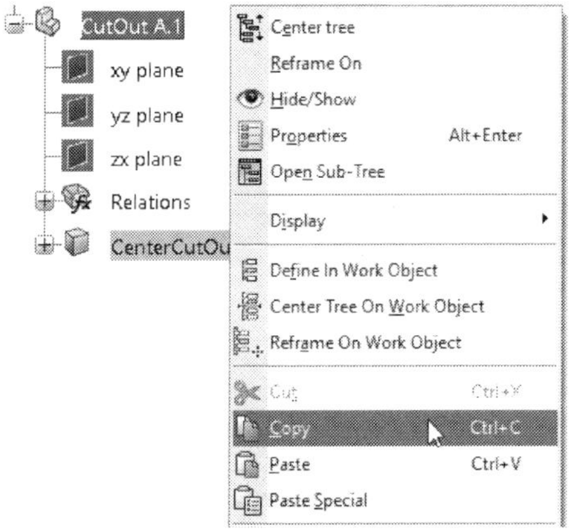


**Figure 20–45**

4. Select the **JCS31-3** tab.

5. Paste **CenterCutOut** body into the 3DShape in the specification tree, as shown in Figure 20–46.

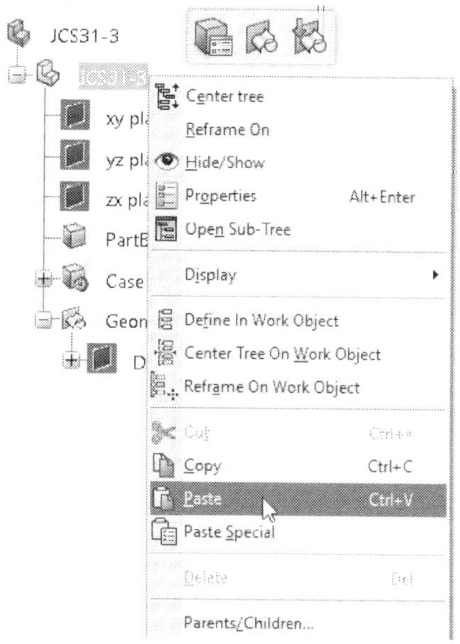


Figure 20–46

The body displays at the bottom of the specification tree.

6. Zoom in and note the pasted geometry, as shown in Figure 20–47.

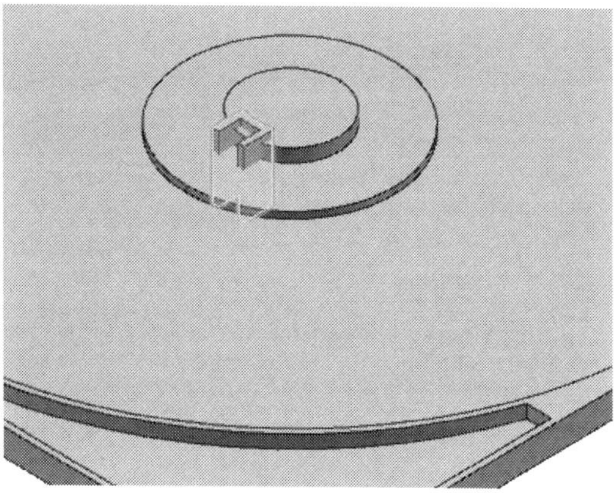

Figure 20–47

## Task 13 - Create a pattern.

1. Select the Pad feature under the pasted **CenterCutOut** body, as shown in Figure 20–48.

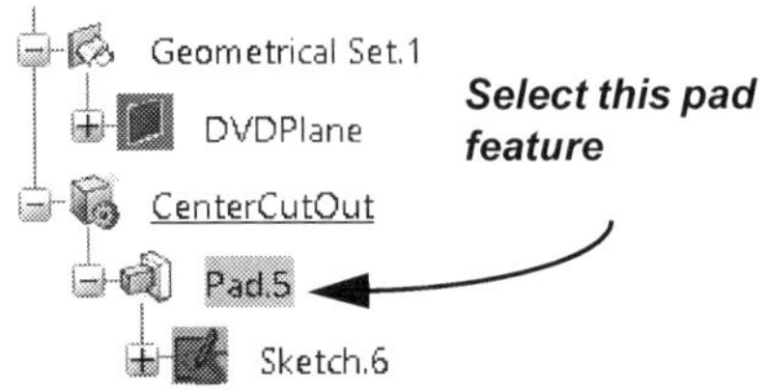


**Figure 20–48**

2. In the *Essentials* section of the Action Bar, click (Circular Pattern).

3. Specify the pattern using the following values:

   - *Parameters:* **Complete crown**
   - *Instance(s):* **3**
   - *Reference element:* as shown in Figure 20–49

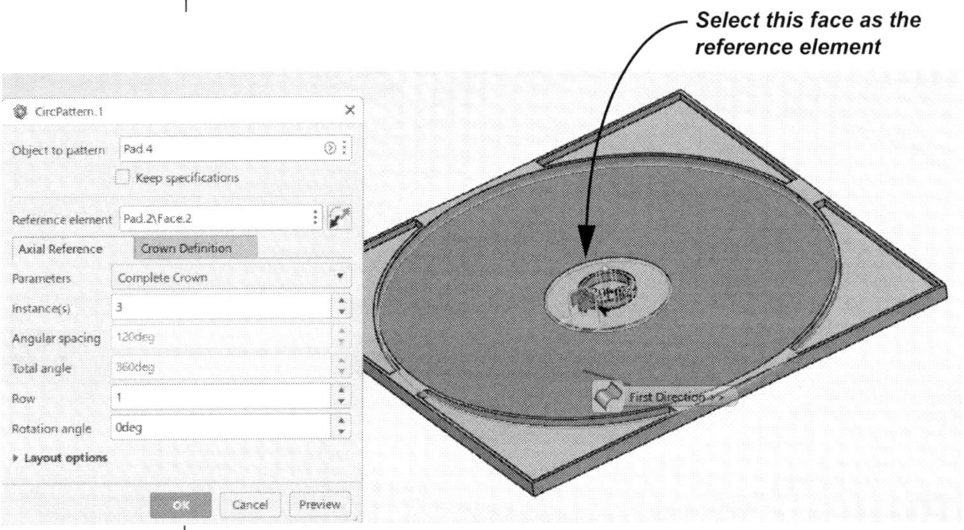


**Figure 20–49**

4. Click **OK**.

5. The pattern displays as shown in Figure 20–50.

 

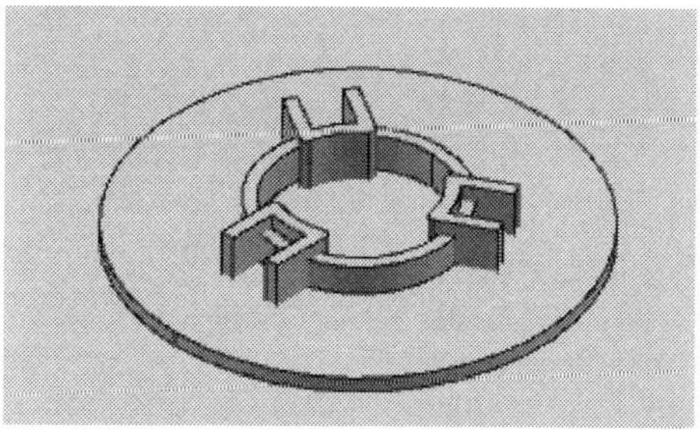

Figure 20–50

6. Remove the **CenterCutOut** body from the **Case** body. The model and the specification tree display, as shown in Figure 20–51.

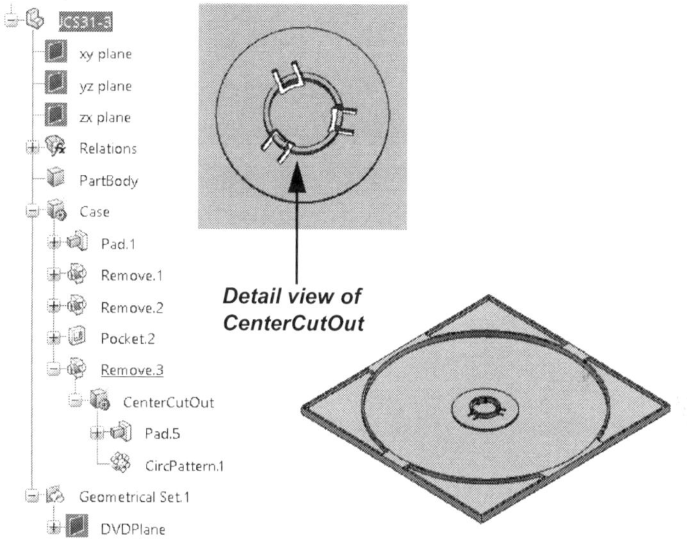


Figure 20–51

7. Save the model and close the tabs.

# Chapter Review Questions

1. Multiple bodies are combined using _________ operations.
   a. Combine
   b. Boolean
   c. Merge
   d. None of the above.
2. Advantages of using boolean operations include:
   a. The creation of the part model becomes easier when the model is divided into smaller, functional areas.
   b. Features can be grouped by function or area, making the model structure easy to interpret.
   c. Update times are reduced.
   d. All of the above.
3. One of the advantages of using the multi-body approach is that you can hide geometry in specific bodies while viewing others.
   a. True
   b. False
4. To locate a feature in the specification tree, right-click on the feature in the model display and select which of the following options?
   a. Search
   b. Center tree
   c. Reframe on
   d. Name

5. Looking at Figure 20–52, if (Only Current Operated Solid) were clicked, **Pad.1**, **Multi-pad.1**, and **Edgefillet.1** would display.

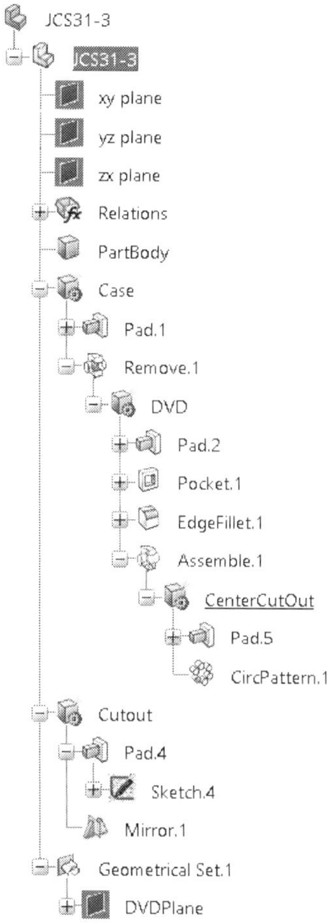


**Figure 20–52**

a. True

b. False

6. Looking at Figure 20–52, if (Only Current Body) were selected, only features in the Center CutOut body would display.

a. True

b. False

**Answers:** 1b, 2d, 3a, 4b, 5b, 6a

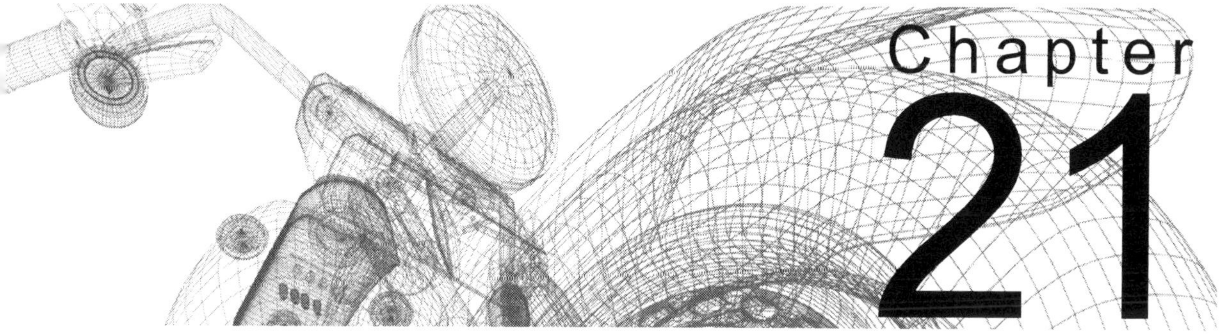


# Assembly Design

This chapter covers how to activate the Assembly Design app and access assembly-specific options. This chapter also guides you through the process of creating an assembly and describes the available assembly constraints.

## Learning Objectives in This Chapter

- Learn about the Assembly Design app interface.
- Create an assembly and add components to it.
- Understand product properties and assembly product structure.
- Use the compass to move components.
- Automatically snap objects to the compass.
- Understand the various constraints available for parametrically locating components.

# 21.1 Assembly Design App

*The terms **Product** and **Assembly** can be used interchangeably.*

In the Part Design app, features are created in the model to build the final part. In the Assembly apps, components can be added to a product file to create an assembly.There are two apps for working with Assemblies:

- (Product Structure): This app is for the creation and manipulation of the Product Structure. It is primarily used for Top-Down Design planning purposes, rather than for assembly design purposes.

- (Assembly Design): This app is for the design of assemblies in cooperation with the Part Design and Drafting apps. This is the app you would typically be using.

Components can be added to a product using either the Product Structure or the Assembly Design apps:

- In the compass shown in Figure 21–1, click **3D**. Then select (Assembly Design). Fill in the applicable information in the Physical Product dialog box.

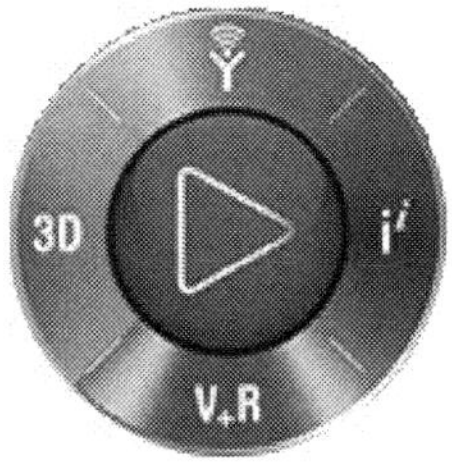


**Figure 21–1**

- Alternatively, select (Add)>**Physical Product in the Top Bar**. Fill in the applicable information in the Physical Product dialog box.

In either case, the Physical Product dialog box displays as shown in Figure 21–2.

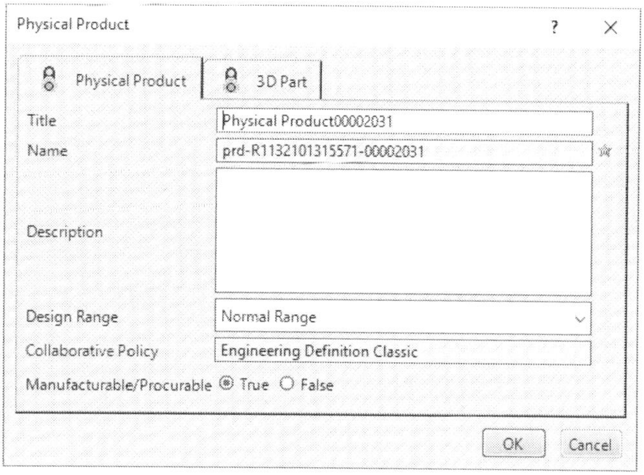


**Figure 21–2**

The *3D Part* tab, shown in Figure 21–3, enables you to also create a new part model as the first component in the assembly.

*3D Shape is the form of the part and the features that make up the shape. A 3D Part has the form information and the location of the geometry in the assembly.*

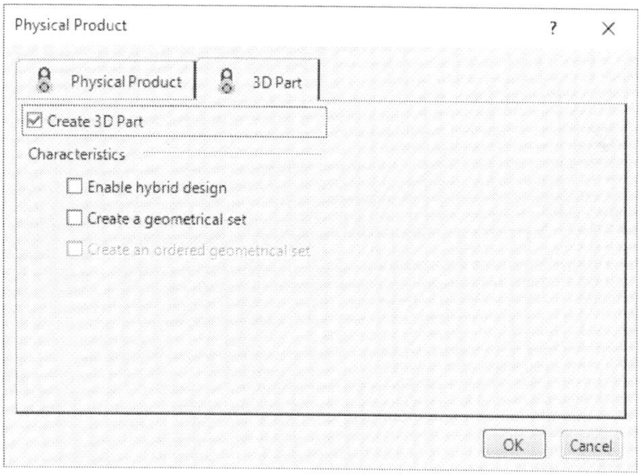


**Figure 21–3**

## Commonly Used Tools

The *Assembly* section of the Action Bar is shown in Figure 21–4.

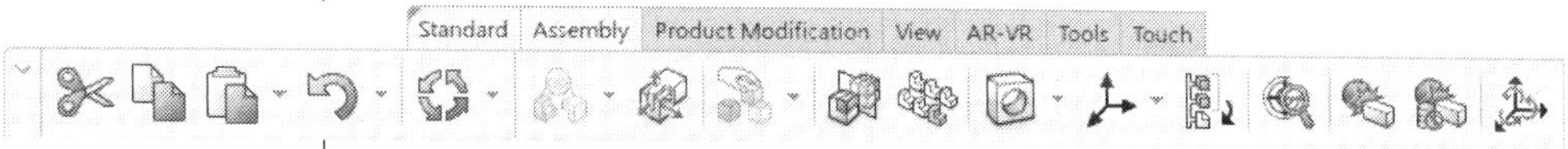


**Figure 21–4**

The (Engineering Connection) option controls the relative position of components in the assembly.

The (Update) option updates the position of components as assembly Engineering Connections are applied or if Engineering Connections have been modified.

In the *Tools* section of the Action Bar are the Measure tools, shown in Figure 21–5. These commands enable various analyses to be performed within the assembly.

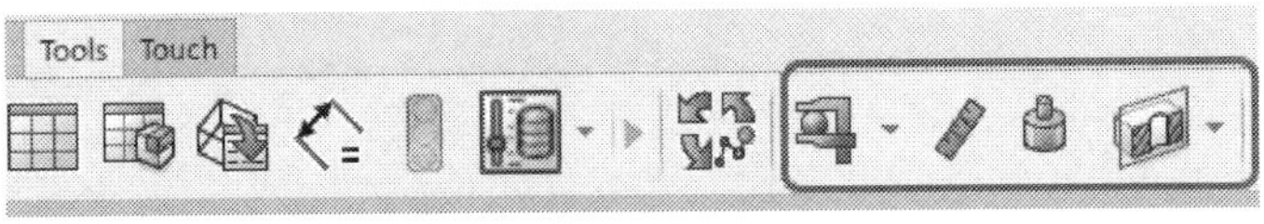


**Figure 21–5**

# 21.2 Create an Assembly

Use the following steps to create a new assembly:

1. Create a new product file by activating the Assembly Design app.
2. Modify any product properties (i.e., Title, Version Comments, or Description).
3. Add components to the assembly using the Assembly Tools.
4. Position components using the compass and/or using Engineering Connections.
5. Add assembly features to the model or modify parts within the context of the assembly.
6. Analyze and extract any critical information from the assembly.

## Product Properties

When a new product file is created, the system assigns an automatically-generated Name, which uniquely identifies the product within the engineering database. You can change the Title and add a Description, as well as set other options, as shown in Figure 21–6.

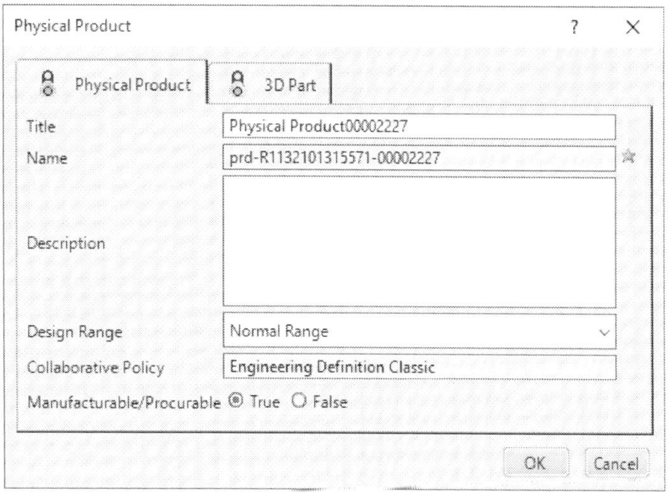


Figure 21–6

## Adding Components

A component is an object that is added to an assembly. The following components can be added to an assembly for product design purposes.

- Product
- 3D Part
- 3D Shape

Components can be added to the assembly in the following ways:

- Select the *3D Part* tab in the Physical Product dialog box and enable **Create 3D Part**.This will create a new part assembled to the assembly.
- Select the assembly in the specification tree and use the right-click menu.
- Use the icons in the *Product Edition* section of the Action Bar.

The following table describes some of the icons found in the *Product Edition* section of the Action Bar:

| Icon | Option | Description |
|---|---|---|
|  | **New Product** | Creates a new subassembly within the top-level assembly with its own Product file. |
| 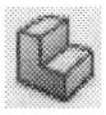 | **New 3D Part** | Creates a new 3D Part within the top-level assembly containing a 3D Shape. |
|  | **New 3D Shape** | Creates a new 3D Shape within the top-level assembly without the creation of a 3D Part. |
|  | **Existing Product** | Adds a product to the assembly whose file already exists within the engineering database. |

When using the **Existing Product** option, multiple objects can be added to the assembly at the same time by pressing <Ctrl> or <Shift> while selecting objects.

 

## Product Structure

The product structure of an assembly consists of the top level assembly (Product), components (3D Parts), and subassemblies (Products) as shown in Figure 21–7.

The active level in the product structure is highlighted in blue in the specification tree. When performing actions on a top level or subassembly (such as **Inserting Components**), the active level of the product structure is affected by the actions performed.

To activate a subassembly, double-click on it in the specification tree.

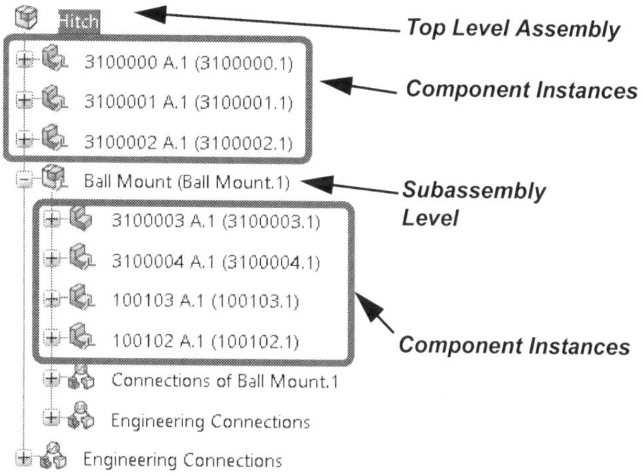


**Figure 21–7**

Once components have been added to the assembly, they display in the specification tree. The part name and the instance name in parenthesis are listed.

# 21.3 Engineering Connections and Constraints

Engineering Connections parametrically control the location and orientation between components using the **Constraints** and **Interferences** tools.

Constraints are specified to locate components parametrically with respect to existing components. Any references made to other components when constraining creates parent/child relationships.

Constraints are created using the Engineering Connections Definition dialog box.

The constraint definition can be streamlined using the predefined templates as follows:

1. Expand the Connection **Type** drop-down menu as shown in Figure 21–8.

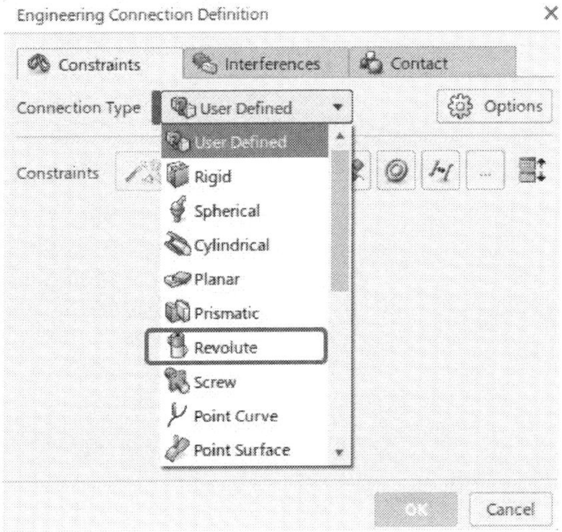


**Figure 21–8**

 

2. The available Engineering Connection templates are described in the table below.

| Name | Icon | Description |
|---|---|---|
| **User-Defined** |  | A combination of constraints, which is incompatible with the predefined engineering connection types. |
| **Rigid** |  | *Welds* components together. |
| **Spherical** |  | Point-Point constraint enabling free rotation about the common points. |
| **Cylindrical** |  | Axis-Axis/Line-Line constraint permitting relative motion along the constrained entities. |
| **Planar** |  | Plane-Plane constraint permitting sliding and rotation relative to the constrained entities. |
| **Prismatic** |  | A constraint group permitting relative translation along a single degree of freedom. |
| **Revolute** |  | A constraint group permitting one degree of rotational freedom. |
| **Screw** |  | A constraint group that creates a relation between a translational and a rotational degree of freedom between constrained entities. (i.e. Bolt & Nut) |
| **PointCurve** |  | A constraint permitting a point to be constrained to a linear or non-linear curve. |
| **PointSurface** |  | A constraint permitting a point to be constrained to planar or non-planar curve. |
| **Gear** |  | A Coupling Engineering connection that links two engineering connections containing an angle constraint each. |
| **Rack** |  | A Coupling Engineering connection that links two engineering connections containing an offset constraint and an angle constraint. |
| **Cable** |  | A Coupling Engineering connection that links two engineering connections containing an offset constraint each. |
| **Universal** |  | A constraint that allows for two relative rotations between components along a shared point. |

| Name | Icon | Description |
|---|---|---|
| **Roll Curve** |  | Allows two curves that are constrained to maintain contact at a single point. Translation of one curve effects an equivalent translation on the other curve. (i.e Wheel rolling down a path) |
| **Slide Curve** |  | Allows for two curves to be constrained to maintain contact with each other at a single point. Translation of curves is independent as long as contact at point is maintained. (i.e Cam and Follower) |
| **Fix** |  | Fastens a component to its current position in the assembly space. It has no other constraints to components. |
| **Free** |  | |
| **Symmetry** |  | A constraint relating two axis systems, in which symmetry can be specified along either the X,Y or Z axis. |
| **Projection** |  | A constraint typically used for positioning of a Spot Fastener Instance. |

Constraints are controlled by three factors:

- Type
- Options
- Mode

## Constraint Type

Constraint Type controls the geometric relationship behavior with the most commonly used Constraints.

Constraint Types can be inserted from the Engineering Connections Definition Dialog box as shown in Figure 21–9.

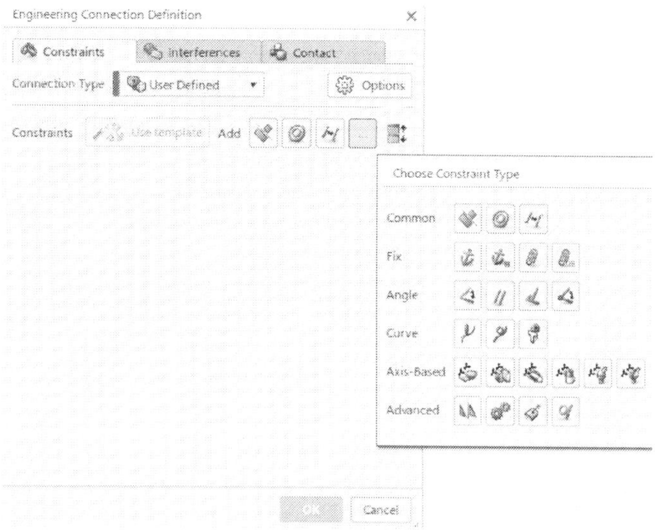


Figure 21–9

### Coincidence

Once additional components have been added to the assembly, how they are constrained depends on their geometry. Coincidence can be used to align points, axes and planes. For example, the T-brace shown in Figure 21–10 is positioned over the mounting block using the coincidence constraint and selecting the axis of the holes.

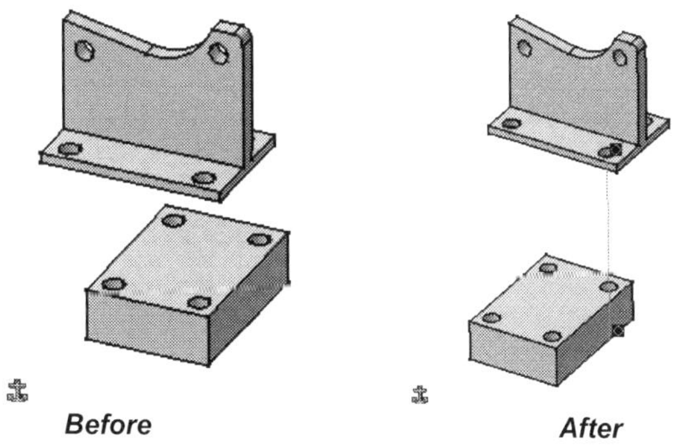


Figure 21–10

The T-brace can be further constrained using the coincidence constraint and selecting planar surfaces by selecting an appropriate Alignment option, as shown in Figure 21–11.

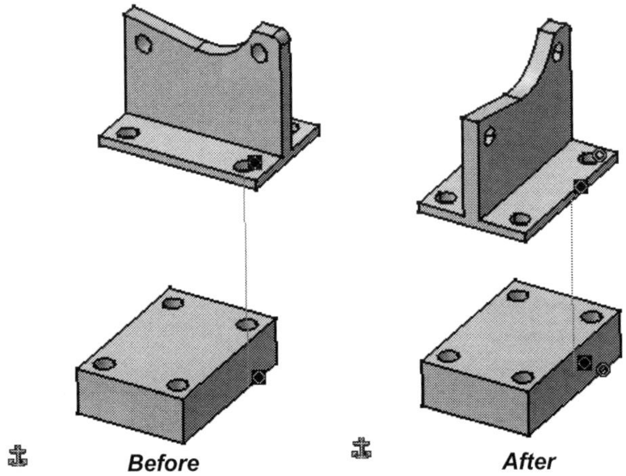


**Figure 21–11**

When specifying the coincidence constraint with planar surfaces, you can change the orientation of the surfaces, as shown in Figure 21–12.

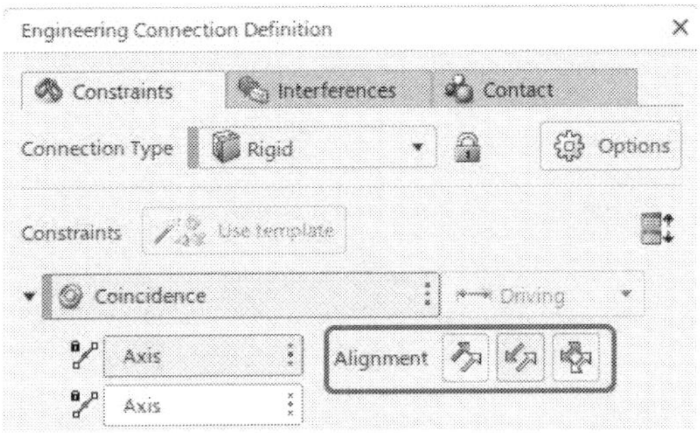


**Figure 21–12**

## Contact

Contact mates two surfaces. The T-brace shown in Figure 21–13 is fully constrained after mating the top surface of the mounting block with the underside surface of the T-brace.

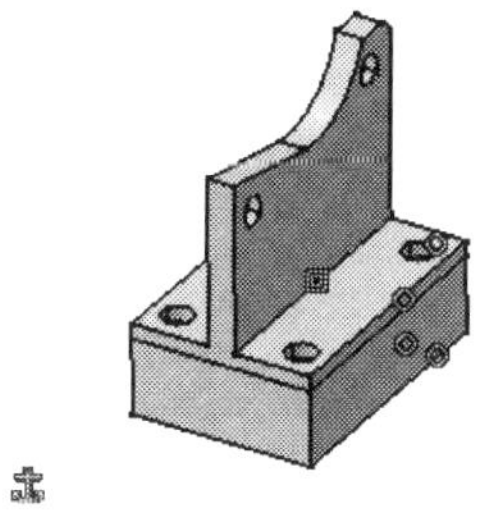

Figure 21–13

## Offset

Offset behaves like contact or coincidence with planar surfaces, without the selections being coplanar. The selections are parallel with a specified offset distance. The bolt shown in Figure 21–14 is offset from the T-brace to permit space for future washer placement. Similar to coincidence, the direction of orientation can be specified.

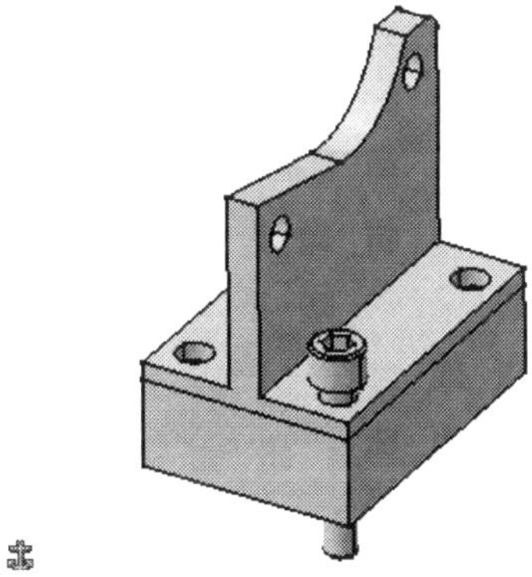

Figure 21–14

## Angle

The Angle Constraint contains four sub-types:

- **Angle:** Enables selection of two lines or planes controlled by an angle dimension between entities.
- **Parallelism:** Enables selection of two lines or planes controlled by a 0 or 180 degree relationship between entities.
- **Perpendicularity:** Enables selection of two lines or planes controlled by a 90 degree relationship between entities.

- **Hinge:** Enables selection of two lines or planes controlled by an angle dimension between entities and the selection of the hinge axis.

In the example shown in Figure 21–15, the finger is assembled with a coincidence constraint. Note the intersecting geometry.

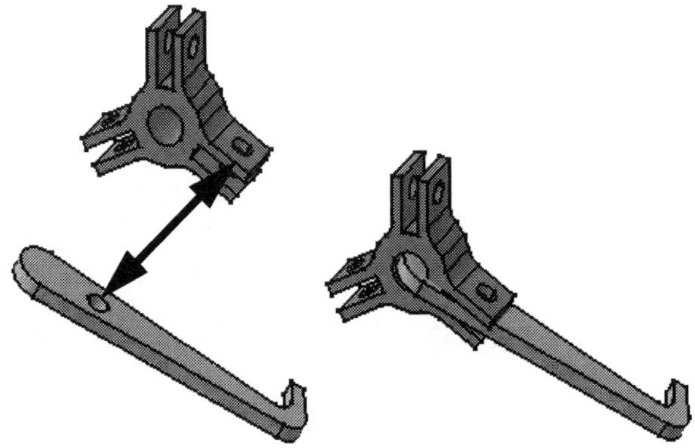

**Figure 21–15**

The angle constraint is used to indicate the correct orientation of components. The example shown in Figure 21–15 indicates that interference exists. The finger component is under-constrained. Therefore, a parallel or angle constraint must be added. The parallel and angle options are shown in Figure 21–16.

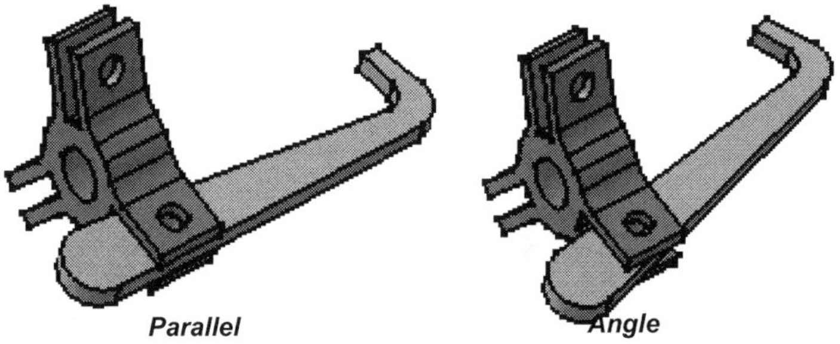


**Figure 21–16**

## Fix Component

In CATIA, the base component is usually constrained to be fixed. This essentially creates a zero position of reference. Once constrained to be fixed, the *Engineering Connections* section displays in the specification tree, as shown in Figure 21–17.

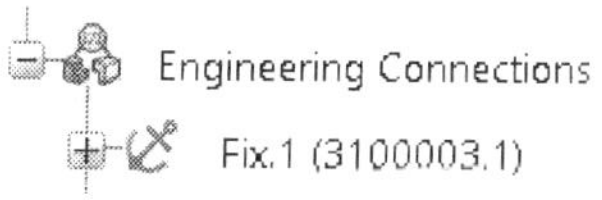


**Figure 21–17**

### Fix Together

Fix together is normally used to fix any remaining degrees of freedom from an under-constrained component. The components behave as a single body in space.

When moving components assembled with a fix together constraint, press <Shift> while using the robot. This forces 3DEXPERIENCE to obey the assembly Engineering Connections during the move. If a component is moved without pressing <Shift>, the fix together constraint updates based on the new locations.

## Constraint Options

Constraint Options are only activated when the orientation of the selected elements is available for the constraint type.

Plane geometry orientation options include plane normal vector relationship options:

- **Undefined:** Plane orientation is undefined and can be modified during update.
- **Same Orientation:** Plane orientations are the same (aligned).
- **Opposite Orientation:** Plane orientations are opposite (mated).

Line geometry orientation options include line vector relationship options:

- **Undefined:** Line orientation is undefined and can be modified during update.
- **Parallelism:** Lines are parallel but line vectors are not oriented.
- **Same Orientation:** Line vector orientations are the same.
- **Opposite Orientation:** Line vectors orientations are opposite.

Hinge constraint orientation options include the four quadrants of angular representation:

- Direct angle
- Angle + 180deg
- 180deg - Angle
- 360deg - Angle

Axis System orientation options include the axes of the cartesian coordinate system:

- X axis
- Y axis
- Z axis

## Constraint Mode

The Constraint Mode controls measurement behavior that is associated with a constraint. The three Constraint Modes available are:

- **Driving:** Constraint definition value is applied to the product during update.
- **Measurement:** Constraint value is a result of the constraint definitions and any other constraints in the product during update.
- **Controlled:** Permits the constraint to be restricted between upper and lower bounds for use in kinematics.

## Change Type

You can change the type of the constraint by selecting it in the Engineering Connection Definition dialog box and selecting the replacement constraint in the flyout, as shown in Figure 21–18.

**Figure 21–18**

## Assembly Considerations

When modeling parts, consider which feature form best captures the design intent of the base feature. When working with assemblies, consider which component is best suited for use as the base component.

Also consider the active level of the product structure. If the top level of the structure is active (highlighted in blue), then the constraint you are creating is going to be grouped with the top level assembly Engineering Connections.

If you want to create an Engineering Connection specific to the components in a subassembly, double-click on the subassembly level in the specification tree to activate it. When you create the Engineering Connection, it is grouped with the subassembly Engineering Connections. The product structure, top level assembly Engineering Connections, and subassembly Engineering Connections are shown in Figure 21–19.

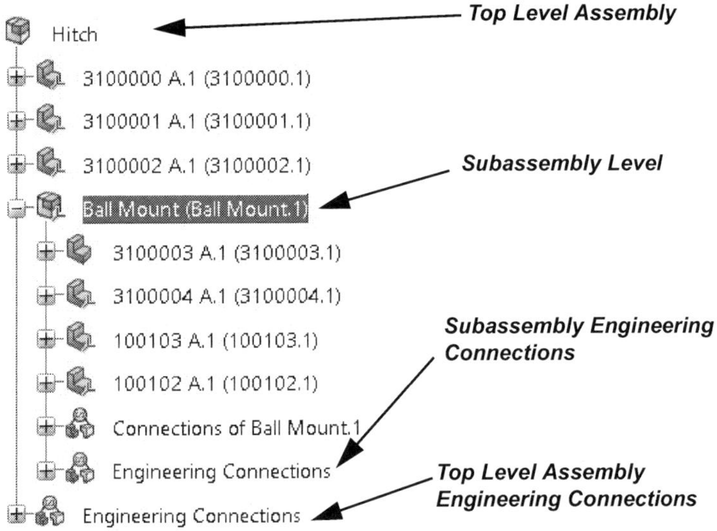


**Figure 21–19**

# 21.4 Use the Robot

Once existing components have been added to the assembly, the components are displayed in the default position and orientation. The robot is used to move components within the main window.

To move a selected component, place the cursor over the center dot as shown in Figure 21–20. Press the left mouse button to move the robot.

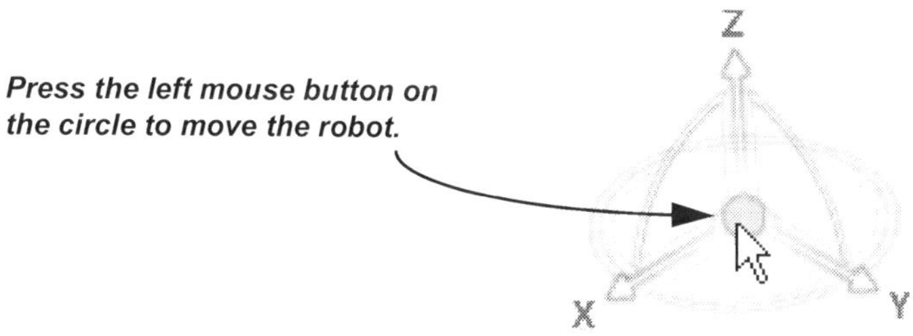


Figure 21–20

Drag the robot to the component to be moved. The robot snaps and reorients to geometry belonging to the component, as shown in Figure 21–21. When the orientation is correct, release the left mouse button to place the robot.

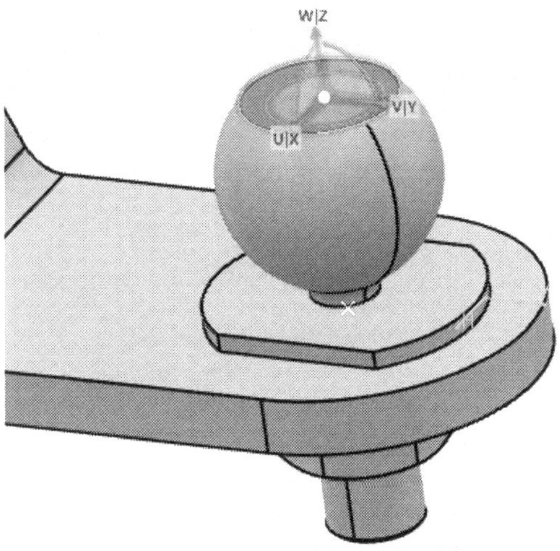


Figure 21–21

Once the robot has snapped to a component, the robot turns orange. If it does not turn orange:

1. Verify that the active model in the specification tree is an assembly.
2. Select the component in the model or specification tree to activate movement of the selected component.

You can activate any component for movement; it does not need to be the component to which the robot is snapped. You can also activate multiple components by selecting them while pressing <Ctrl>.

## Automatic Snap

You can automatically snap the robot to a selected object by right-clicking and selecting **Snap Automatically to Selected Object**, as shown in Figure 21–22.

*Turn off this option once you have finished moving components.*

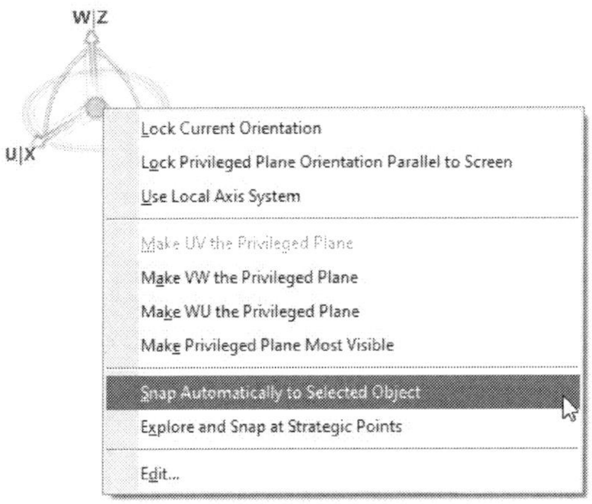


**Figure 21–22**

Once the option has been activated, select the component you want to move from the model or specification tree. The robot automatically snaps to the selected component, as shown in Figure 21–23.

*The system automatically selects the orientation of the robot based on the origin of the selected component.*

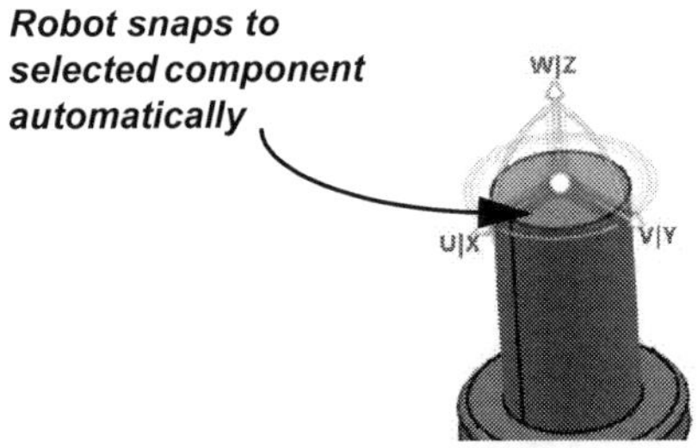


**Figure 21–23**

Once the robot has been activated on the component, only robot movements control the selected component(s).

If you want to move components while accounting for the placement constraints, hold down <Shift> while pressing the left mouse button. Note that more than one component might move, depending on how the constraints are defined.

More precise movements of a component can be achieved by right-clicking on the robot and selecting **Edit**. The Parameters for Robot Manipulation dialog box, shown in Figure 21–24, enables you to enter exact translation or rotation increment values for precise movements.

*It is recommended that you restore any changed values to 0 once you have completed the* ***Move*** *operation. This ensures that further operations do not snap to the previous increment values.*

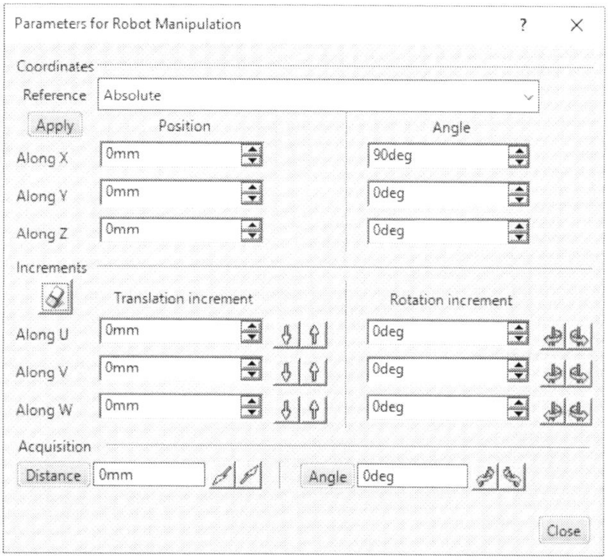


**Figure 21–24**

Once the component has been moved to the correct location, complete the movement by selecting another component to move or clicking anywhere on the screen to deactivate the robot control of the component. The robot returns to its default color and controls the entire assembly. To return the robot to its default position, right-click and select **Display > Reset Robot**, or drag the robot away from the model and move it anywhere in the background of the screen.

# Practice 21a Creating Assemblies I

## Practice Objectives

- Change product properties.
- Move components with the robot.
- Apply assembly Engineering Connections.

In this practice, you will create a new ball mount assembly, as shown in Figure 21–25. You will use constraints to assemble the four components of the assembly. The ball mount assembly that you create is a subassembly of a larger assembly.

**Figure 21–25**

## Task 1 - Import Components.

1. Import **Creating_Assemblies_I.3dxml**. A folder is imported containing the models needed for this practice. If you expand the folder, it will display as shown in Figure 21–26.

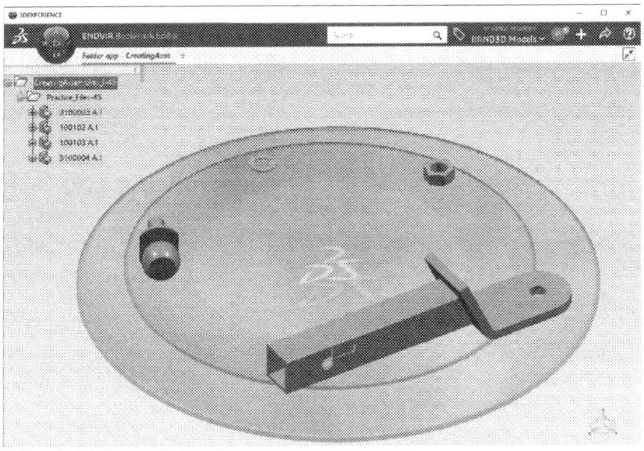

**Figure 21–26**

 

## Task 2 - Create a new Product file.

1. **In the Top Bar**, select (Add) **> Physical Product**.
2. In the Physical Product dialog box, type ***Your_Initials*_Ball Mount** in the *Title* field.
3. In the *Description* field, type **Ball Mount for Hitch**.
4. Click **OK**.

## Task 3 - Assemble the first component and fix it.

1. Ensure that you are in the Assembly Design app.
2. Right-click on the top level assembly (Ball Mount) in the specification tree and select **Insert** > **Existing Product**, as shown in Figure 21–27.

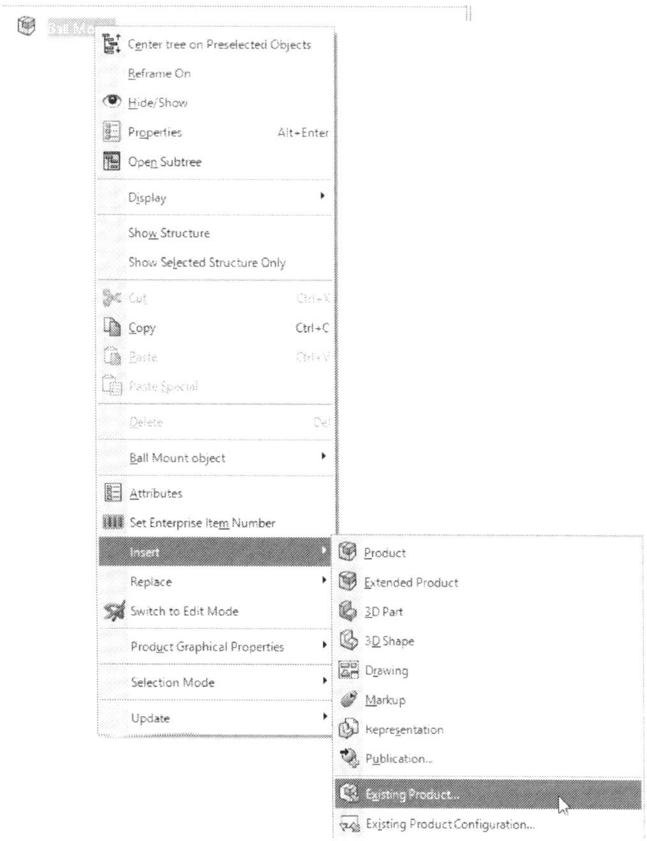


**Figure 21–27**

3. Select the *Folder app - CreatingAssemblies_I* tab and select **3100003** in the specification tree.

4. The system returns you to the *Ball Mount* assembly tab.Click on the screen to temporarily place the component. The component needs to be fixed.

5. Select the component, on screen or in the specification tree, and select  (Fix) from the context toolbar.

6. This component is now fixed. Note the *Engineering Connections* section in the specification tree, as shown in Figure 21–28.

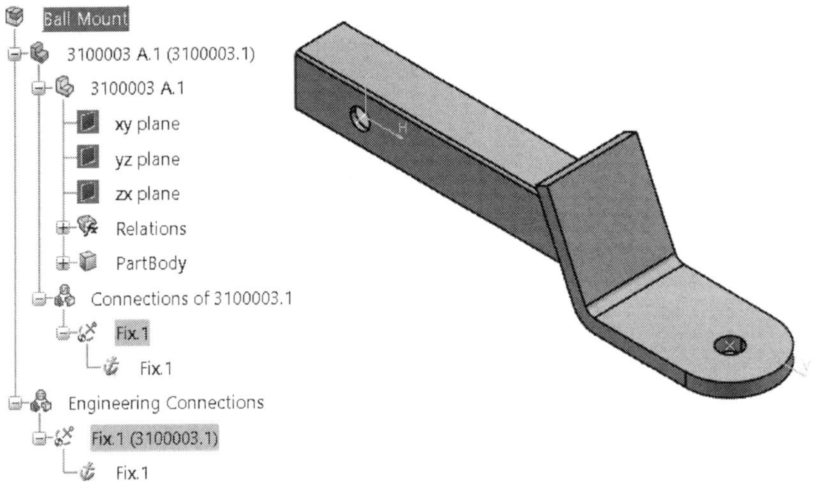


**Figure 21–28**

## Task 4 - Add the second component in a free position.

1. Bring another component into the assembly. Select **Ball Mount** in the specification tree, right-click and select **Insert>Existing Product**.

2. Select the *Folder app - CreatingAssemblies_I* tab and select **3100004** in the specification tree.

3. Note that the **3100004 (Ball)** part is brought into the assembly and placed in the default position, so it intersects the **3100003** component.

 

4. To view the **3100004 (Ball)** geometry, the part needs to be moved away from the fixed assembly. Drag the **U** axis of the robot on the **Ball** part as shown in Figure 21–29.

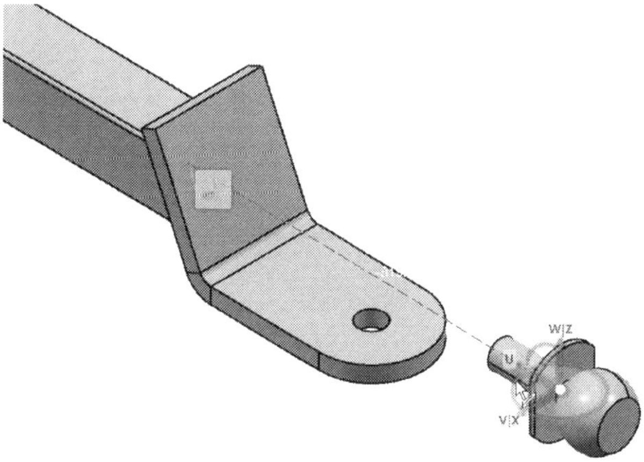


**Figure 21–29**

## Task 5 - Constrain the 3100004 (Ball) part.

1. Click on the screen to temporarily place the component.
2. In the *Assembly* section of the Action Bar, click  (Engineering Connection).
3. In the Engineering Connection Definition dialog box that opens, select Coincidence constraint, as shown in Figure 21–30.

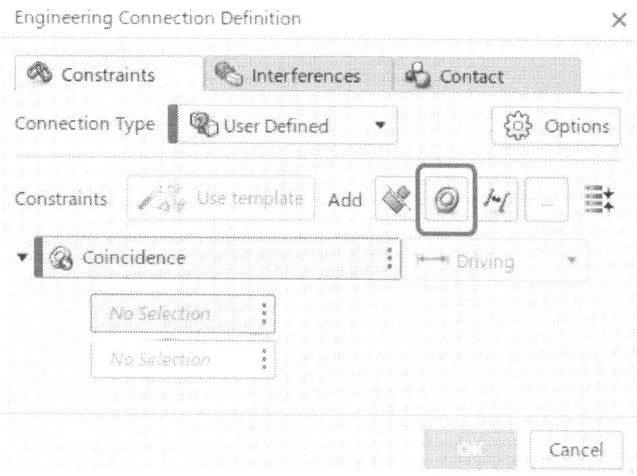


**Figure 21–30**

4. Select the axis of the Ball stem by selecting the cylindrical surface, as shown in Figure 21–31. You might need to zoom into the part.

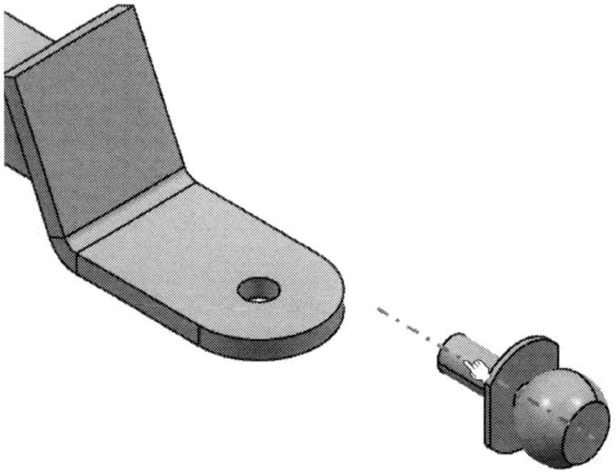

**Figure 21–31**

5. Select the axis on the base part by selecting the inner cylindrical surface of the hole, as shown in Figure 21–32.

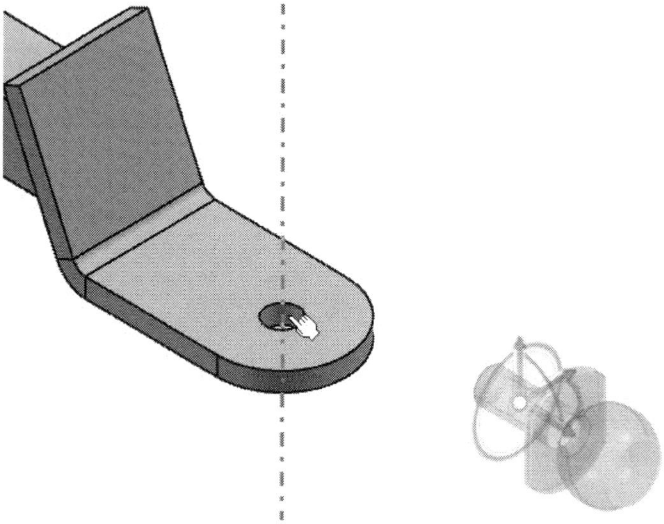

**Figure 21–32**

6. Part **3100004** is now partially constrained. The assembly updates the position of all of the components. The assembly displays similar to Figure 21–33.

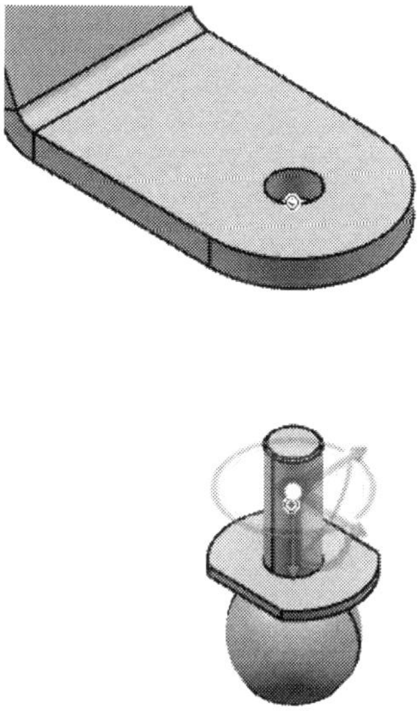

**Figure 21–33**

7. To control the orientation of the axial Vectors, select  (Opposite) as shown in Figure 21–34.

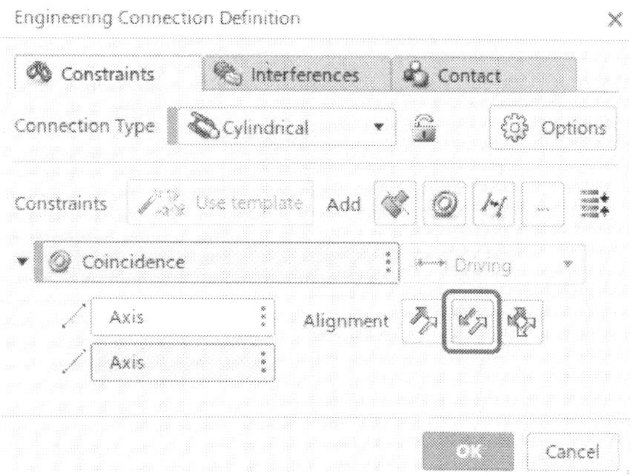


**Figure 21–34**

8. The assembly updates the position of all of the components. The assembly displays similar to Figure 21–35.

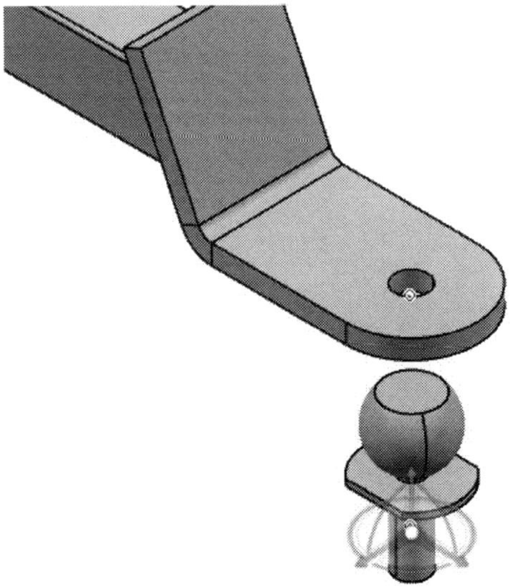

Figure 21–35

## Design Considerations

The **Ball** (Part **3100004**) is only constrained along its axis. Therefore, it can still be translated and rotated on its axis.

9. To lock the position of the Ball along the coincident axis, in the Engineering Connection dialog box, click the Contact constraint icon, as shown in Figure 21–36.

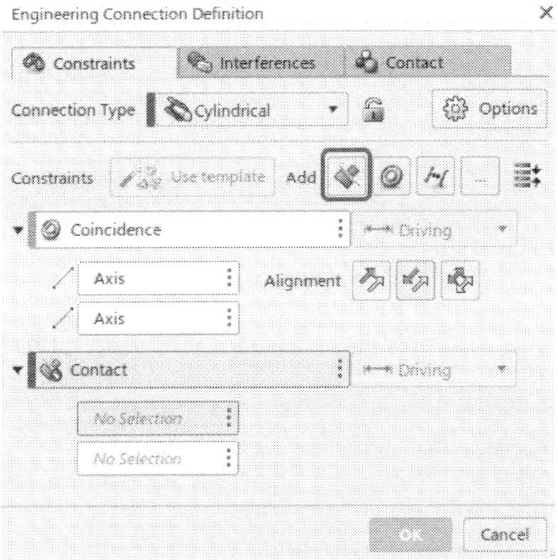


Figure 21–36

10. Select the mating surface of the slide, as shown in Figure 21–37.

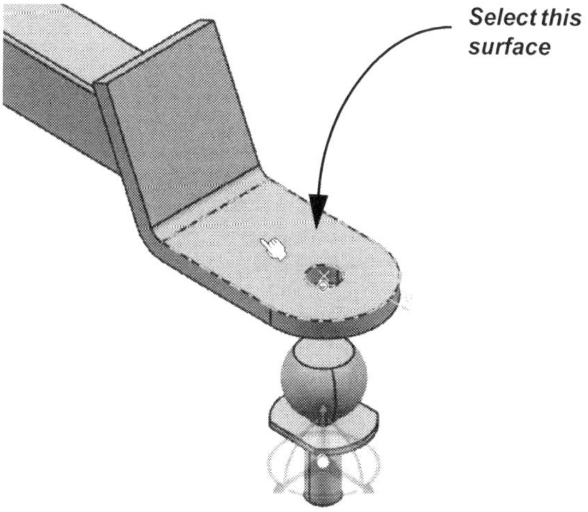


**Figure 21–37**

11. Select the underside surface of the **Ball**, as shown in Figure 21–38.

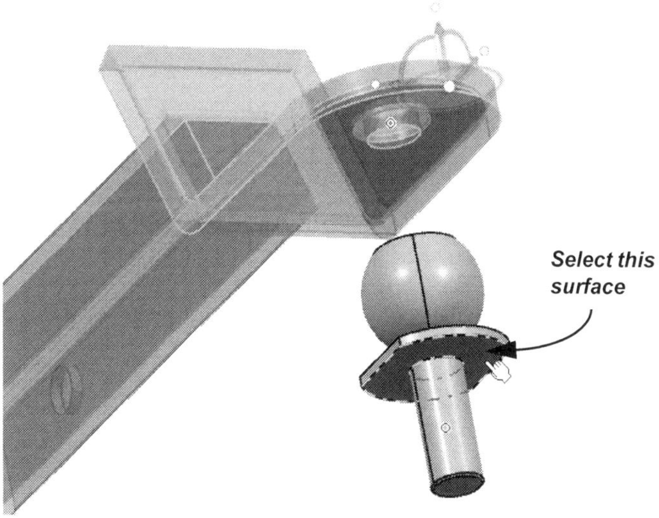


**Figure 21–38**

12. The position of the components updates, as shown in Figure 21–39.

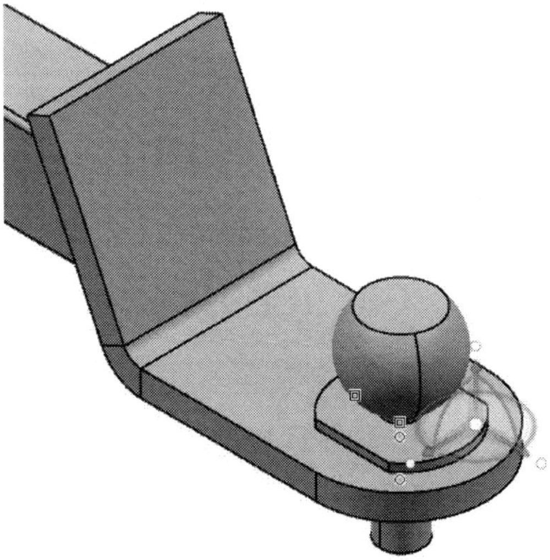

Figure 21–39

13. The **Ball** can still rotate about the coincident axis. Add an angle constraint to the still open Engineering Connection dialog box to fully constrain the ball by clicking the Show all possible constraints icon, and then the Parallelism icon, as shown in Figure 21–40.

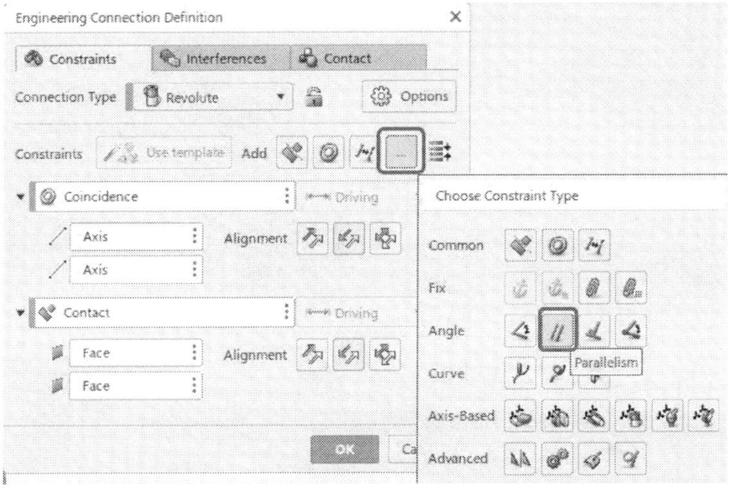


Figure 21–40

14. Select the two surfaces shown in Figure 21–41.

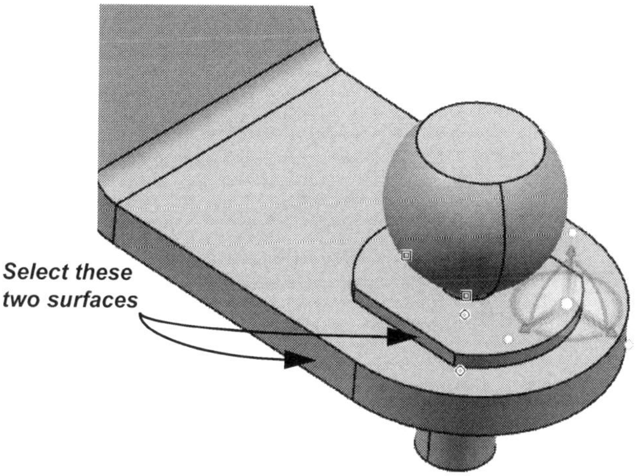


Figure 21–41

15. To control the orientation of the planes' Normal Vectors, select  (Same), as shown in Figure 21–42.

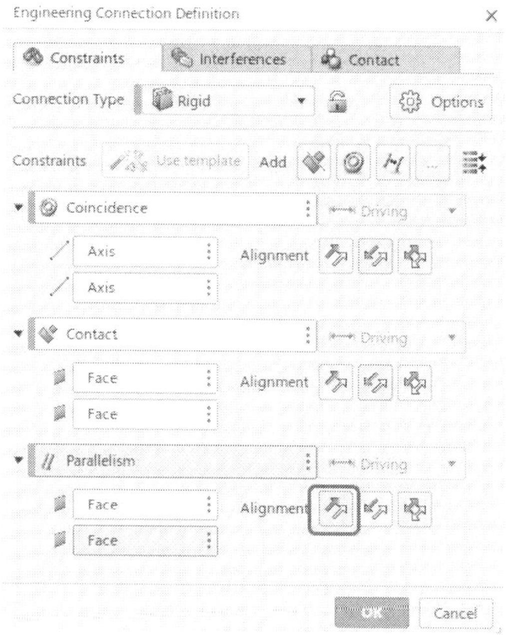


Figure 21–42

16. Click **OK** to finalize the Constraints and close the Engineering Connection Definition dialog box.

17. A dialog box reporting *Undefined Interference Specifications* will open. Click **No** to omit creation of the Interference specification, as shown in Figure 21–43.

*To avoid seeing this warning, disable Check interferences at validation under* ***Me>Preferences>App Preferences>3D Modeling>Mechanical System>Assembly Design****.*

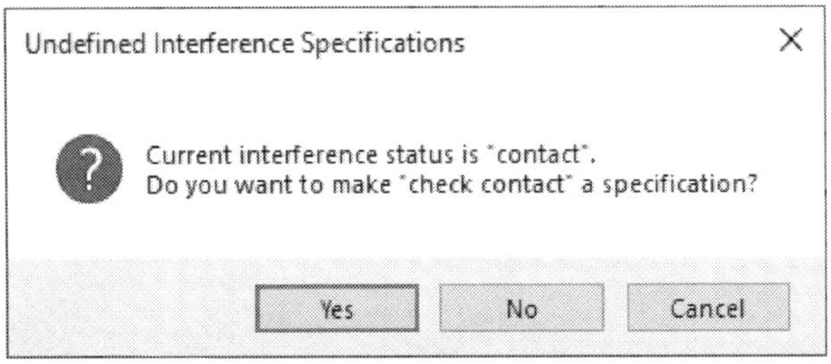


**Figure 21–43**

18. The **Ball** component is now fully constrained, and displays as shown in Figure 21–44.

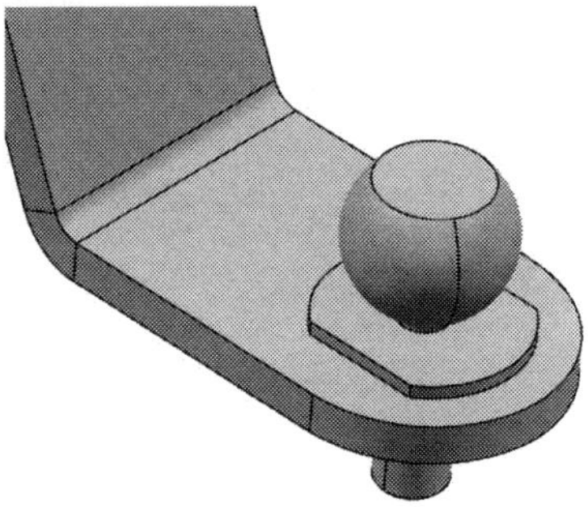

**Figure 21–44**

## Task 6 - Assemble the washer.

1. Right-click on Ball Mount and selecting **Insert > Existing Product**.
2. Select the *Folder app - CreatingAssemblies_I* tab and select **100103** in the specification tree.
3. The system switches back to the *Ball Mount* tab.

4. Use the robot axes to move the washer to a position clear of the Product (as shown in Figure 21–45), then click on the screen to temporarily locate the washer.

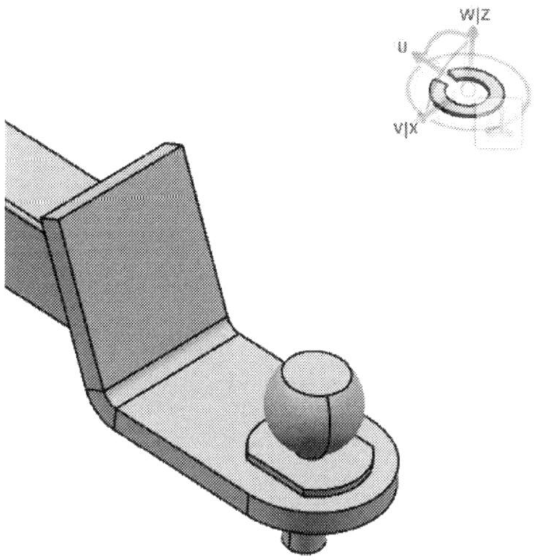


**Figure 21–45**

5. In the *Assembly* section of the Action Bar, click  (Engineering Connection).

6. In the Engineering Connection Definition dialog box, click  (Coincidence).

7. Click **Options** and in the Movable component drop-down list select **Second**, as shown in Figure 21–46, to enable part **100103** to be positioned relative to the product.

Figure 21–46

8. Select the axis of the ball first, then zoom in and select the axis of the washer. Selecting the cylindrical surface will select the axis.

9. Click **OK** to finalize the Constraint and close the Engineering Connection dialog box.

10. Click **No** to omit creation of the Interference specification.

11. Click  (Engineering Connection).

12. In the Engineering Connection dialog box, select  (Contact) to create a Contact Constraint.

13. Select the surface of the washer and the underside surface of the slide, as shown in Figure 21–47.

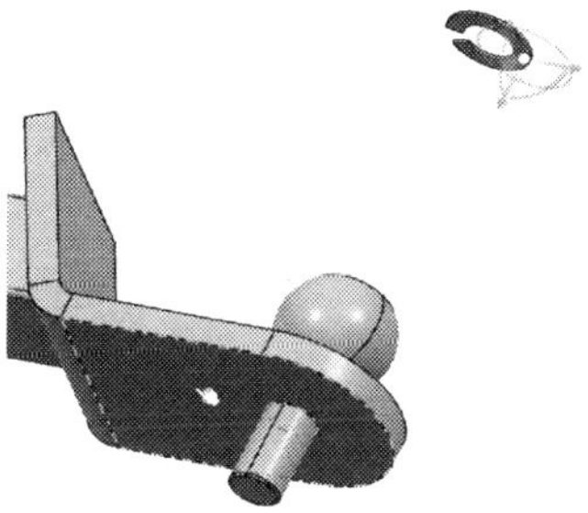

Figure 21–47

14. Click **OK** to finalize the Constraint and close the Engineering Connection Definition dialog box.

15. Click **No** to omit the creation of the Interference specification.

16. To update the position of the components, click  (Update).

17. The washer still has a degree of freedom to rotate about the coincident axis. Double-click on the 3rd Engineering Connection in the specification tree to re-open it.

18. Select **User Defined** as the *Connection type*. Click  (Show all possible constraints) and select  (Parallelism), as shown in Figure 21–48.

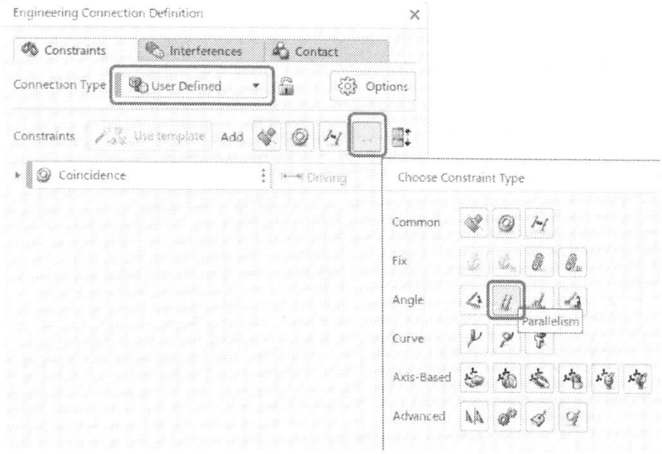


Figure 21–48

19. Select the two surfaces shown in Figure 21–49.

**Figure 21–49**

20. Click **OK** to close the dialog box.

21. Update the assembly, if necessary.

## Task 7 - Add the nut (100102) component.

1. Insert **100102** (**Nut**) into **Ball Mount** by right-clicking on Ball Mount and selecting **Insert > Existing Product**.
2. Select the *Folder app - CreatingAssemblies_I* tab and select **100102** in the specification tree.
3. The system switches back to the *Ball Mount* tab.
4. Use the robot to place the new component in open space, as shown in Figure 21–50.

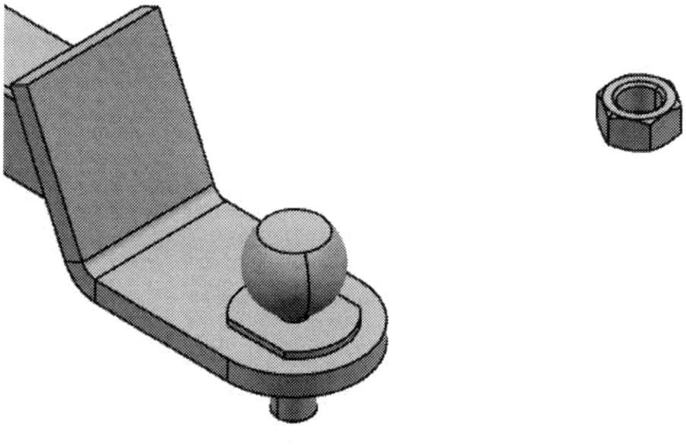

**Figure 21–50**

5. Click (Engineering Connection).
6. In the Engineering Connection dialog box, select **Options > Movable components > First**.
7. In the Engineering Connection Definition dialog box, select (Coincidence). Select the axis of the nut first, then the axis of the ball, as shown in Figure 21–51.

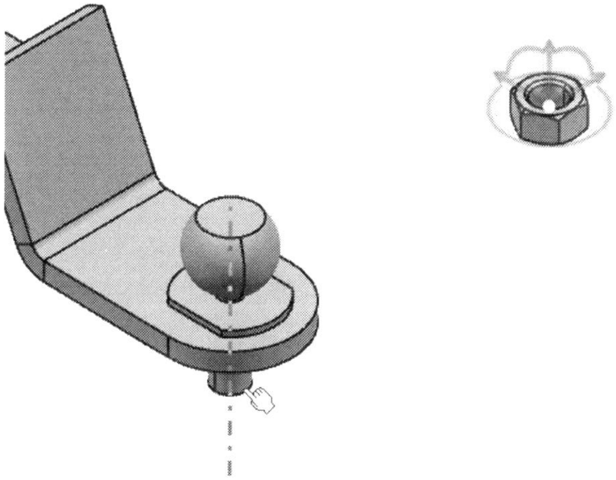

**Figure 21–51**

8. Click **OK** to finalize the Constraint and close the Engineering Connection dialog box.
9. Click **No** to omit the creation of the Interference specification.
10. Click (Engineering Connection).
11. Select (Contact) to create a Contact Constraint.

12. Select the flat surface of the nut and the surface of the washer, and the position updates as shown in Figure 21–52.

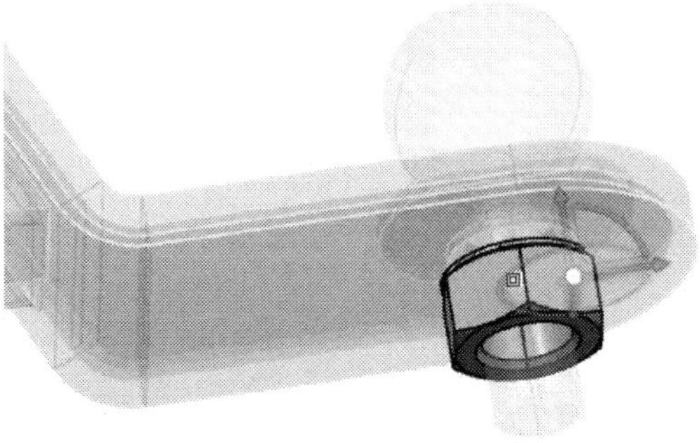

**Figure 21–52**

13. The nut still has a degree of freedom to rotate about the coincident axis. In the Engineering Connection dialog box, select  (Show all possible constraints) and select  (Fix together) and select both the nut and the washer parts to fix them together.

14. Click **OK** to finalize the Constraint and close the Engineering Connection dialog box.

15. Click **No** to omit the creation of the Interference specification.

16. Save the assembly and close all tabs.

 

# Practice 21b Creating Assemblies II

## Practice Objectives

- Apply Engineering Connections.
- Insert a subassembly.

In this practice, you will create the assembly shown in Figure 21–53. This assembly will consist of various parts and the subassembly that you created in a previous practice.

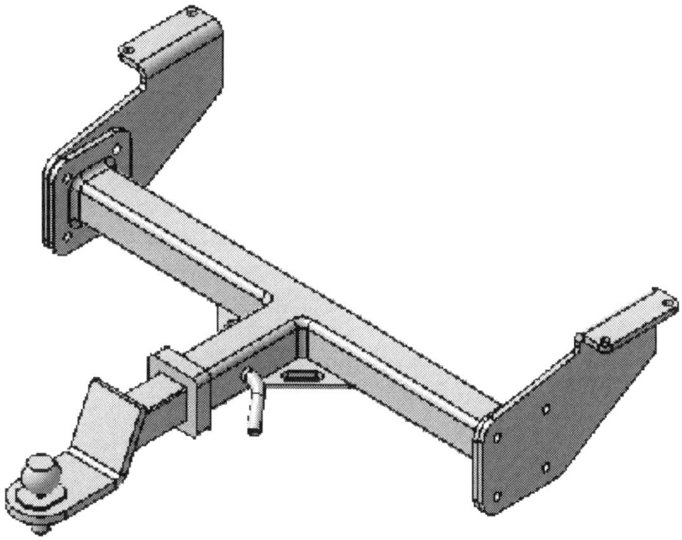

**Figure 21–53**

### Task 1 - Create a new Product file.

1. Import **Creating_Assemblies_II.3dxml**.
2. **In the Top Bar**, select  (Add)>**Physical Product**.
3. In the Physical Product dialog box, type ***Your_Initials*_Hitch** in the *Title* field.
4. In the *Description* field, type **Main Hitch Assembly**
5. Click **OK**.

## Task 2 - Assemble the first component and fix it.

1. Right-click on the top level assembly (Hitch) in the specification tree and select **Insert > Existing Product**.
2. Select the *Folder app - Creating_Assemblies_II* tab and select **310000** in the specification tree.
3. Select **310000** in the specification tree and click  (Fix) from the context toolbar.
4. This component is now fixed. Note the *Engineering Connections* section in the specification tree.

## Task 3 - Assemble the braces.

1. Insert the **3100001** component into **Hitch** using the same method as in Task 2, steps 1 to 3.
2. Use the robot to drag and rotate the model into the approximate orientation shown in Figure 21–54, Use the arrows to drag translation and the arcs to drag rotation.

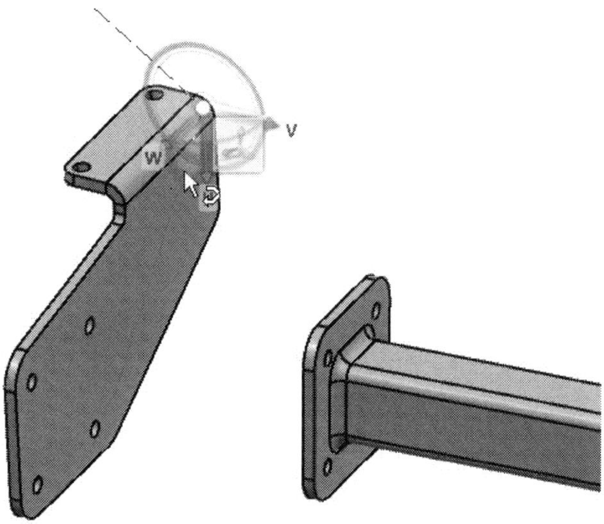


**Figure 21–54**

3. Click on the screen to temporarily place the component.

 

4. Create an  (Engineering Connection) and insert a  (Coincidence) constraint between the axes, as shown in Figure 21–55. The assembly updates automatically.

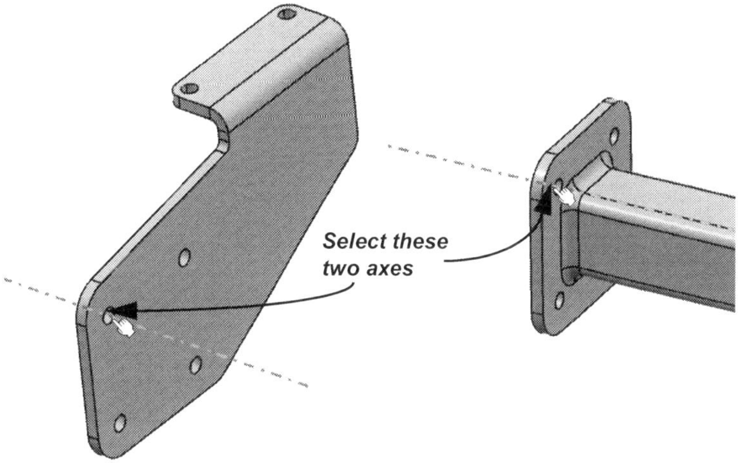


**Figure 21–55**

5. Within the same Engineering Connection, insert a  (Contact) constraint between the surfaces shown in Figure 21–56.

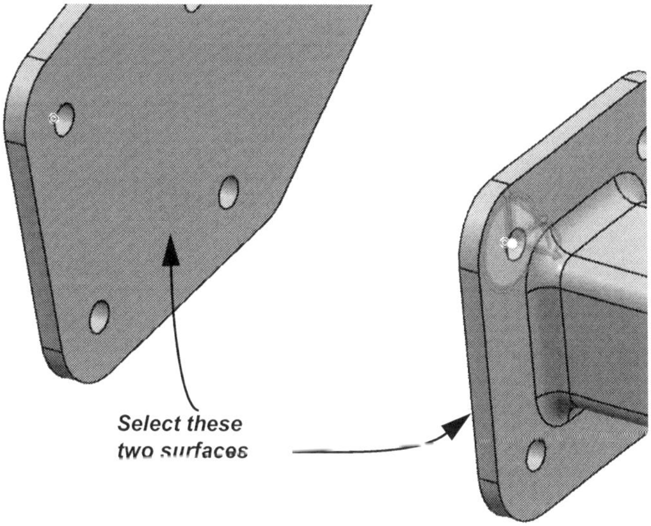


**Figure 21–56**

6. The assembly updates automatically. Within the same Engineering Connection, select (Show all possible constraints) and select (Parallelism) constraint option between the surfaces shown in Figure 21–57. The assembly updates automatically.

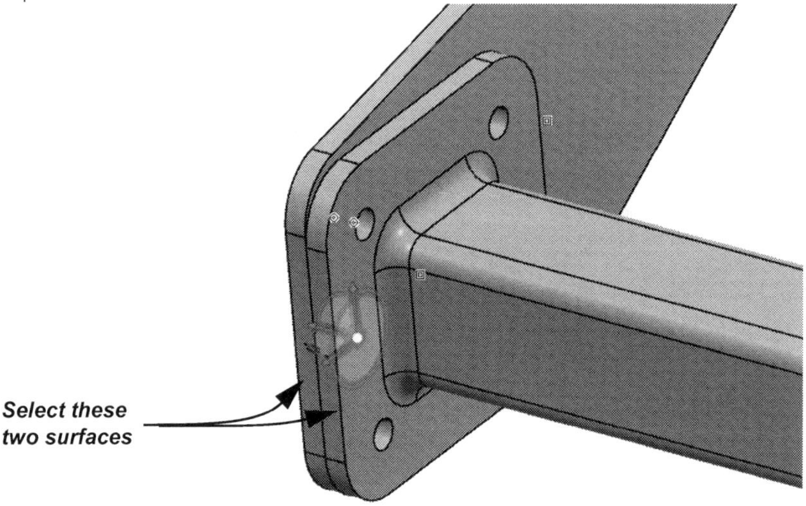


**Figure 21–57**

7. Select **OK** and **No** to complete the Engineering Connection.
8. Assemble **3100002** using Steps 1-7 described in this Task. The assembly displays as shown in Figure 21–58.

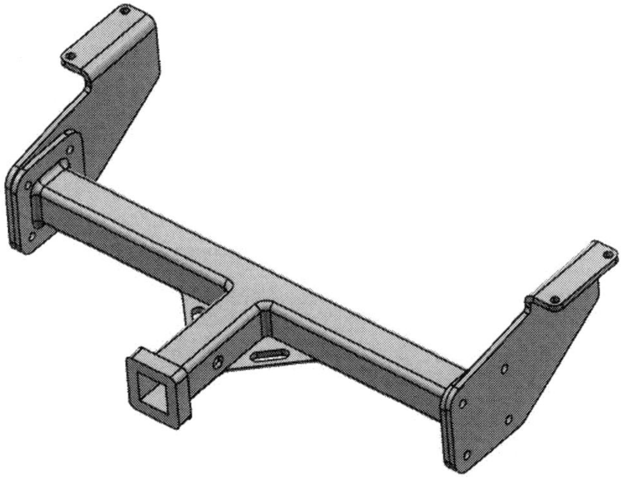

**Figure 21–58**

## Task 4 - Assemble the Ball_Mount subassembly.

1. Insert the **65100010** assembly into **Hitch** by right-clicking on Hitch and selecting **Insert > Existing Product**.
2. Select the *Folder app - Creating_Assemblies_II* tab and select **65100010**.
3. Drag the **Ball_Mount** assembly away from the model and use the robot to manipulate the sub-assembly into a similar position as shown in Figure 21–59. Click to drop it into the product.

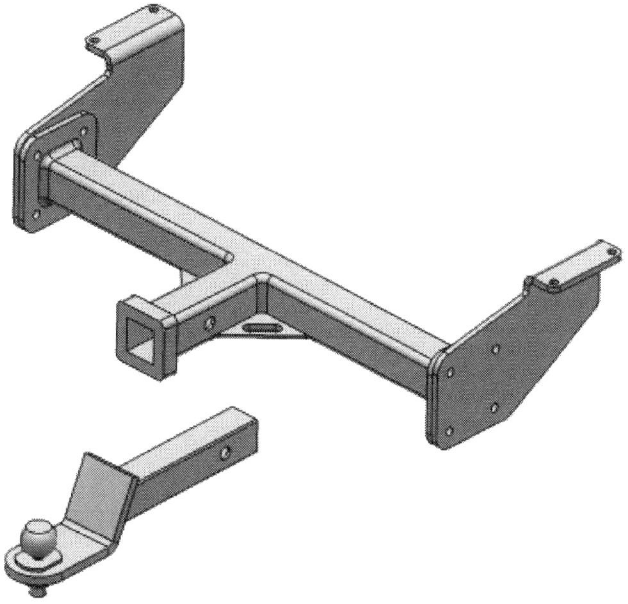

**Figure 21–59**

4. Select (Engineering Connection). With the Engineering Connection Definition dialog box open, insert a (Coincidence) constraint between the axes as shown in Figure 21–60. The assembly updates automatically.

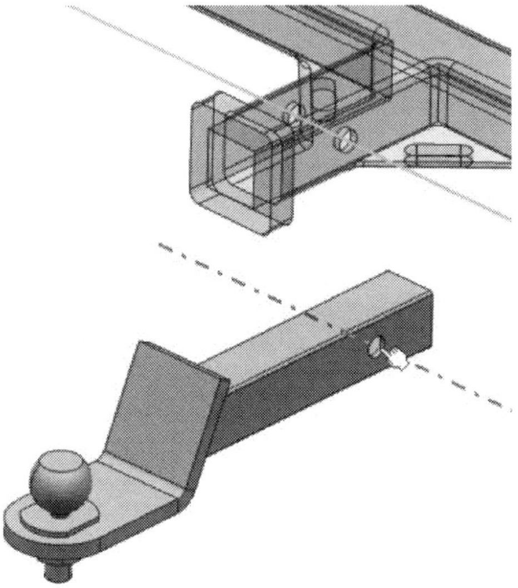

**Figure 21–60**

5. **65100010** is now partially constrained. Insert an (Offset) constraint to position along the axis by offsetting two surfaces.

6. Select the surface on the **Slide** and on the **T-Support**, as shown in Figure 21–61.

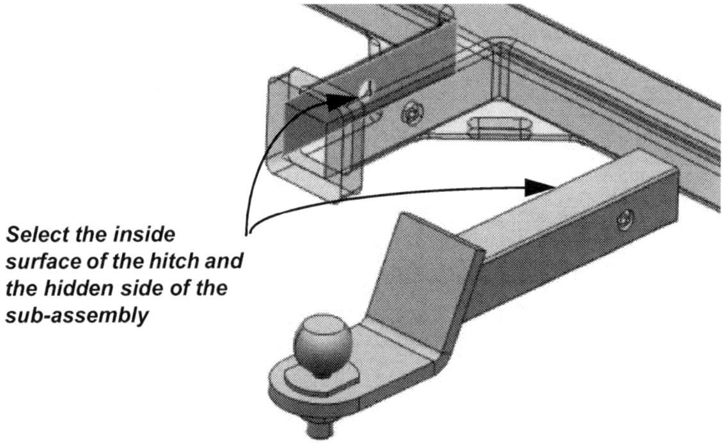


**Figure 21–61**

7. Within the Engineering Connection Definition dialog box, ensure that *Alignment* is set to  (Opposite) for each reference and enter a *Distance value* of [0.4] as shown in Figure 21–62.

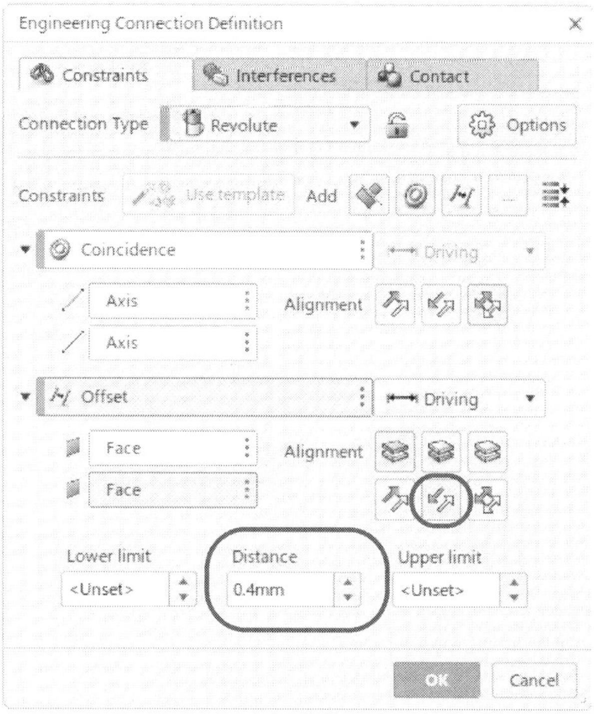


**Figure 21–62**

8. Insert an Angle Constraint using the  (Show all possible constraints) icon. Click  (Parallelism) and reference the surfaces shown in Figure 21–63.

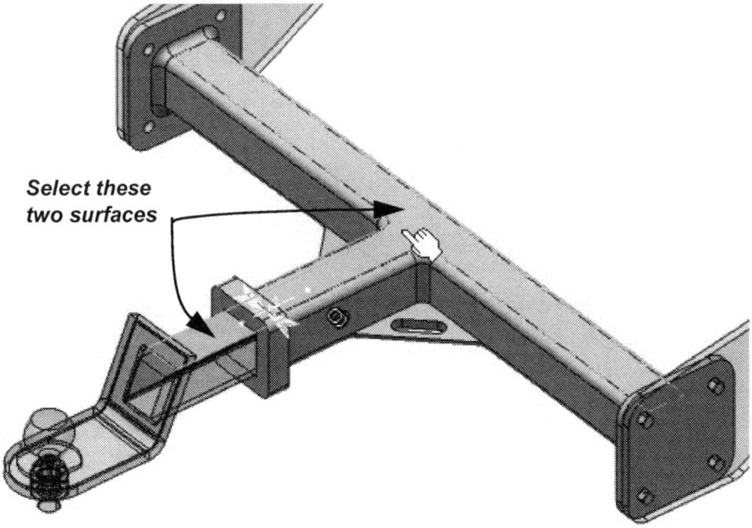


**Figure 21–63**

9. Click **OK** to finalize the Constraint and close the Engineering Connection Definition dialog box.

10. Click **OK** to omit the creation of the Interference specification. Update the assembly. The model displays as shown in Figure 21–64.

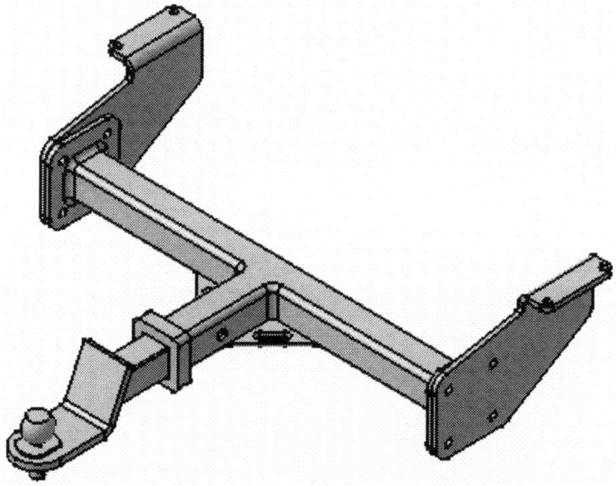

**Figure 21–64**

## Task 5 - Assemble the pin.

1. Insert **3100005** into **65000011** by right-clicking on **Hitch** and selecting **Insert > Existing Product**.

2. Drag the pin away from the model and use the robot to manipulate the component into a similar position as shown in Figure 21–65. Click to drop it into the product.

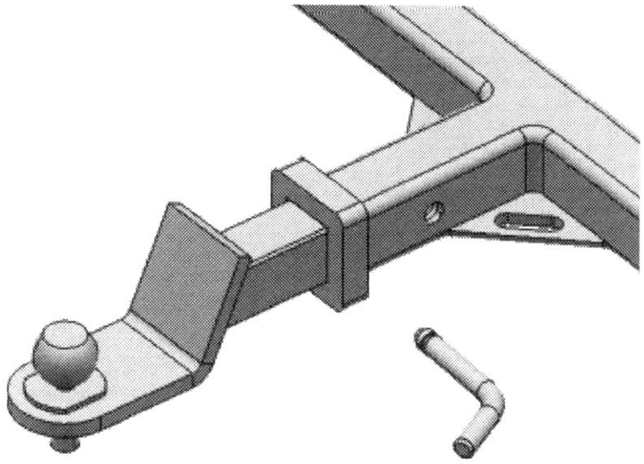

**Figure 21–65**

3. Select  (Engineering Connection) and insert a  (Coincidence) constraint between the hole of the **T-Support** and the axis of the **Pin**, as shown in Figure 21–66.

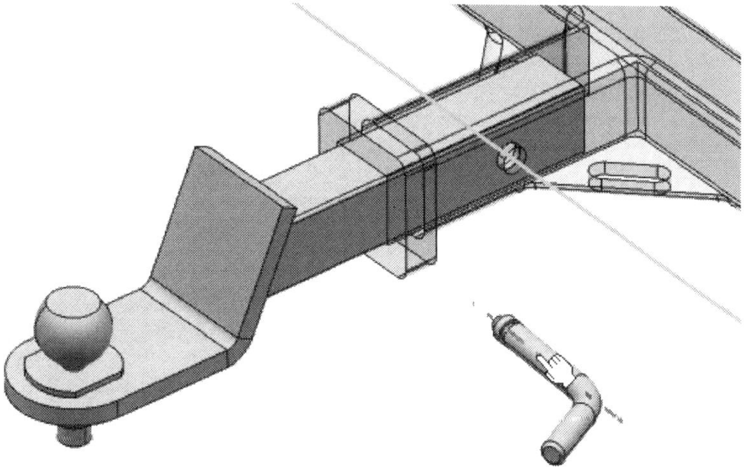

**Figure 21–66**

4. In the active Engineering Connection Definition dialog box, insert an  (Offset) constraint and select the face of the Pin shown in Figure 21–67.

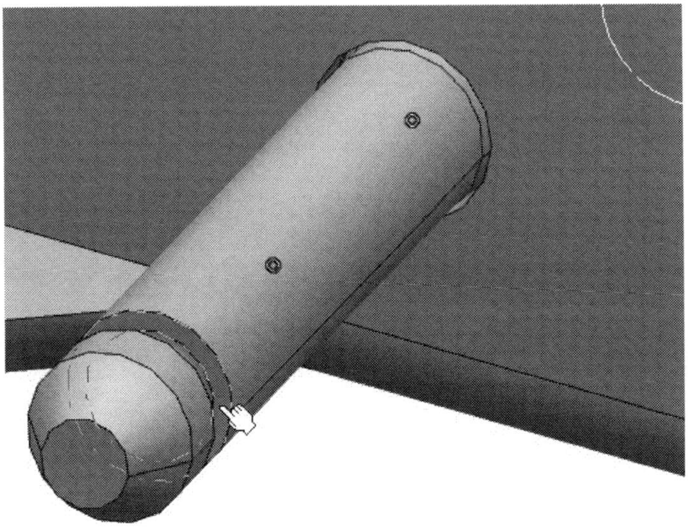

**Figure 21–67**

5. Select the face of **T-Support** as shown in Figure 21–68.

   Ensure that the *alignment* is set to  (Same) and enter an *offset value* of [0].

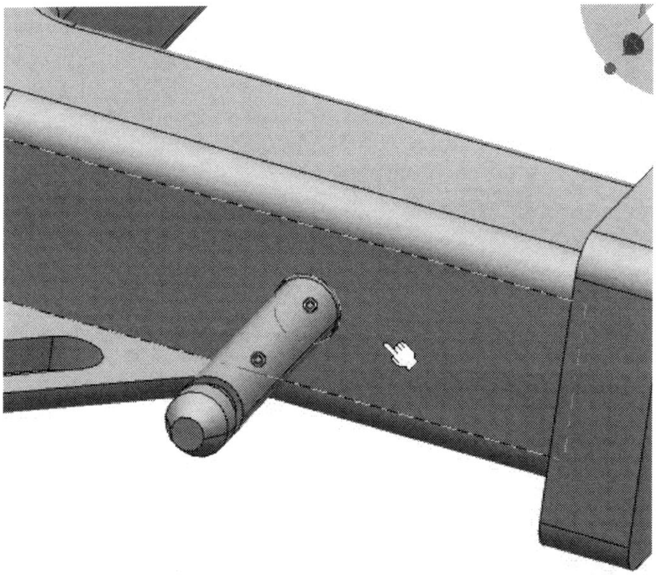

**Figure 21–68**

6. Select **OK** and (Update) the assembly. The model displays as shown in Figure 21–69.

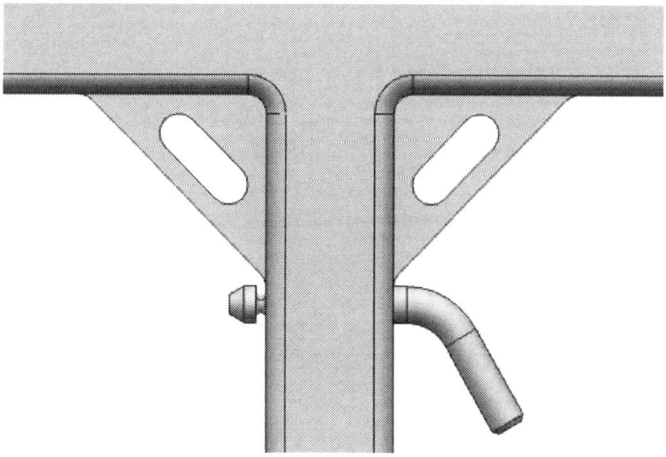

**Figure 21–69**

**Task 6 - Assemble the Retaining Pin (3100006).**

1. In this task, you will position the **Retaining Pin** model in the assembly and then constrain its location by fixing it to the **Pin** model.

2. Insert **3100006** into **65000011** by right-clicking on **Hitch** and selecting **Insert > Existing Product**.

3. Drag the retaining pin away from the model and use the robot to manipulate the component into a similar position as shown in Figure 21–70. Click to drop it into the product.

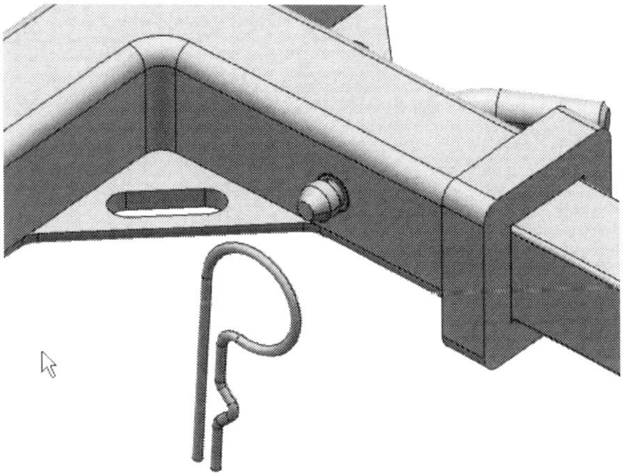

**Figure 21–70**

## Design Considerations

Note the curved geometry of the **Retaining Pin**. Few references can be selected from the model to position it relative to the **T-Support** and **Pin**. For this reason, reference elements have been added to the model that will assist during constraint creation.

4. Show the **RefGeom** geometrical set under **Retaining Pin** (**3100006**) and **Pin** (**3100005**) in the specification tree. The **Retaining Pin** model contains two reference planes and a reference point, as shown in Figure 21–71. The **Pin** model contains a reference plane located at the center of the groove.

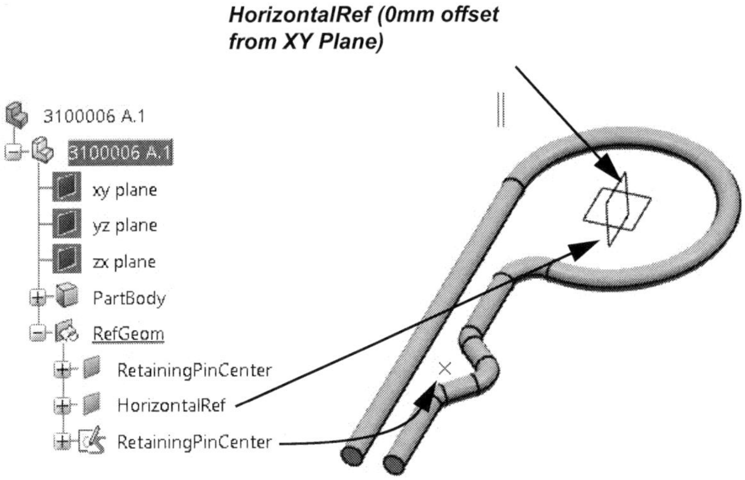


Figure 21–71

5. Using two Engineering Connections, insert the constraints listed in the table below using Figure 21–72 as a guide. The parallelism constraint will require its own Engineering Connection due to referencing the **T-Support**. Modify the vectors of the parallelism constraint to match the **Retaining Pin** orientation as shown in Figure 21–72.

| No. | Constraint | Reference 1 | Reference 2 |
|---|---|---|---|
| 1 | (Coincident) | Axis of Pin | RetainingPinCenter (sketched point) of Retaining Pin |
| 2 | (Offset) (0mm) | GrooveCenter (plane) of Pin | RetainingPinCenter (plane) of Retaining Pin |
| 3 | (Parallelism) | Face of T-Support | HorizontalRef (plane) of Retaining Pin |

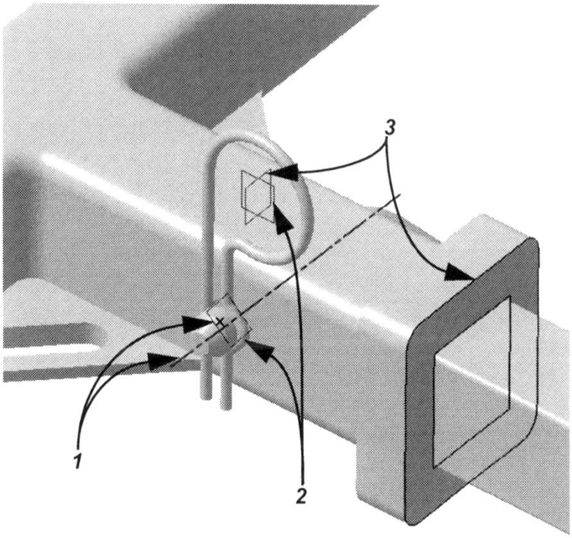


**Figure 21–72**

6. Update the assembly and hide RefGeom from **Retaining Pin**. The completed model displays as shown in Figure 21–73.

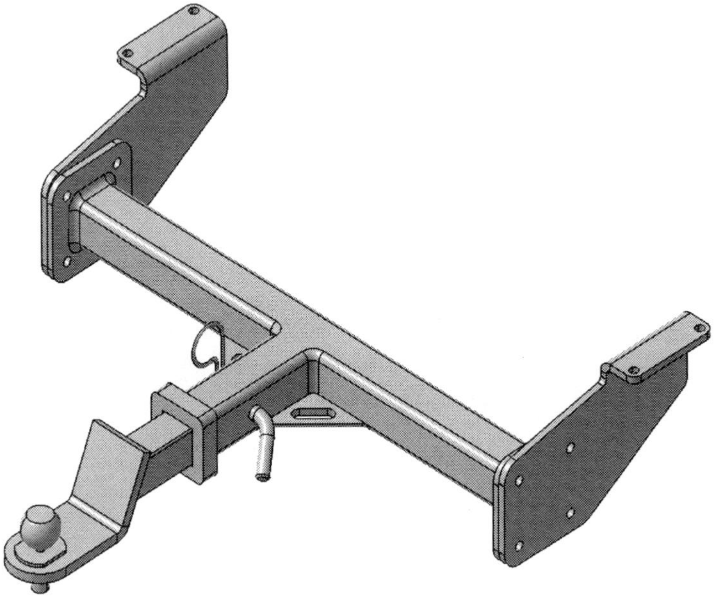

**Figure 21–73**

7. Save the assembly and close all tabs.

# Practice 21c Creating Assemblies III

## Practice Objectives

- Create a new product.
- Apply Engineering Constraints.

In this practice, you will create the assembly shown in Figure 21–74.

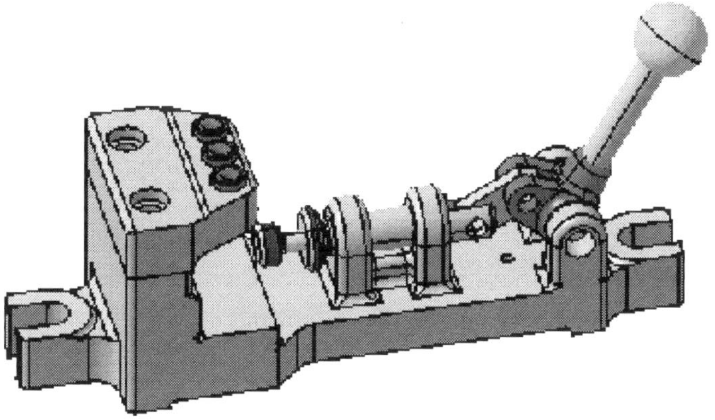

**Figure 21–74**

## Task 1 - Import Components.

1. Import **Bore_Device_Create.3dxml**.
2. In the specification tree, right-click **Bore_Device_Assembly** and select **Open**.
3. In the *View* section of the Action Bar, click  (Fit All In).

4. The assembly displays as shown in Figure 21–75. Note that the components are placed in the assembly but have not been constrained.

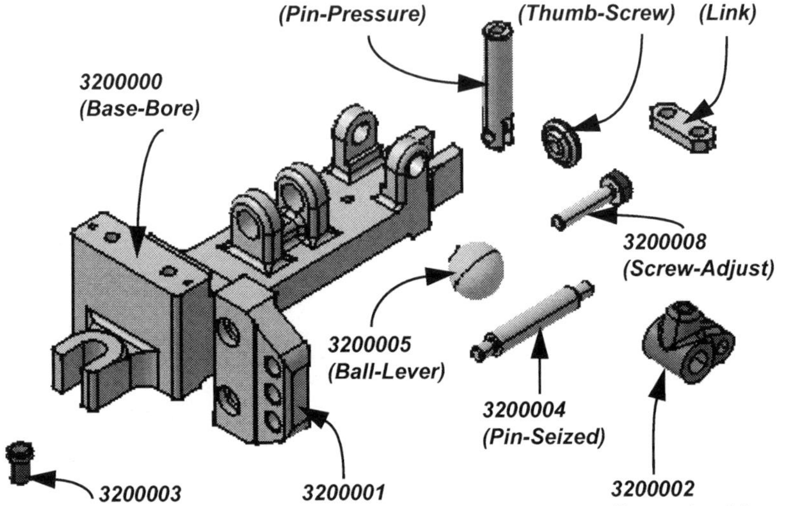


Figure 21–75

## Task 2 - Assemble the components.

1. Select the **Base-Bore(3200000)** part and select  (Fix) using the context menu that appears, as shown in Figure 21–76.

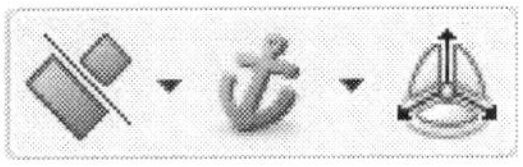

Figure 21–76

2. Assemble the **Drill Fixture(3200001)**, to the base shown in Figure 21–77. Instead of using the  (Engineering Connection) command, preselect the references of the components you want to constrain. Then, select the Constraints from the Context menu that appears. Use  (Coincidence),  (Contact), and  (Parallel) constraints to Assemble the **Drill Fixture**.

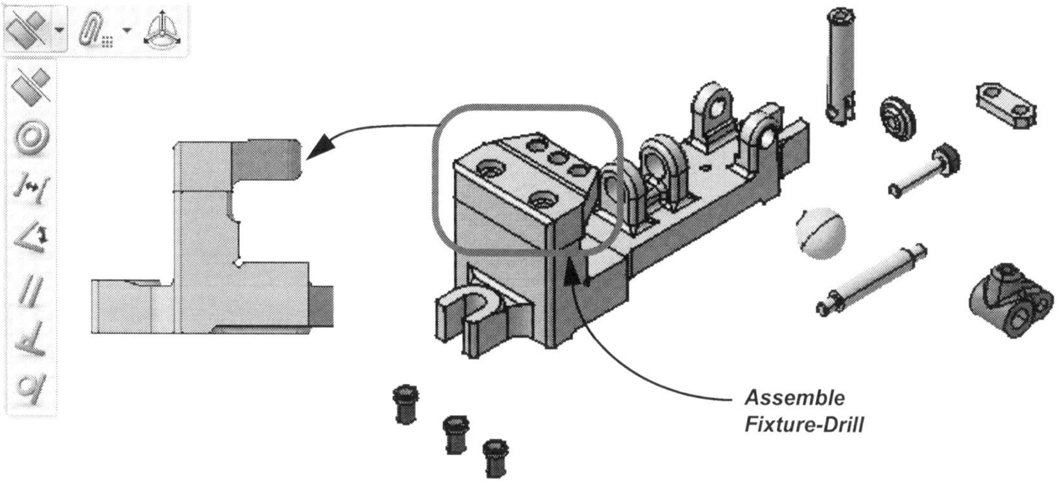


**Figure 21–77**

3. Assemble the three drill bushings into the drill fixture.

4. Assemble the **Ball-Lever 3200005**, **Pin-Seized 3200004**, and **Lever-Angle 3200002**, as shown in Figure 21–78.

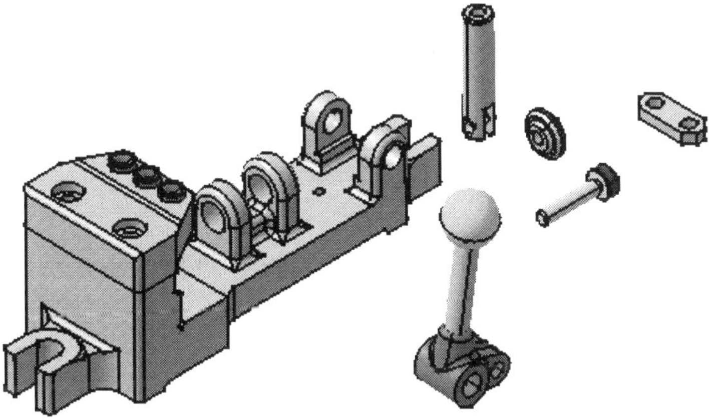

**Figure 21–78**

5. Assemble **Lever-Angle-3200002**, **Link-3200007**, and **Pin-Pressure 3200006**, as shown in Figure 21–79.

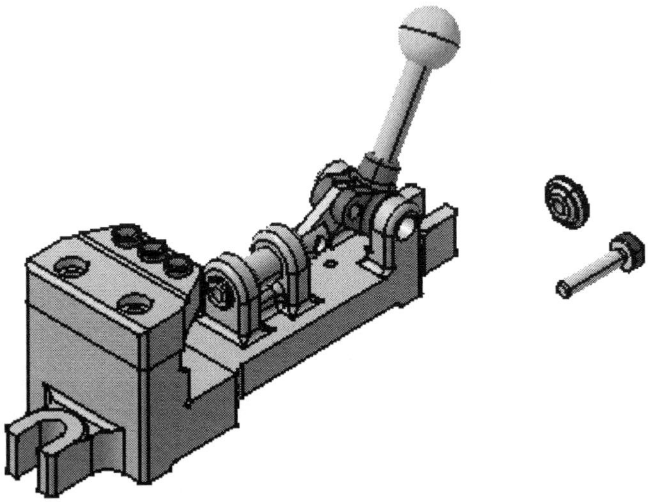

**Figure 21–79**

6. Assemble the remaining components, as shown in Figure 21–80.

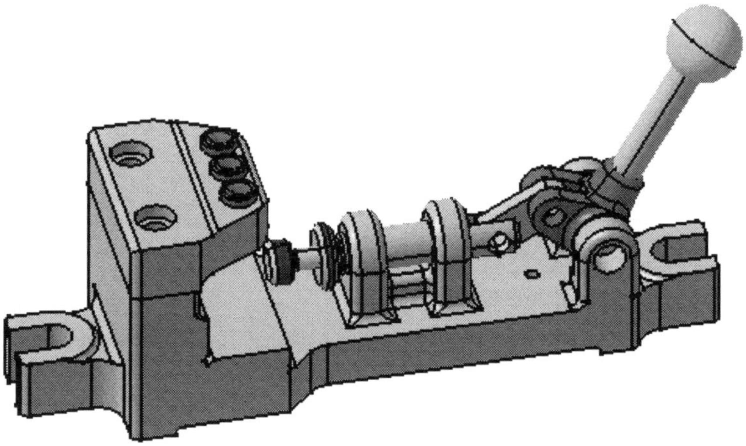

**Figure 21–80**

7. Save the file and close the assembly.

**NOTE:** An additional assembly practice is found in Practice B17 at the end of this guide.

# Chapter Review Questions

1. Parent/child relationships cannot exist between the components in an assembly.
   a. True
   b. False
2. What types of components can be added to a product? (Select all that apply.)
   a. Parts
   b. Products
   c. Drawings
3. Multiple components can be added to an assembly at the same time.
   a. True
   b. False
4. Which constraint can be used to constrain a component so that two surfaces are mated but you maintain the flexibility of entering an offset value if the design intent changes?
   a.  (Contact)
   b.  (Offset)
   c. 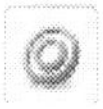 (Coincidence)
   d.  (Angle)

5. Which of the assemblies shown in Figure 21–81 could have used the coincidence constraint to constrain surfaces C and 2 and surfaces A and 3? (Select all that apply.)

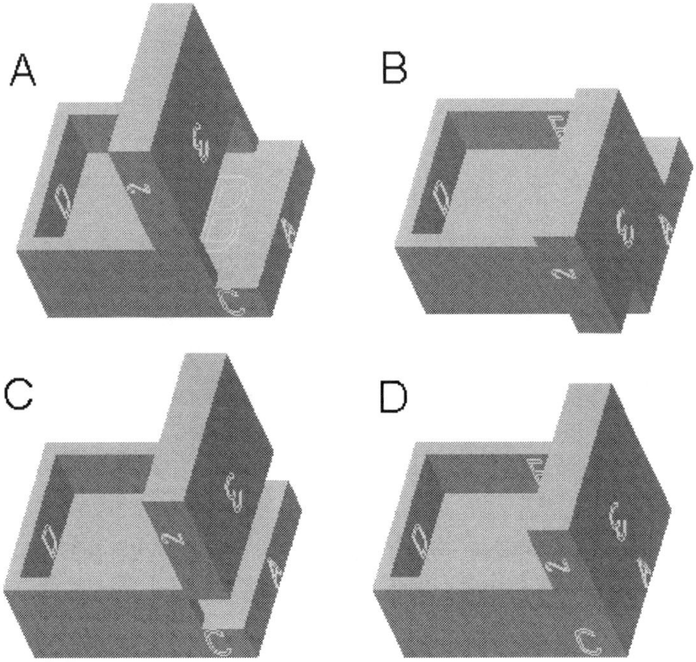


**Figure 21–81**

   a. A
   b. B
   c. C
   d. D

6. Once a constraint is created, the only way to change it to another type is to delete it and recreate it.
   a. True
   b. False

7. How can you force CATIA to obey the assembly constraints while moving components using the compass?
   a. Press and hold <Ctrl> while using the compass.
   b. Press and hold the middle mouse button while using the compass.
   c. Press and hold <Shift> while using the compass.
   d. Constraints cannot be obeyed when using the compass to move components.

**Answers:** 1b, 2ab, 3a, 4b, 5cd, 6b, 7c

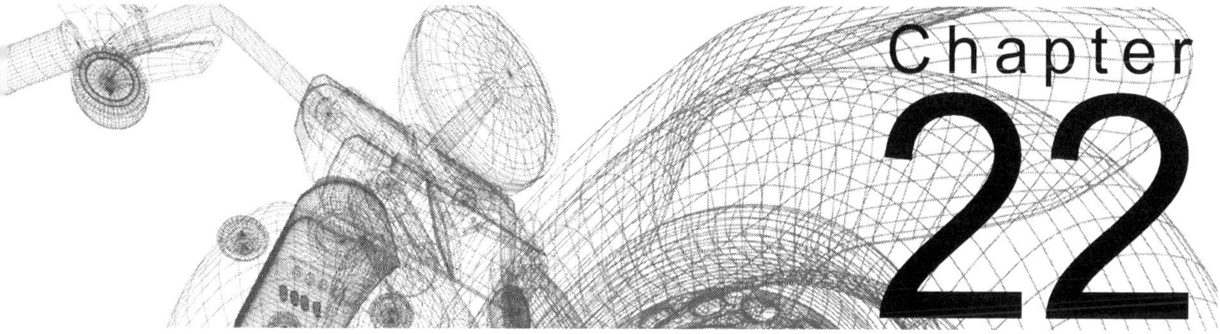


# Assembly Techniques

Knowledge on additional assembly techniques, as well as how to design in context enables designers to work with greater efficiency. Additionally, designing in the context of an assembly simulates a top-down design philosophy.

## Learning Objectives in This Chapter

- Place components using the **Copy** and **Paste** commands.
- Apply the **Assembly Pattern** command to quickly assemble components by referencing patterns.
- Use external references.

# 22.1 Additional Placement Options

If a component is used more than once in an assembly, you can add the components and position them accordingly using the Copy/Paste.

## Copy and Paste

Copy and Paste is an easy way to duplicate a component in an assembly. Select the required component from the specification tree, right-click and select **Copy**. Select the assembly that you want to copy into, right-click and select **Paste**. A duplicate instance of the component now exists. The instance name changes and can be modified, as shown in Figure 22–1.

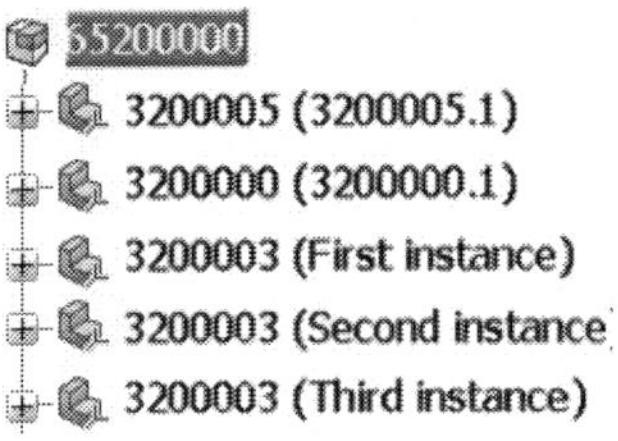


Figure 22–1

Copied components display directly *on top of* the original component in the assembly display. A copy (instance) must then be moved using the compass. Once moved, constraints can then be applied to position the copied component.

## Assembly Patterns

If a component is assembled by referencing the initial feature of a pattern, that pattern can be reused to quickly assemble more components. For example, the bolt shown in Figure 22–2 is assembled to the hole in the plate. This hole is the original hole that was patterned.

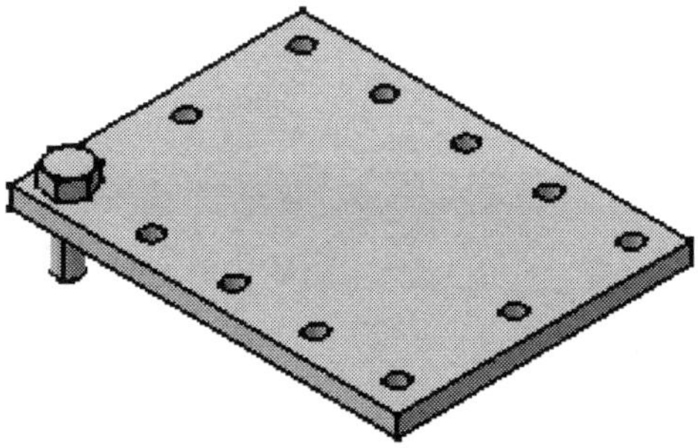

Figure 22–2

1. Click 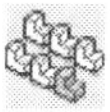 (Assembly Pattern).
2. Select the corresponding pattern in the specification tree of the plate to place a bolt at each hole, as shown in Figure 22–3.

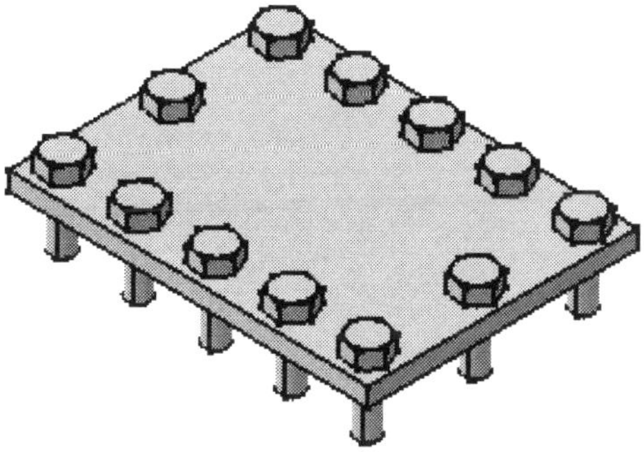

**Figure 22–3**

3. Select **OK** or click in the background to complete the operation.

## 22.2 Designing in Context

A powerful aspect of 3DEXPERIENCE is the ability to design in the context of an assembly. Parts and subassemblies can be created or modified in the presence of other components. Working in the context of the assembly is often referred to as *top-down design*.

While creating and/or editing components in the context of an assembly, external references can be created automatically. It is important to understand how external references are created. Therefore, carefully consider the selection of the following items:

- Selection of sketching planes
- Dimensional references
- Constraints
- Depth option

### External References

External references come from another part or product file. When designing in the context of the assembly, you can create external references depending on a configuration setting. If the reference changes position or shape, the feature making the reference associatively updates. To turn on external references, select **Me> Preferences > Common Preferences > Object Properties > 3D Shape Infrastructure > General**. Select the **Keep link with selected object** option to enable external references as shown in Figure 22–4.

*Discuss the recommended setting of this option with your system administrator.*

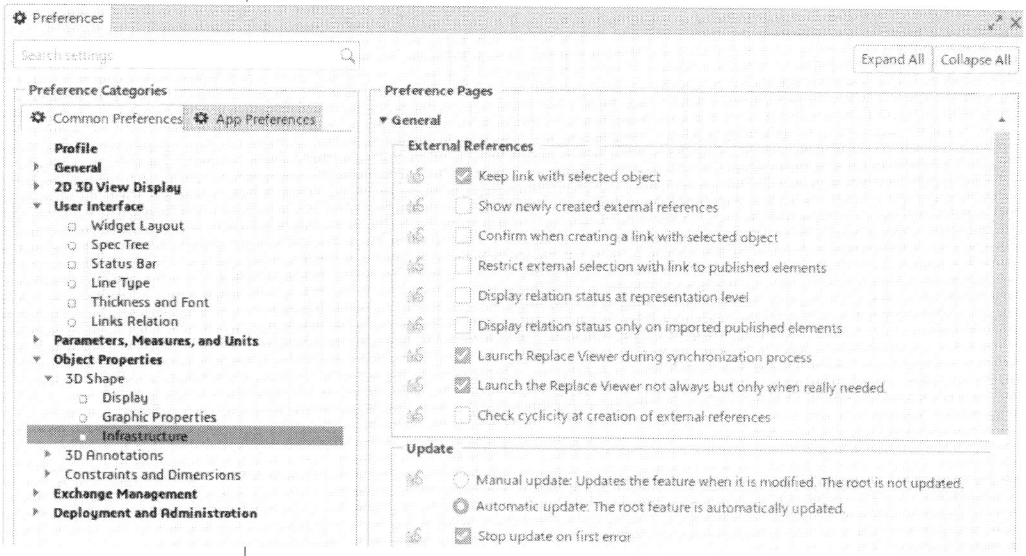


**Figure 22–4**

If external references are not enabled, any references that result in external references are copied to the part as a geometrical set, and do not associatively update with changes.

- To edit a part in the context of the assembly, expand the 3D part in the specification tree and double-click on the 3D Shape level to make it the active object (blue). Once active, the Part Design app is loaded. All other assembly components are still visible and available for reference selection (provided external references have been enabled).

# 22.3 Assembly Holes

Assembly Hole functionality enables you to create Hole features in the context of an assembly. This enables the creation of Hole features that are:

- Controlled from a common location
- Capable of removing material from multiple components simultaneously.

Assembly holes are created in the context of an assembly, resulting in the creation of external references. It is important to carefully consider the following items:

- Selection/Creation of the 3DShape
- Dimensional references
- Constraints
- Depth option
- Impacted representations

The following steps are used to create an Assembly Hole:

1. In the *Assembly* section of the Action Bar, click  (Assembly Hole).
2. Select or create a 3DShape as shown in Figure 22–5. The 3DShape used to store the Assembly Hole feature and its accompanying reference information. To use an existing 3DShape, select a component from the specification tree. To create a new 3DShape, click **OK**.

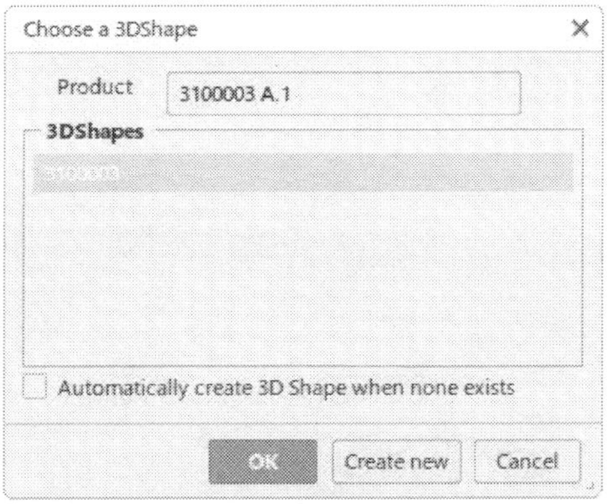


Figure 22–5

3. If you create a new 3DShape, the 3D Shape/Physical Representation dialog box opens. Enter a name as shown in Figure 22–6.

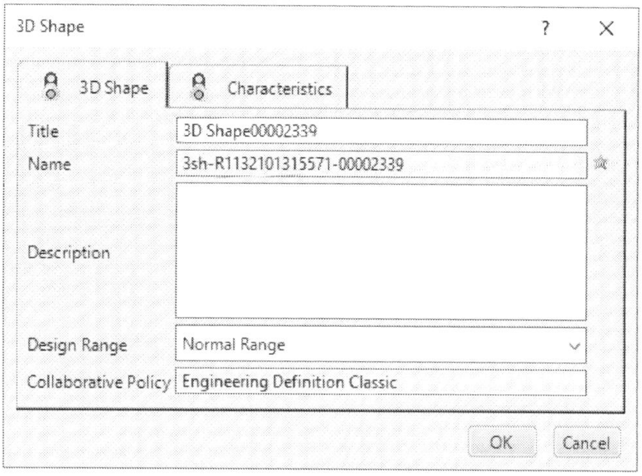


**Figure 22–6**

4. Select the hole placement location. If the selected geometry belongs to a 3DShape other than the one in which the Assembly Hole is located, a warning is generated as shown in Figure 22–7. This warning is only intended to remind you that the action is going to result in the creation of an external reference. Click **OK** to continue.

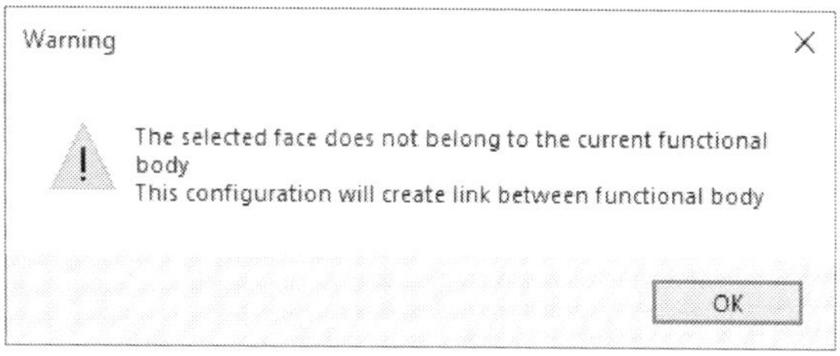


**Figure 22–7**

5. The Hole Definition dialog box opens. Configure the **Limit Type**, **Main Diameter**, **Type**, and **Positioning Sketch** options.

6. After clicking **OK** in the Hole Definition dialog box, the Assembly Feature Definition dialog box opens as shown in Figure 22–8.

    - To manually select impacted files, select the geometry from the screen or specification tree.

- To permit CATIA to calculate intersected, click  (Preset By Clash).

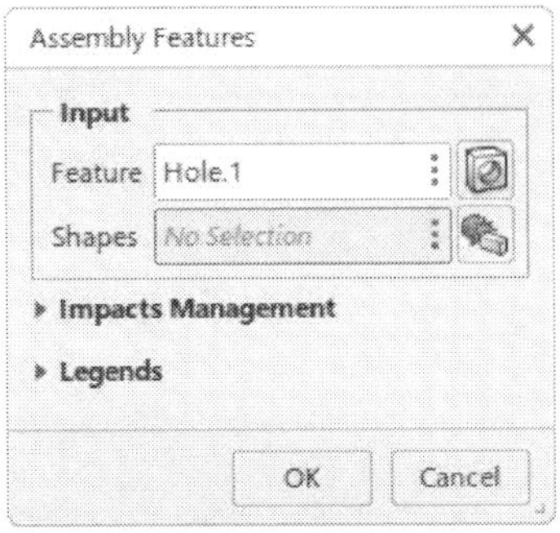


**Figure 22–8**

7. Click **OK** to close the Assembly Feature Definitions dialog box. Once the hole has been created, the following is true:

   - A Solid Functional Set containing the Hole feature in the 3DShape that *owns* the Assembly Hole as shown in Figure 22–9.
   - A Rep Impact Feature within the affected component(s) as shown in Figure 22–10.

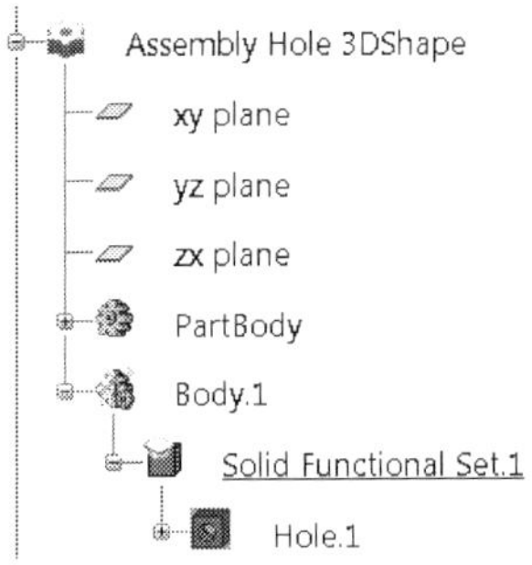


**Figure 22–9**

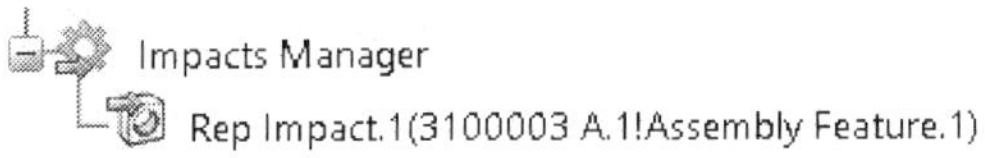


**Figure 22–10**

Manipulation of the Assembly Hole occurs at different levels within the specification tree, depending on the required change:

- To manipulate the Assembly Hole geometry (size, shape, type, or limits) after creation, the 3DShape should be activated. Double-click on the Hole in the specification tree as shown in Figure 22–9 to open the Hole definition dialog box.

- To manipulate the affected components, expand the Assembly features branch in the specification tree. Double-click on the Assembly feature to open the Assembly Feature Definition dialog box.

# Practice 22a Repeating Component Placement

## Practice Objectives

- Use the Snap Constrain method.
- Create an assembly pattern.

In this practice, you will complete the **Hitch** assembly by adding the remaining hardware. The completed assembly displays as shown in Figure 22–11. You will use the Snap Constrain method and Assembly Patterns to efficiently constrain a number of small identical parts.

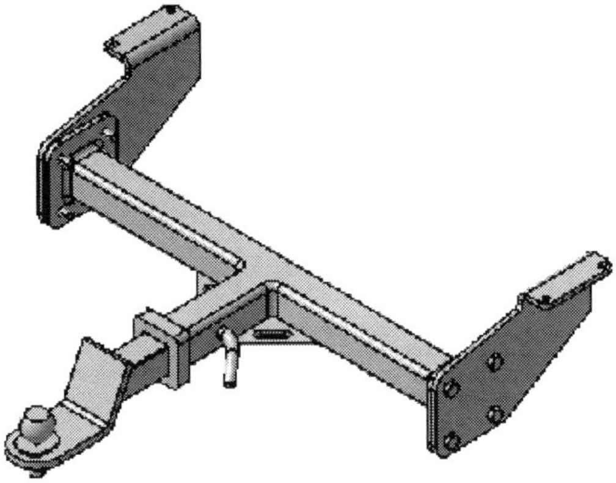

Figure 22–11

## Task 1 - Import the Hitch assembly.

1. Import **Hitch_Repeat.3dxml**.
2. Select **OK** to the Import 3D XML window, and **OK** to the Operation report.
3. Right-click **65100011R** in the specification tree and select **Open**.
4. In the *View* section of the Action Bar, click  (Fit All In).

**Task 2 - Add the bolts to the left side.**

1. Note the bolt is placed but not constrained in the position shown in Figure 22–12.

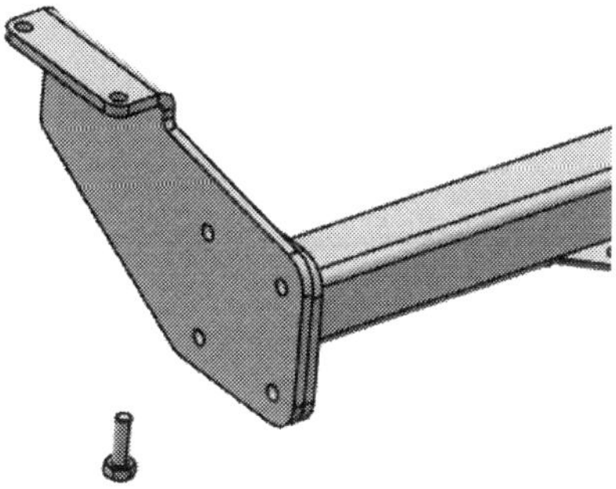

**Figure 22–12**

2. One more bolt is needed. Select **100100** in the specification tree and select  (Copy).
3. Select the top level assembly, **65000011R**, in the specification tree and select  (Paste). Another instance displays in the specification tree.
4. Move the copy to the position shown in Figure 22–13.

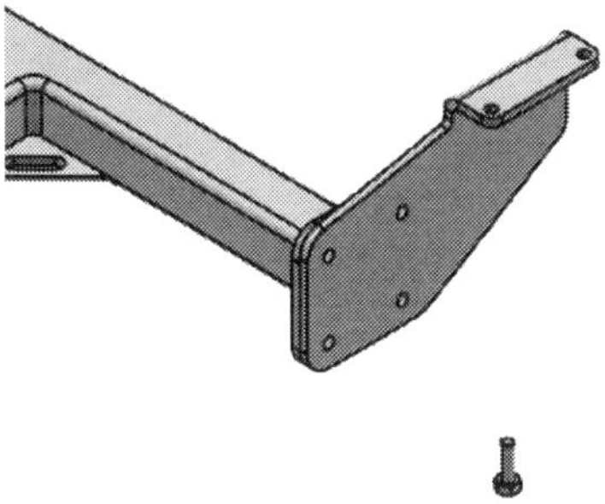

**Figure 22–13**

**Task 3 - Add the bolts for the left side using the Reuse Pattern tool.**

In this task, you will reuse a pattern developed in a part model to position bolts within the assembly. Before you begin to assemble the bolts, you will first investigate the pattern.

 

1. Expand **3100001** in the specification tree to display the features within the **PartBody**, as shown in Figure 22–14.

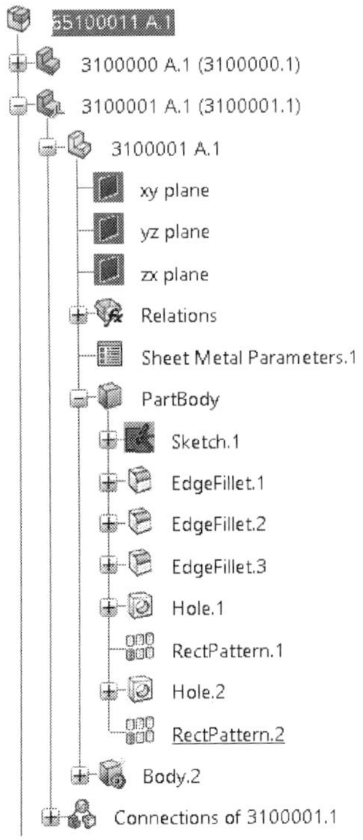


Figure 22–14

2. Select **Hole.1** in the specification tree and note the Hole feature that highlights on the model, as shown in Figure 22–15. This feature is termed the lead pattern feature, because it is the feature that was patterned.

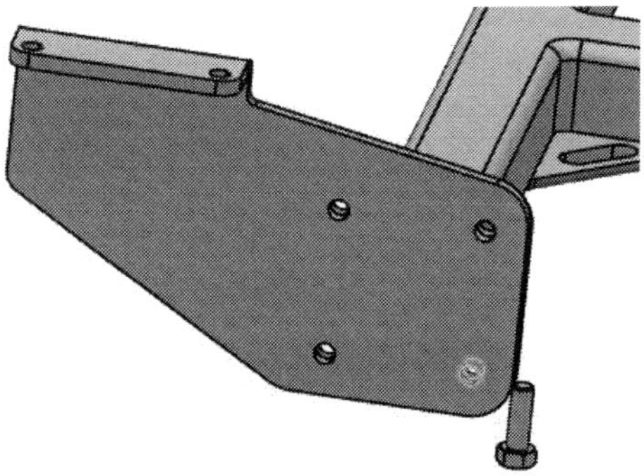

Figure 22–15

3. Select **RectPattern.1** and note that the remaining three holes are highlighted on the model.

4. In the *Assembly* section of the Action Bar, click  (Engineering Connection). You will use a 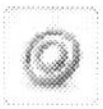 (Coincidence) to assemble the bolt to the Lead Pattern feature in **3100001**.

5. Click 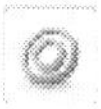 (Coincidence) from within the Engineering Connection window.

6. Select the axis of the bolt as shown in Figure 22–16.

7. Select the axis of the hole as shown in Figure 22–16.

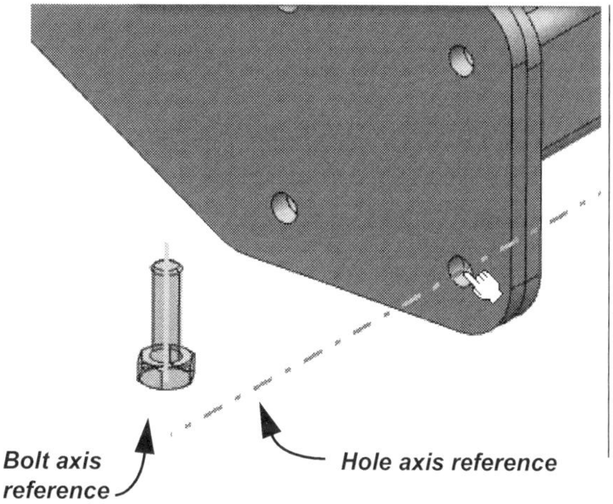


**Figure 22–16**

8. Once the second reference has been selected, the bolt will snap into alignment with the axis of the hole. The Engineering Connection Definition should look as shown in Figure 22–17.

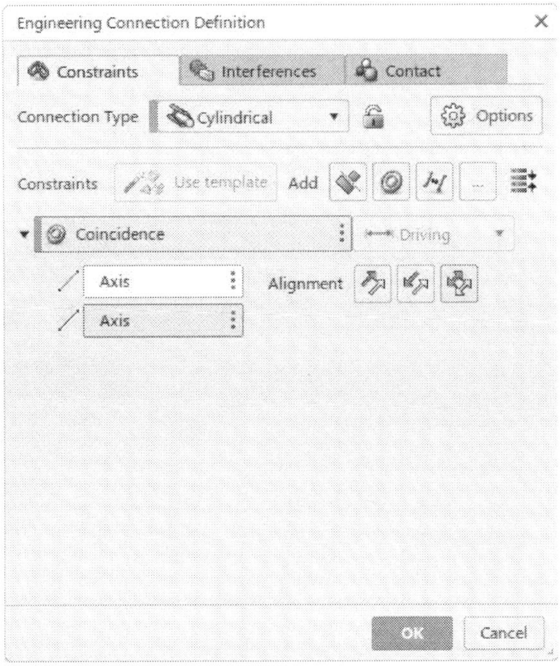


**Figure 22–17**

9. Select  (Contact) from within the Engineering Connection window to add a contact constraint.

10. Select the underside surface of the bolt head as shown in Figure 22–18 as the first reference.

*Robot removed from display for clarity.*

11. Select the surface of **3100001** as shown in Figure 22–18 as the second reference of the contact constraint. Note that in this case, you should press and hold <Alt> when selecting the surface, and ensure that you are selecting the face of the solid body and not that of the rectangular pattern.

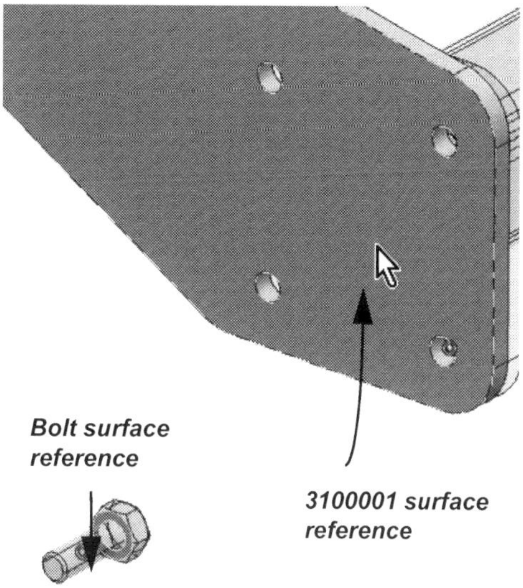


**Figure 22–18**

12. Click **OK** to finalize the Constraints and close the Engineering Connection dialog box.

13. Click **No** to omit creation of the Interference specification. The bolt is now constrained and displays as shown in Figure 22–19.

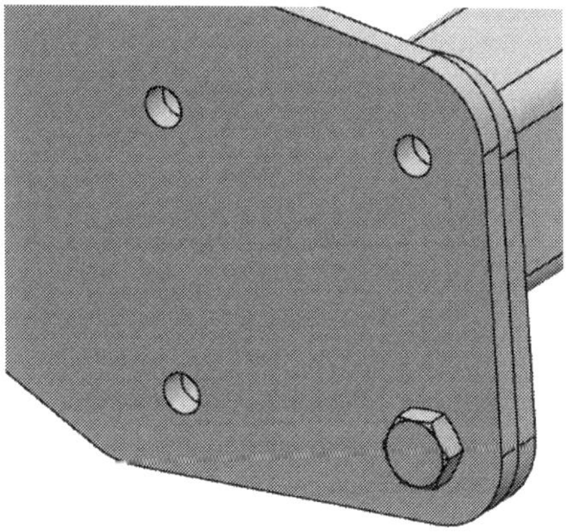

**Figure 22–19**

14. Select the newly constrained bolt.

15. Click  (Assembly Pattern) in the Assembly toolbar.

16. Select **RectPattern.1** under **3100001**.Click **OK** to accept the selection. The model displays as shown in Figure 22–20.

    Alternatively, when the curse displays with a check mark , you can click in the background to confirm the Assembly Pattern.

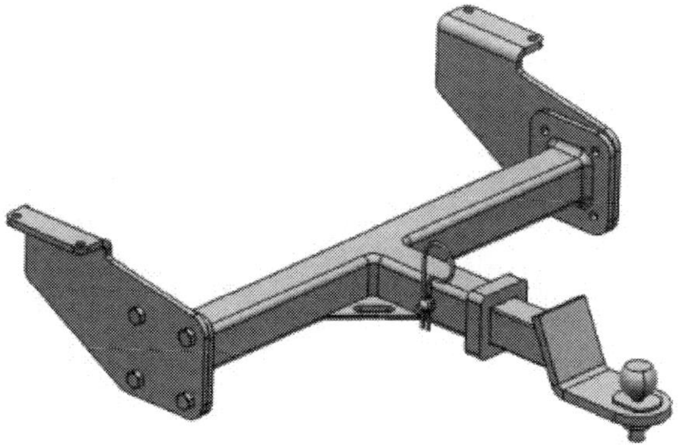

**Figure 22–20**

## Task 4 - Assemble the remaining hardware.

1. Repeat the previous steps to assemble the bolt on the other side of the assembly. Assemble it to **3100002**.

2. Save the assembly and close the window.

# Practice 22b Assembly Features

## Practice Objective

- Add features to an assembly.

In this practice, you will modify **an** assembly shown in Figure 22–21 by adding holes at the assembly level. By creating the holes at the assembly level, all parts affected by the hole creation are automatically updated to reflect the creation of the holes.

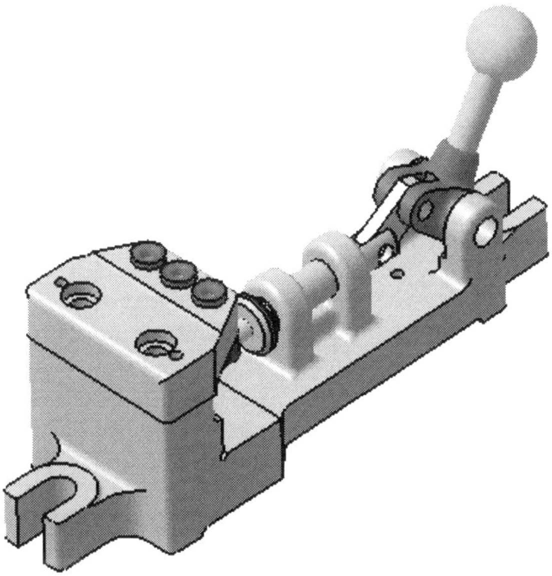

Figure 22–21

### Task 1 - Open the Product and investigate some parts using Open Advanced.

1. Import **Bore-Device-2.3dxml**.
2. In the specification tree, right-click **65200000** and select **Open With** > **Open Advanced**.

3. Enable the **With expanded children** and **Without any representation option**, as shown in Figure 22–22, and click **OK**.

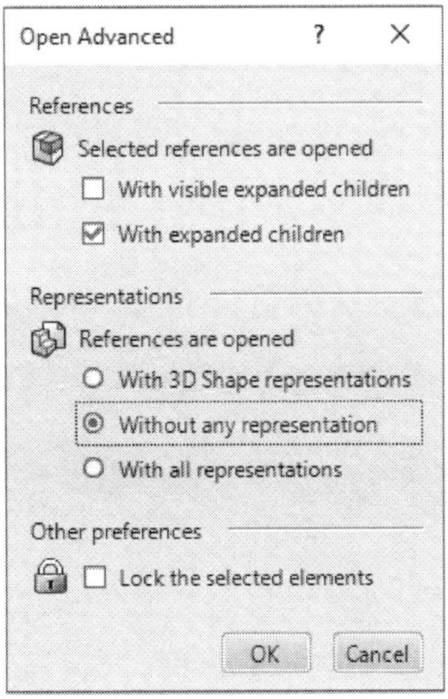


Figure 22–22

4. The specification tree loads, but no geometry is visible.

   Select the **3200000** object and click (Manage Representation) in the *Tools* section of the Action Bar.

5. Ensure that **Load all Representations under selected object** is selected, and then select **Next** as shown in Figure 22–23.

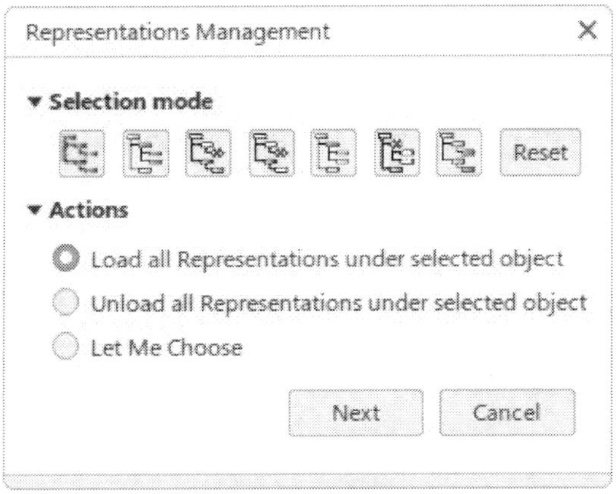


Figure 22–23

6. Select **OK** to the Manage Representations window.

7. The model displays in the window. Note that it has two small holes, as shown in Figure 22–24.

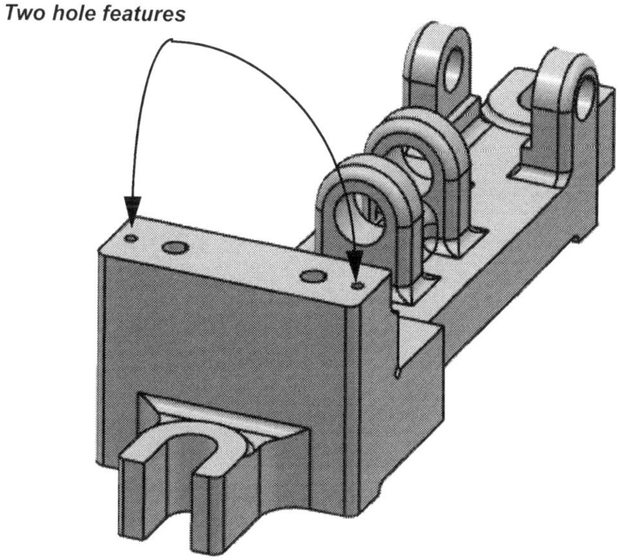


**Figure 22–24**

8. You will reference these holes to create the holes in another part, so in the *Product Modification* tab of the Action Bar, click  (Create a Publication).

9. Select the surface of the hole shown in Figure 22–25.

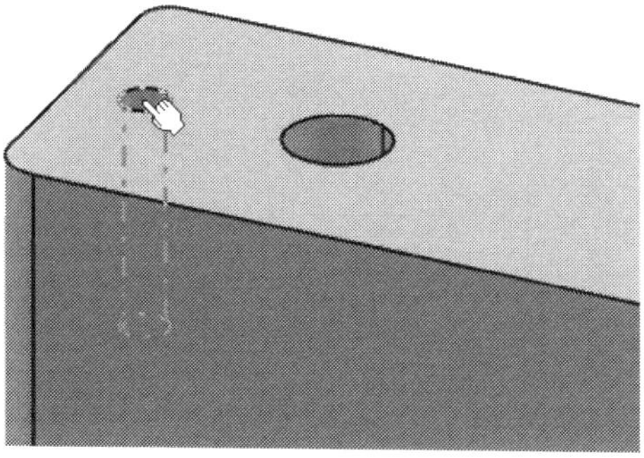

**Figure 22–25**

10. For the Title in the Publication dialog box, enter **Axis_1** and click **OK**.

11. Click  (Create a Publication).

 

12. Select the surface of the hole shown in Figure 22–26.

Figure 22–26

13. For the Title in the Publication dialog box, enter **Axis_2** and click **OK**.

14. Select the *Tools* tab in the Action Bar.

15. Select the **3200001** object and click  (Manage Representation) in the *Tools* section of the Action Bar.

16. In the Representations Management dialog box, ensure that **Load all Representations under selected object** is selected and then click **Next**.

17. Select **OK** in the Manage Representations window to confirm the process and load the part.

18. Note the 3200001 part does not have the required holes to match the other part, as shown in Figure 22–27.

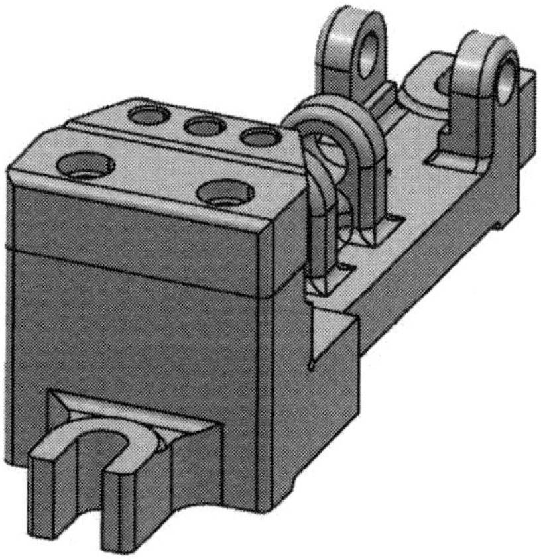

Figure 22–27

## Task 2 - Publish the surfaces to use for the hole starting surface and depth.

1. In the *Product Modification* tab of the Action Bar, click (Create a Publication).

2. Select the surface shown in Figure 22–28.

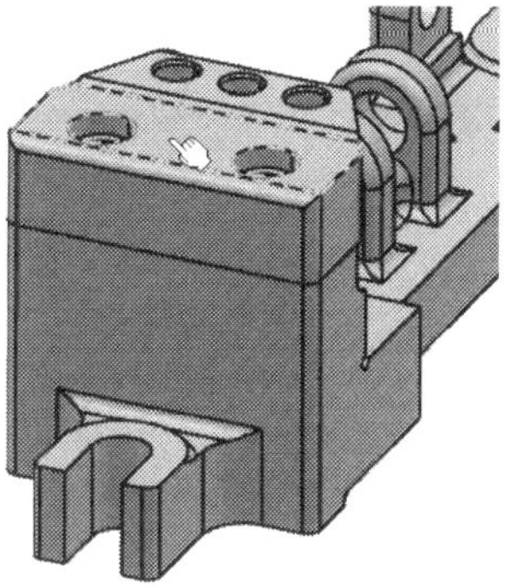

**Figure 22–28**

3. Enter **Start_Surface** as the Title and click **OK**.

4. Click (Create a Publication).

5. Press and hold <Alt> and select the surface shown in Figure 22–29. Click the selection shown in Figure 22–29.

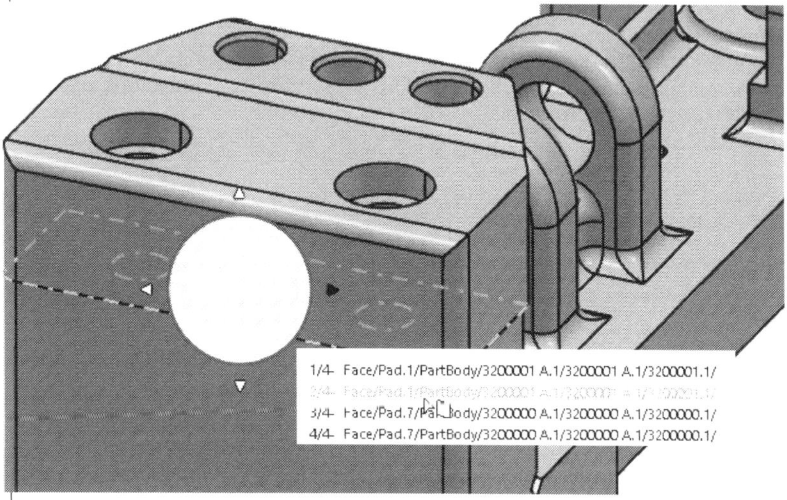


**Figure 22–29**

6. Enter **End_Surface** as the Title and click **OK**.

## Task 3 - Create holes at assembly level.

1. Ensure the external reference settings are correct by selecting **Me> Preferences > Common Preferences > Object Properties > 3D Shape Infrastructure > General** and selecting the **Keep link with selected object** option, as shown in Figure 22–30.

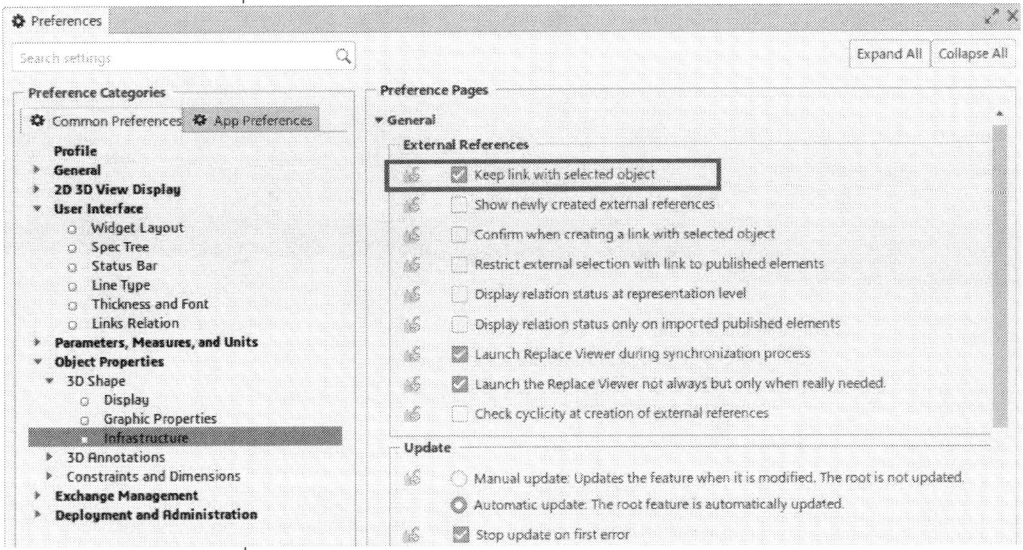


**Figure 22–30**

2. Click **OK**.

3. Change the display mode to wireframe by clicking  (View Mode) in the *View* section of the Action Bar, and then choosing  (Wireframe).

4. In the *Assembly* tab of the Action Bar, click  (Assembly Hole) to create a Hole feature.

5. In the Choose a 3DShape dialog box, click **Create new**.

6. Enter **Drilled Holes** for the Title and click **OK**.

7. In the specification tree, select **Start_Surface**, as shown in Figure 22–31.

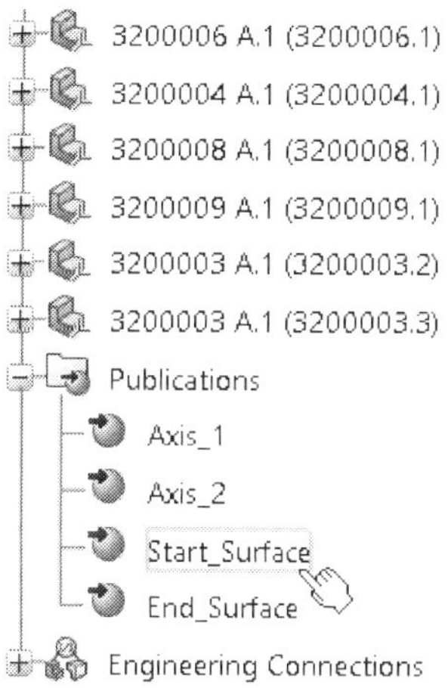


**Figure 22–31**

8. Click **OK** in the Warning dialog box, indicating that a link will be created.

9. Change the orientation to  (* top).

10. In the Hole Definition dialog box, click  (Positioning Sketch).

11. Select the locating point shown in Figure 22–32.

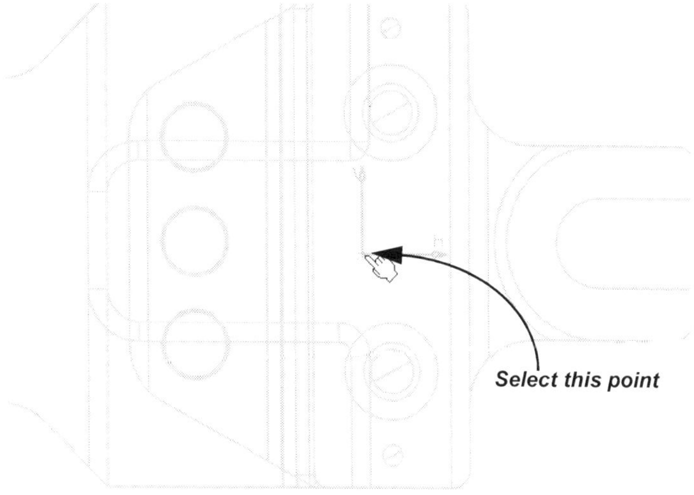


**Figure 22–32**

12. Click (Constraint) and select **Axis_2** in the specification tree.

13. Right-click and select **Coincidence**.

14. Click (Exit App) to complete the sketch.

15. Change the display mode to Shading with Edges by clicking (View Mode) and, in the *View* section of the Action Bar, selecting (Shading With Edges).

16. In the Hole dialog box, click (Reverse) for the Direction.

17. Edit the Main diameter to **5**.

18. Set the *Limit Type* to **Up to Surface** and select **End_Surface** in the specification tree.

19. Click **OK** in the Warning dialog box, indicating that a link will be created.

20. Click **OK** in the Hole Definition dialog box.

21. When the Assembly Feature Definition dialog box opens, select **3200001** from the specification tree.

22. Click **OK**.

23. The hole is initially not visible. Select the *65200000 (Explore)* tab, right click **6520000** in the specification tree and select **Open**. This brings all objects into session.

24. In the *Assembly* tab of the Action Bar, click (Update).

25. In the *Assembly* tab of the Action Bar, click (Hole) to create a Hole feature.

26. In the Choose a 3DShape dialog box, select the **Drilled Holes** 3DShape listed and click **OK**.

27. In the specification tree, select **Start_Surface**, as shown in Figure 22–33.

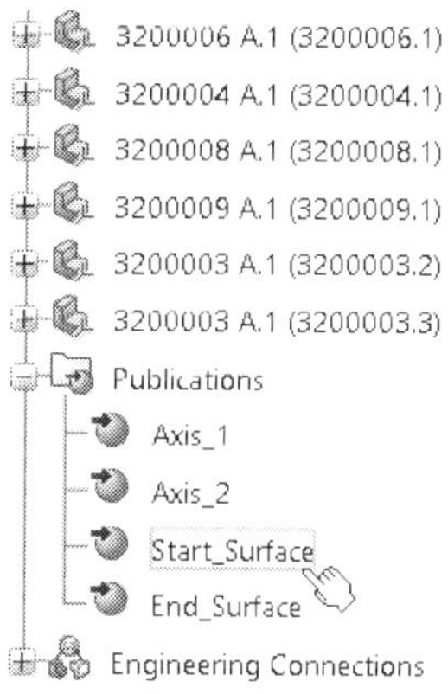


**Figure 22–33**

28. Click **OK** in the Warning dialog box, indicating that a link will be created.

29. Change the orientation to  (* top).

30. In the Hole Definition dialog box, click  (Positioned Sketch).

31. Select the locating point shown in Figure 22–34.

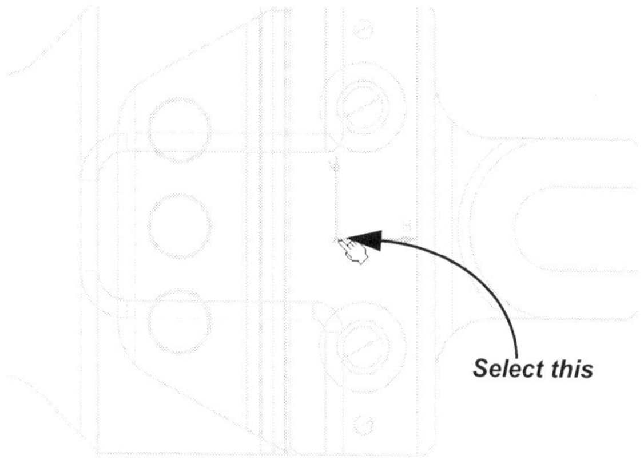


**Figure 22–34**

32. Click 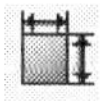 (Constraint) and select **Axis_1** in the specification tree.

33. Right-click and select **Coincidence**.

34. Click (Exit App) to complete the sketch.
35. Change the display mode to Shading with Edges by clicking (View Mode) and, in the *View* section of the Action Bar, selecting (Shading With Edges).
36. In the Hole dialog box, click (Reverse) for the Direction.
37. Edit the Diameter to **5**.
38. Set the *Limit Type* to **Up to Surface** and select **End_Surface** in the specification tree.
39. Click **OK** in the Warning dialog box, indicating that a link will be created.
40. Click **OK** in the Hole Definition dialog box.
41. When the Assembly Feature Definition dialog box opens, select **3200001** from the specification tree.
42. Click **OK**.
43. The hole is initially not visible. Select the *65200000 (Explore)* tab, right click **6520000** in the specification tree and select **Open**. This brings all objects into session.
44. In the *Assembly* tab of the Action Bar, click (Update). The model displays as shown in Figure 22–35.

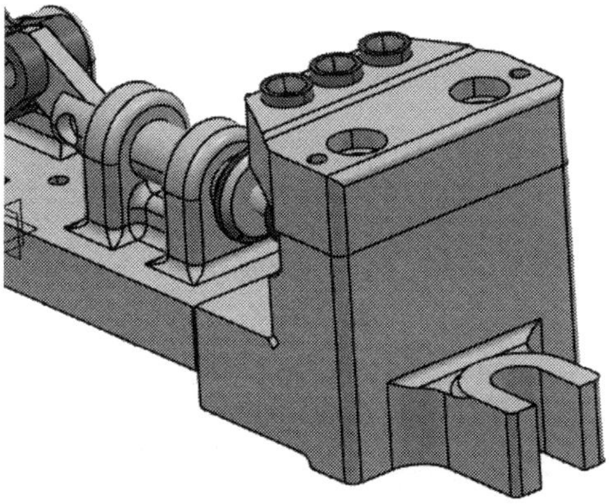

**Figure 22–35**

## Task 4 - Incorporate design changes.

1. A design change requires that the position of the referenced hole feature be modified. Double-click **3200000** in the specification tree.

2. Modify **Sketch.23** of **Hole.4**. Change the *5 dimension* to [7.5], as shown in Figure 22–36. Exit the sketch.

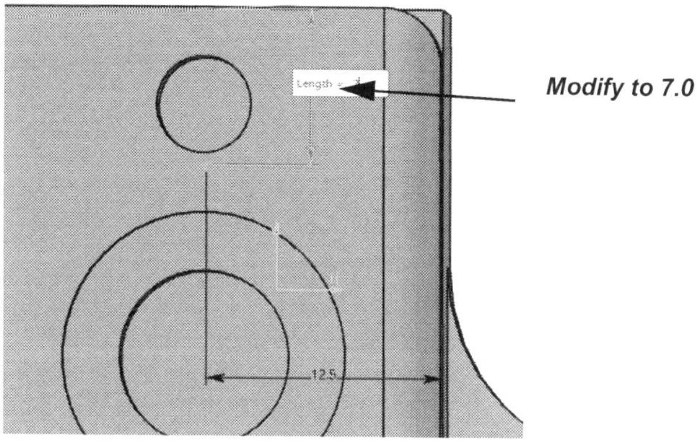


**Figure 22–36**

3. Complete the edit.

4. Activate the Top Level of the assembly.

5. Click (Update) to update the assembly.

6. The assembly displays as shown in Figure 22–37. View the assembly and note the updated position of the holes.

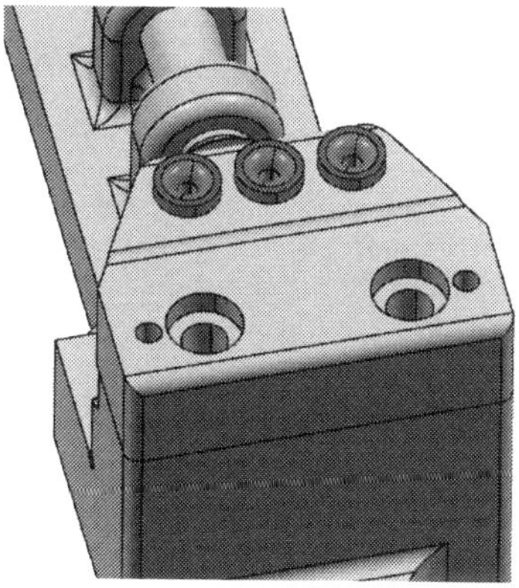

**Figure 22–37**

7. Save the assembly and close all tabs.

# Chapter Review Questions

1. To use the **Assembly Pattern** tool, the component to be patterned must be constrained relative to the initial feature of the pattern.
   a. True
   b. False
2. Where is a copied component placed into the assembly?
   a. At the origin of the assembly.
   b. On top of the original component.
   c. There is no way of knowing, it is random.
   d. In the same location as it would be if it was inserted into the assembly using the **Insert>Existing component** tool.
3. What does the **Keep link with selected object** option do? The option is located in **Me> Preferences > Common Preferences > Object Properties > 3D Shape Infrastructure > General**.
   a. Enables external references.
   b. Disables external references.
   c. Creates a report of external references.
   d. None of the above.
4. Working in the context of an assembly is often referred to as______________________.
   a. Bottom up approach.
   b. Top down approach.
   c. Multi-body approach.
   d. None of the above.
5. Parent/child relationships are created between components when creating external references.
   a. True
   b. False

6. How do you edit a part in the context of the assembly? (Select all that apply.)

   a. Double-click on the part in the specification tree.

   b. Right-click on the part in the specification tree and select **x object>Edit**.

   c. Click .

   d. You cannot edit a part within the context of the assembly.

**Answers:** 1.a, 2.b, 3.a, 4.b, 5.a, 6.ab

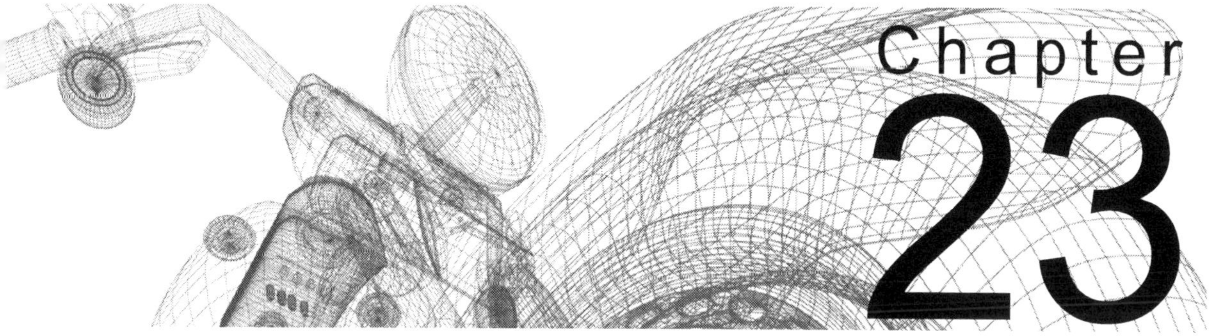

# Chapter 23

# Assembly Information

This chapter covers the techniques that you can use to obtain information about an assembly. The Measure tools enable you to take measurements of the assembly in the same way that you take measurements of parts. The Clash and Clearance Analysis tool enables you to determine whether any interference is present in the assembly.

## Learning Objectives in This Chapter

- Use the measurement options for assembly components.
- Understand how the Clipping Tool works within a Product.
- Determine whether interference exists in an assembly.
- Find how to determine Weight Definition and Weight Distribution.

# 23.1 Measurements

CATIA provides tools to extract important information from your assembly model. The *Tools* section of the Action Bar enables you to perform the following functions:

- Measure the distance between items on different parts.
- Measure the distance between items on a single part.
- Measure the mass properties of the assembly.
- Section the assembly to view internal components

These functions can be accessed using the options shown in Figure 23–1.

**Figure 23–1**

## Component Materials

To assist in the generation of relevant mass properties measurements, materials can be applied to the components of an assembly at the 3D Part level within the Assembly Design app.

Use the following steps to accomplish this:

1. In the *Tools* section of the Action Bar, click  (Material Browser) to open the Materials catalog.
2. Select the material from the Materials dialog box, as shown in Figure 23–2.

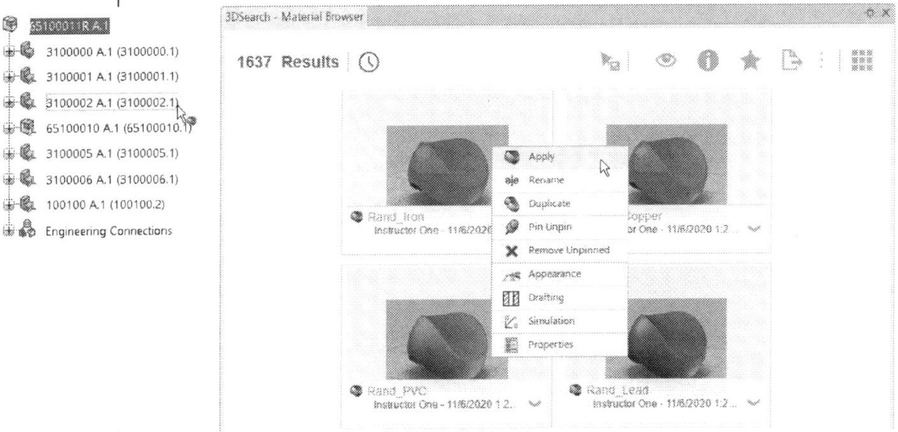


**Figure 23–2**

3. From the specification tree, select the specific component(s) to which the material be applied.

4. Click  (Exit Context Menu).

When this is done, the system considers each component's material property when performing measure inertia calculations.

# 23.2 Clipping Tool

The (Clipping Tool) command enables you to create temporary cut sections in one or more components. You can use this tool to perform the following tasks:

- Examine assembly components' positions.
- View complex 2D cross-sections.
- Verify the internal design considerations of a part.
- View internal clash conditions.

## General Steps

Use the following general steps when using the Clipping Tool.

1. Activate the **Clipping Tool** command.
2. Select the clipping plane to access the context toolbar.
3. Use the context toolbar to customize settings.
4. Complete the clipping operation.

### Step 1 - Activate the Clipping Tool command.

The (Clipping Tool) icon can be found in the *Tools* section of the Action Bar. Selecting this icon will toggle the Clipping Tool on/off. The clipping plane cuts through all components in an assembly by default, as shown in Figure 23–3.

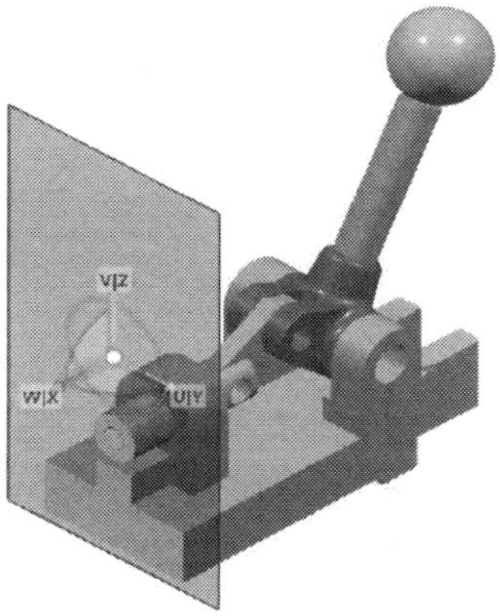


**Figure 23–3**

The first time you select the Clipping Tool, the clipping plane appears and you are in an edit mode. However, if you select the Clipping Tool more than once, it will only toggle the display of the section on/off without putting you into the edit mode. To be able to edit the section after the initial creation, select Edit Clipping by expanding the arrow next to (Clipping Tool), as shown on the left in Figure 23–4. Edit Clipping can also be found by selecting the (Clipping Tool) then right-clicking in the background and selecting **Clipping>Edit Clipping**, as shown on the right in Figure 23–4.

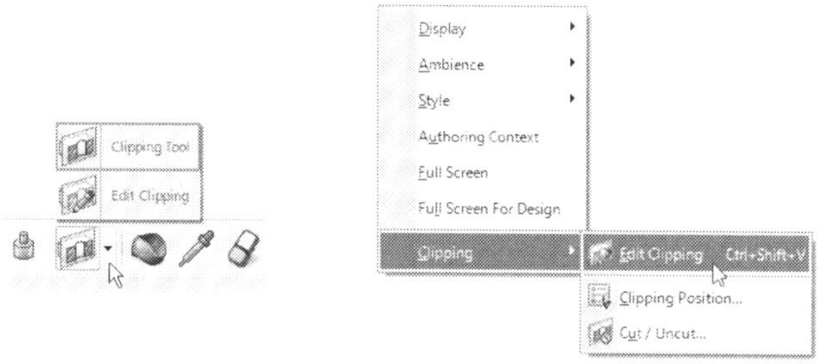


**Figure 23–4**

## Step 2 - Select the clipping plane to access the context toolbar.

Once you see the clipping plane appear, selecting it will display the context toolbar, as shown in Figure 23–5. These options allow you to be able to completely customize the Clipping Tool settings.

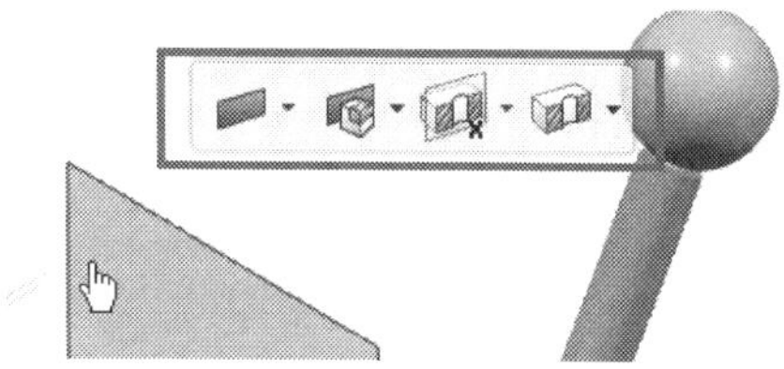

**Figure 23–5**

There are four different groups of icons within the context toolbar. The icons that are displayed before expanding the groups are the current display settings in the clipping.

## Step 3 - Use the context toolbar to customize settings.

The context toolbar has many options for customizing how the Clipping Tool works. Below is a table listing all of the options found within the Clipping Tool. Also note that while many of these commands will reposition the primary clipping plane, you can also click and drag it into a custom position as needed.

## Clipping Tool Options

| Icon | Name | Definition | Example |
| --- | --- | --- | --- |
|  | **Display a Plane** | Region of interest is displayed as a single plane. |  |
| 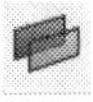 | **Display a Slice** | Region of interest is sliced by two parallel planes. Material is kept between those planes. |  |
|  | **Display a Box** | Region of interest is displayed as a box. |  |
|  | **Define Clipping using Objects selections** | Allows selection of multiple components to define the location of the region of interest. | 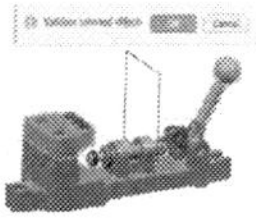 |
|  | **Reset Clipping** | Resets primary clipping plane to default location. | |
|  | **Position clipping along X-axis** | Primary clipping plane is placed normal to the X-axis. |  |
|  | **Position clipping along Y-axis** | Primary clipping plane is placed normal to the Y-axis. | 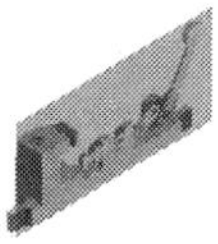 |

 

| | | | |
|---|---|---|---|
| | **Position clipping along Z-axis** | Primary clipping plane is placed normal to the Z-axis. |  |
| | **Specify the position of the clipping precisely** | Allows position of clipping plane to be placed based on selection of other surfaces. | |
| | **Invert Clipping** | Flip which side of the section is displayed or cut. | |
| | **Activate Clipping** | Visually cuts the solid, showing 3D geometry on one side of the cut. | |
| | **De-activate Clipping** | Visually shows both 3D geometry and the region of interest without cutting any away. | |
| | **Only Contour** | Only shows the outline of the section. No solid geometry displayed. | |

## Step 4 - Complete the clipping operation.

Once you have completed customizing the look of the section using the context toolbar, click in the background to finish the command. The clipping view is displayed on the model. As mentioned in Step 1, you can select **Edit Clipping** if you need to modify the look.

There are other options available for editing the look that are not found in the context toolbar. While the clipping view is being displayed, right-click and select **Clipping**. Under this option, you will find the **Clipping Position** and **Cut / Uncut** tools.

## Clipping Position

This tool enables you to adjust the size and location of the primary clipping plane numerically. Type in the values based on robot directions U, V, and W, as shown in Figure 23–6.

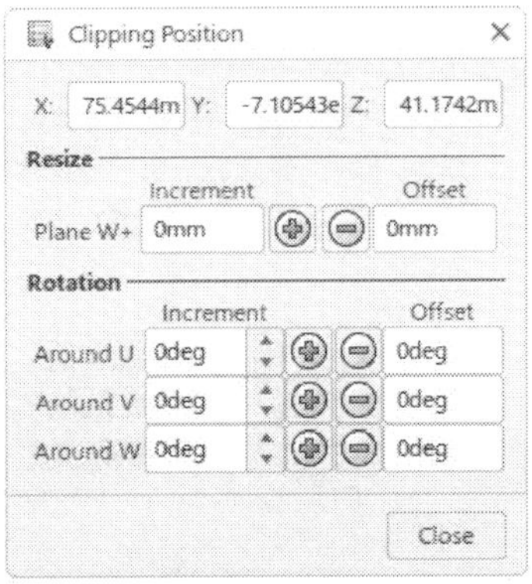


Figure 23–6

## Cut and Uncut

The  (Cut / Uncut) command is only available while the clipping display is applied. It enables you to pick and choose which components are being sectioned, and is only usable when working with a Product. You can pick elements to cut and elements not to cut within the Cut Elements window. An example cutting the larger parts and excluding everything else is shown in Figure 23–6.

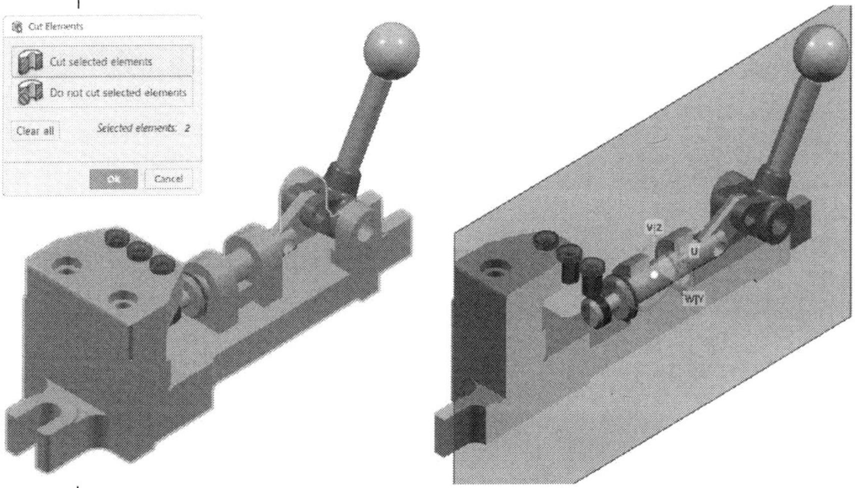


Figure 23–7

# 23.3 Interference

When creating an assembly, the system permits interference between components. There are three tools that are used to evaluate an assembly for interference and related conditions:

- Engineering Connection Interference Checks
- Interference Check App
- Non Persistent Inference Check

## Engineering Connection Interference Check

During the definition of Engineering Connections, the *Interference* tab provides the ability to define a check for clash/contact/clearance conditions between the related components as the Engineering Connection is created. The *Interference* tab displays in the Engineering Connection dialog box as shown in Figure 23–8.

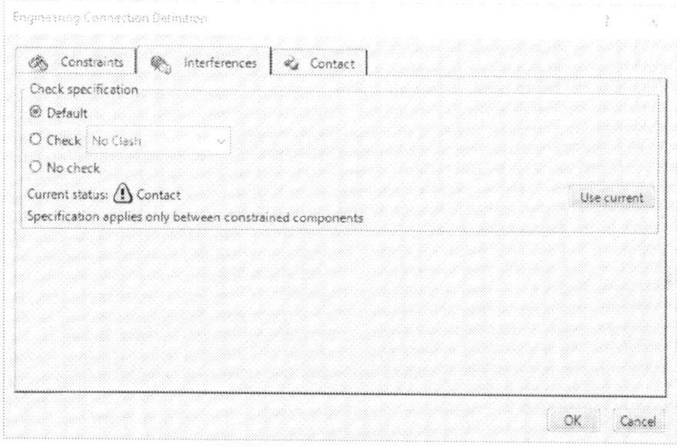


**Figure 23–8**

If the Check Specification value is set to **Default**, the Undefined Interference message box is triggered as shown in Figure 23–9. This enables a warning to be generated if downstream modifications result in the Engineering Connection components violating the check specification condition.

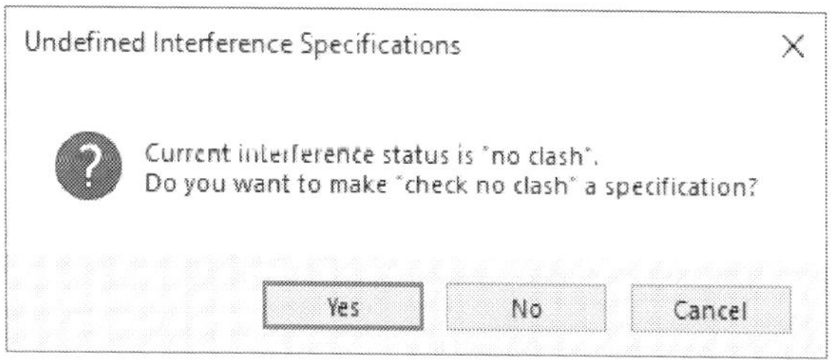


**Figure 23–9**

## Interference Check App

The Interference Check App enables the analysis of conditions including clash, contact and clearance between two or more components.

The Interference Check App is used to determine whether interference exists, and if so, the degree of interference. By using Interference Check App, a Simulation object is created within the system allowing for interference information and additional markup information to be saved for later use.

To access the Interference Check app, click **Roles, Apps & Solutions portfolio** in the compass, as shown in Figure 23–10.

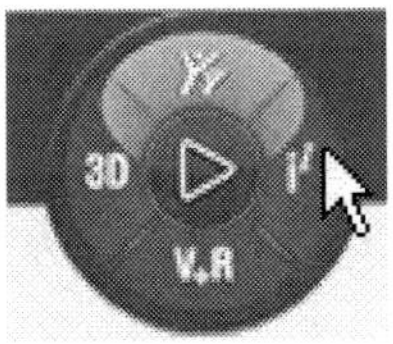


**Figure 23–10**

In the list of apps, click  (Interference Check). An alternative to selecting on the App from the list is to select  (Create Interference Simulation) from the *Assembly* section of the Action Bar. Both of these options will create a Simulation and put you into the same Interferences Check app.

A Interference Simulation window will appear as shown in Figure 23–11, allowing you to fill out any custom specifications you require for your simulation. Select **OK** when finished.

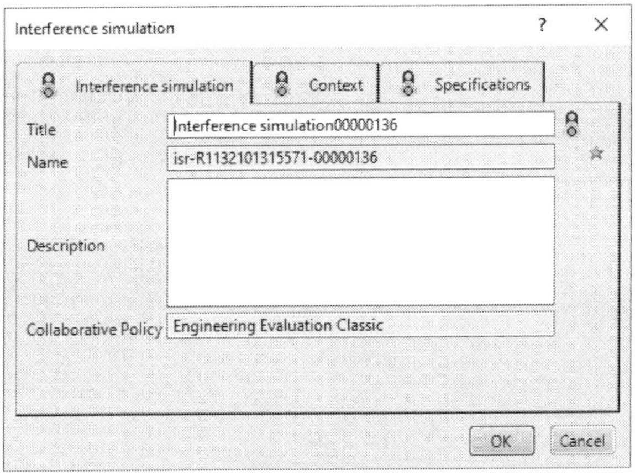


**Figure 23–11**

In the *Interference* section of the Action Bar, click (Analyze Interference). To see the results of this analysis, click , at the bottom center of screen. The results expand and display as shown in Figure 23–12.

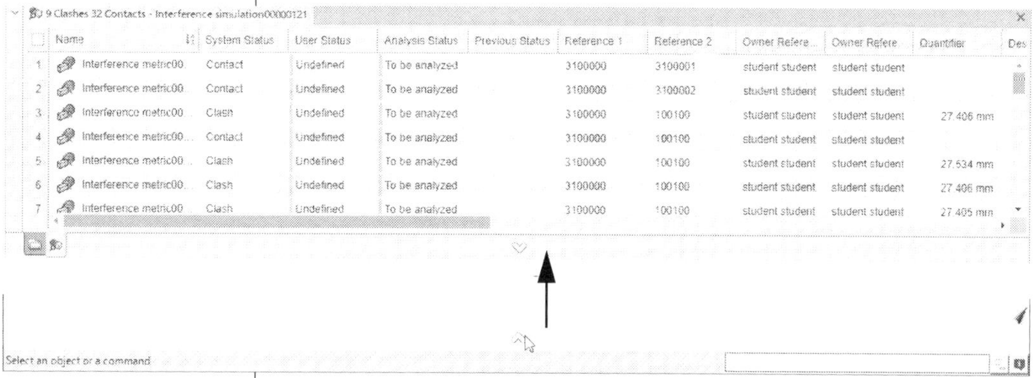


**Figure 23–12**

If any conflicts occur, you can select and view the result as shown in Figure 23–13. The pair of interfering components is visible and all other components are displayed in a transparent state. Transparency can be adjusted by dragging the Context transparency slider.

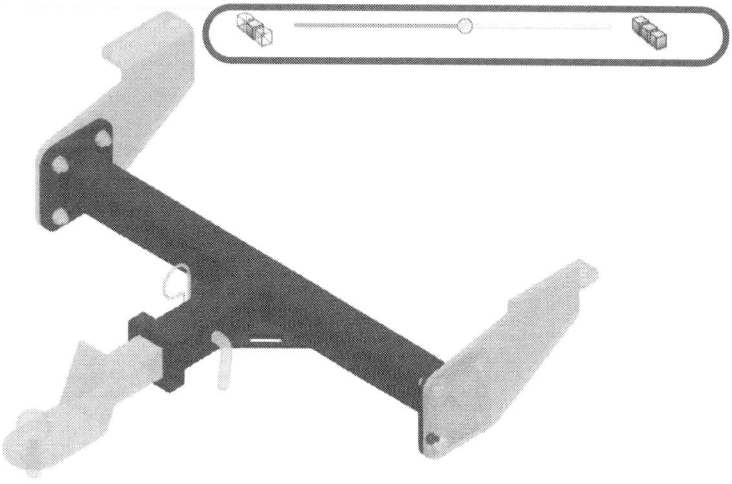

**Figure 23–13**

By default, Interference Analysis checks between all components for **Clash and Contact** (and **Clearance** if selected). The scope of the analysis might be restricted through the options available in the *Specification* tab as shown in Figure 23–14.

To access the Interference Simulation Definition dialog box, click  (Edit Specification) in the *Interference Analysis* section of the Action Bar.

- **Inside Groups:** Checks components selected to belong to Group1 for Contact/Clash/Clearance between them.
- **Groups against groups:** Checks components selected to belong to Group1 for Contact/Clash/Clearance between each other. The selected components belong to Group2.
- **Groups against context:** Checks components selected to belong to Group1 for Contact/Clash/Clearance against the rest of the product.

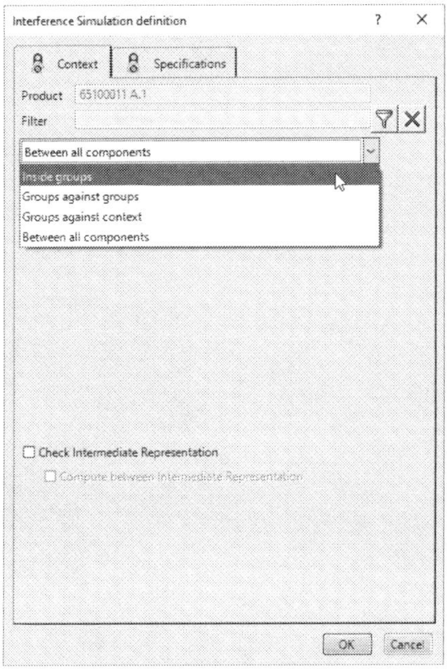


**Figure 23–14**

## Non Persistent Interference Simulation

This is similar to the previously talked about Interference Check App, however the results are displayed within the Assembly and no Simulation object is created. This means that the results are temporary and cannot be saved.

(Non Persistent Interference Simulation) is found in the *Assembly* section of the Action Bar. When selected, a Light Interference Simulation Definition window will appear as shown in Figure 23–15, allowing the user to define all of the criteria for the interference check right away.

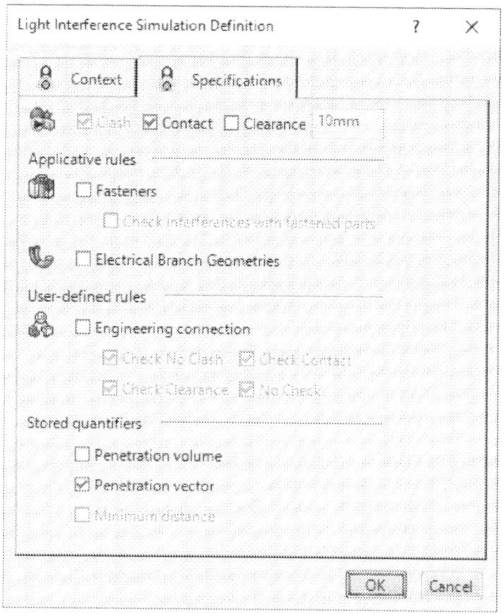


**Figure 23–15**

Once all of the criteria is defined and the **OK** command is selected, the results of the Interference will display at the bottom of the assembly window similar to how they look in a simulation, as shown in Figure 23–16. A major difference is that while these results can be minimized and expanded, once you hit the (close) icon in the corner, the results are deleted and cannot be retrieved again. A new (Non Persistent Interference Simulation) would need to be run.

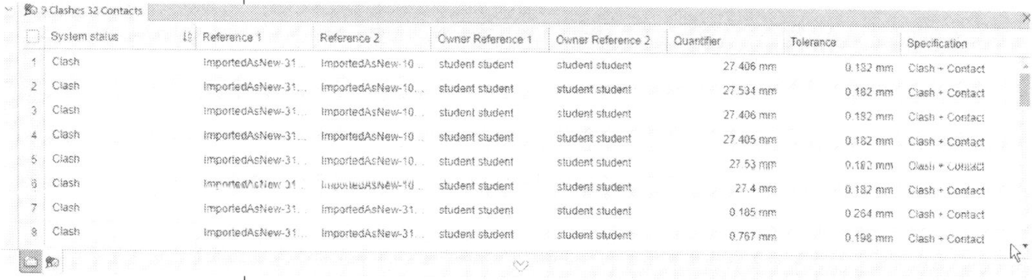

9 Clashes 32 Contacts

| | System status | Reference 1 | Reference 2 | Owner Reference 1 | Owner Reference 2 | Quantifier | Tolerance | Specification |
|---|---|---|---|---|---|---|---|---|
| 1 | Clash | ImportedAsNew-31... | ImportedAsNew-10... | student student | student student | 27.406 mm | 0.182 mm | Clash + Contact |
| 2 | Clash | ImportedAsNew-31... | ImportedAsNew-10... | student student | student student | 27.534 mm | 0.182 mm | Clash + Contact |
| 3 | Clash | ImportedAsNew-31... | ImportedAsNew-10... | student student | student student | 27.406 mm | 0.182 mm | Clash + Contact |
| 4 | Clash | ImportedAsNew-31... | ImportedAsNew-10... | student student | student student | 27.405 mm | 0.182 mm | Clash + Contact |
| 5 | Clash | ImportedAsNew-31... | ImportedAsNew-10... | student student | student student | 27.53 mm | 0.182 mm | Clash + Contact |
| 6 | Clash | ImportedAsNew-31... | ImportedAsNew-10... | student student | student student | 27.4 mm | 0.182 mm | Clash + Contact |
| 7 | Clash | ImportedAsNew-31... | ImportedAsNew-31... | student student | student student | 0.185 mm | 0.264 mm | Clash + Contact |
| 8 | Clash | ImportedAsNew-31... | ImportedAsNew-31... | student student | student student | 0.767 mm | 0.198 mm | Clash + Contact |

**Figure 23–16**

# 23.4 Weight Definition

The **Weight Definition** tool is used to check, calculate, or declare the weight of a part based on its geometry and/or material. This tool is part of the B.I. Essentials tools.

The B.I. Essentials tools are accessed by clicking

 (B.I. Essentials) in the *Tools* tab of the Action Bar. The B.I Essentials dialog box opens. From the Choose information to reveal drop-down list, select **Weight Definition**, as shown in Figure 23–17.

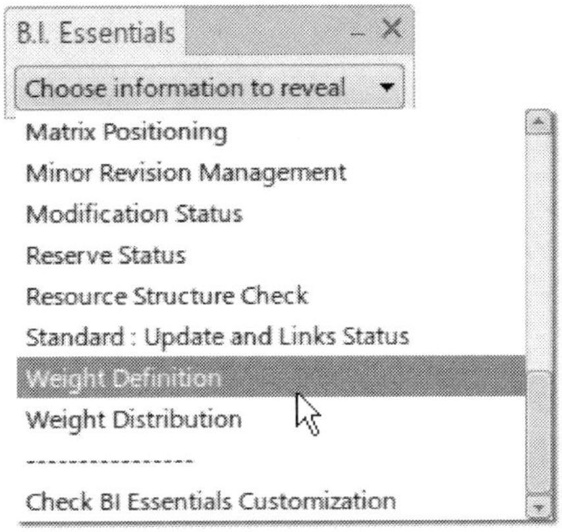


**Figure 23–17**

The Weight Definition tool uses color coding to indicate the status of each component, as shown in Figure 23–18.

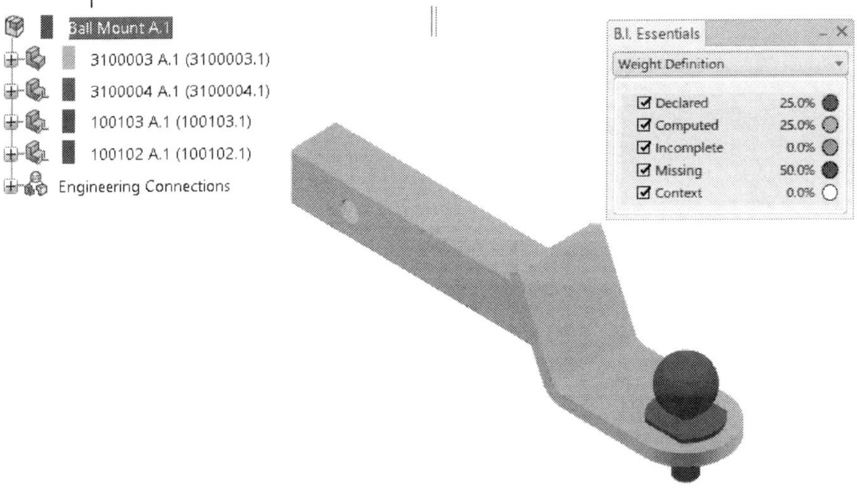


**Figure 23–18**

The color coding is broken into 5 categories:

- Declared (Blue) - Weight is declared manually through the Weight Definition tool.
- Computed (Green) - Weight is computed automatically using the geometry and material properties.
- Incomplete (Orange) - Weight is partially defined.
- Missing (Red) - No weight is assigned or calculated.
- Context (Transparent White) - The assembly as a whole, or elements not taken into account for the weight computation.

The B.I. Essentials dialog box indicates the percentage of components falling into each category. You can select any (or multiple) category in the B.I. Essentials dialog box and the system will remove any components in that category from display, setting the color to transparent, as shown in Figure 23–19.

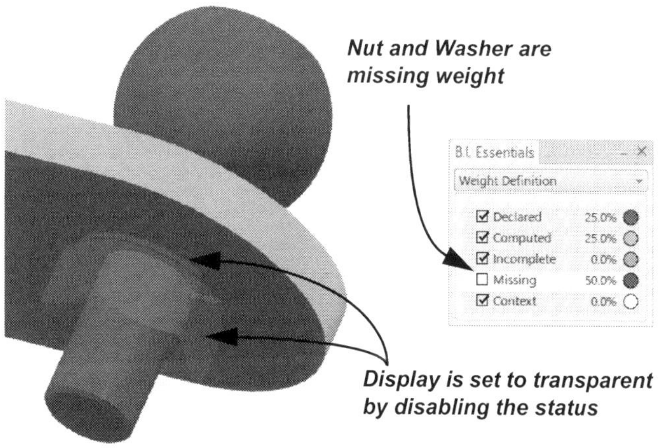


**Figure 23–19**

## Weight Attributes Table

Clicking a component opens a set of hyperlinks on the screen related to declaring or computing the weight. The links displayed depend on the current status of the component. For example, if a component already has a calculated weight, the links are as shown in Figure 23–20.

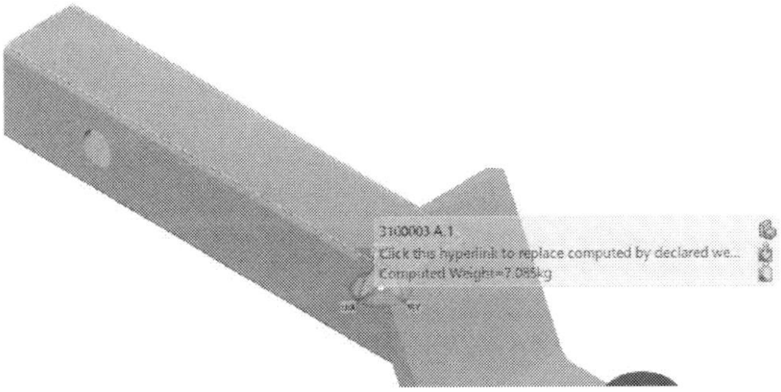


**Figure 23–20**

Clicking the links will open the Weight Attributes table for the component, as shown in Figure 23–21.

| # | Attribute | Value |
|---|---|---|
| 1 | Weight | 0.5kg |
| 2 | Weight Tolerance (±) | 0.05kg |
| 3 | CoG along X | 1.776e-015mm |
| 4 | CoG along Y | 154.05mm |
| 5 | CoG along Z | -32.3mm |
| 6 | CoG Tolerance (±) | 10mm |
| 7 | Moment Ixx / G | 0kgxm2 |
| 8 | Moment Iyy / G | 0kgxm2 |
| 9 | Moment Izz / G | 0kgxm2 |
| 10 | Product of Inertia Ixy / G | 0kgxm2 |
| 11 | Product of Inertia Ixz / G | 0kgxm2 |
| 12 | Product of Inertia Iyz / G | 0kgxm2 |
| 13 | Comment | |

**Figure 23–21**

The weight will be listed in the *Weight* field. For components that do not have a calculated weight, you can declare a weight. This is particularly useful for purchased parts, where you may want to use the manufacturer's declared weight, rather than calculating it from your model.

# 23.5 Weight Distribution

To calculate the weight distribution, access the B.I. Essentials tools by clicking  (B.I. Essentials) in the *Tools* tab of the Action Bar. From the B.I Essentials dialog box, select **Weight Distribution**, as shown in Figure 23–22.

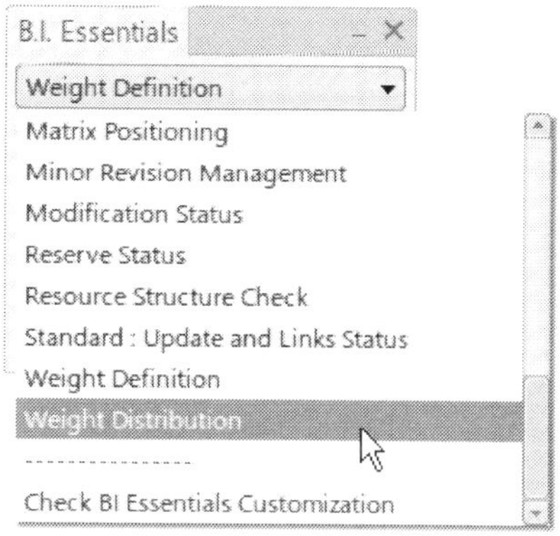


**Figure 23–22**

The Weight Distribution tool uses color coding to review components according to their weight, as shown in Figure 23–23.

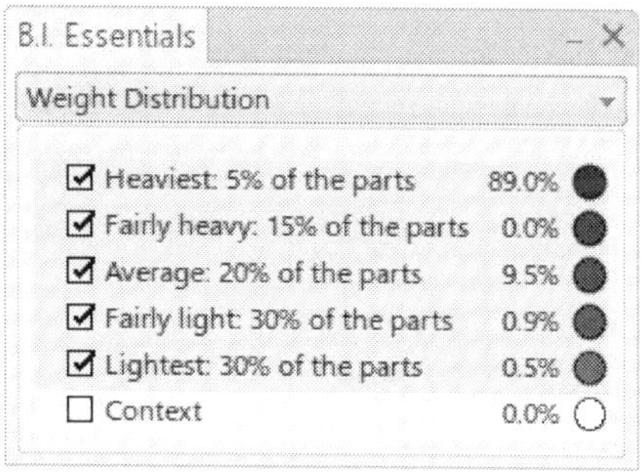


**Figure 23–23**

The Weight Distribution tool provides insights into your model weight so you can make informed decisions about adjusting components or materials.

# Practice 23a Assembly Information

## Practice Objectives

- Extract measurements from the assembly.
- Calculate interference.

## Task 1 - Import the Hitch assembly.

1. Import the **Hitch_Complete.3dxml** assembly from the *Hitch* folder. If prompted with an Import 3D XML window referencing legacy Flexible or Graphic Property data, click **OK**. This will not affect our exercise.
2. Click **OK** to the Operations report.
3. Right-click **65100011** and select **Open**.
4. In the *View* section of the Action Bar, click  (Fit All In).
5. Fit the model to the display area and activate the Isometric view. The assembly displays as shown in Figure 23–24.

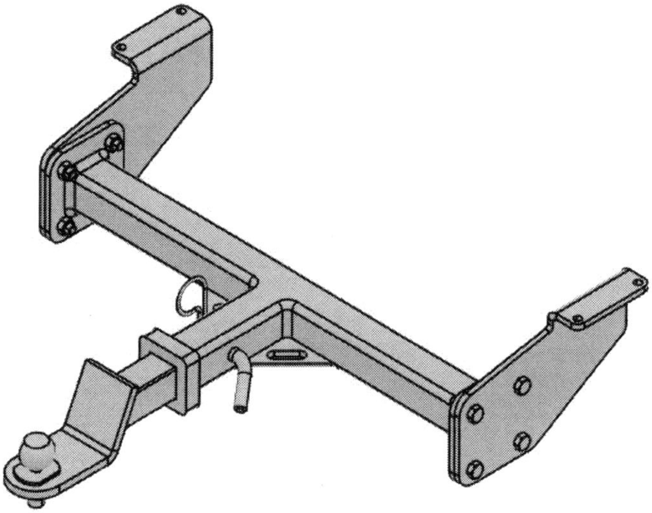

Figure 23–24

## Task 2 - Check for interference.

1. Click (Non Persistent Interference Simulation) in the *Assembly* section of the Action Bar.

2. When the Light Interference Simulation Definition window appears, ensure that both Clash and Contact have a check mark, as shown in Figure 23–25.

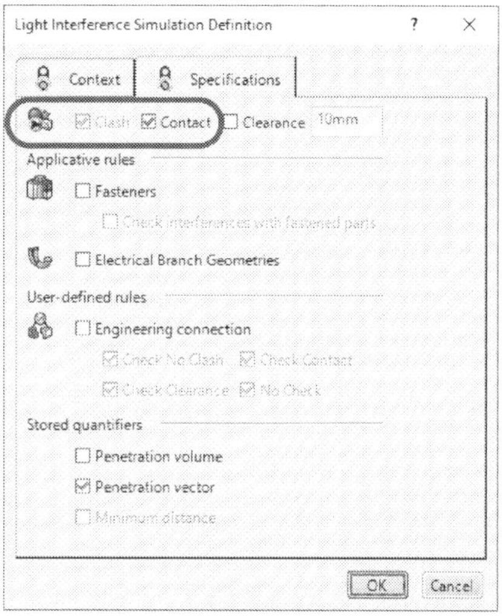


**Figure 23–25**

3. Click **OK** in the Light Interference Simulation Definition dialog box.

4. Click at the bottom center of the screen, if required. The results of the Interference Analysis are shown in Figure 23–26.

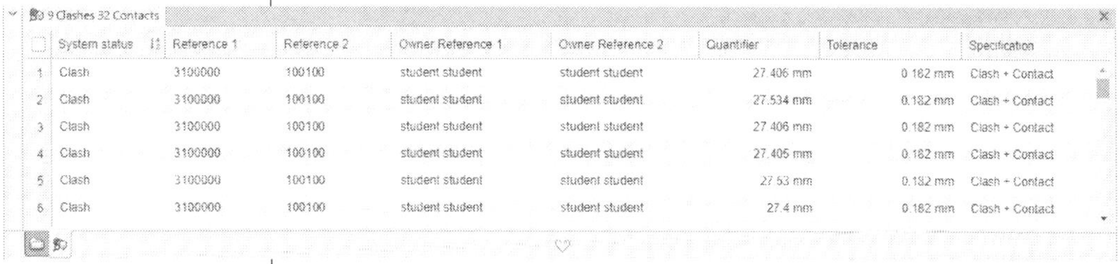
9 Clashes 32 Contacts

| | System status | Reference 1 | Reference 2 | Owner Reference 1 | Owner Reference 2 | Quantifier | Tolerance | Specification |
|---|---|---|---|---|---|---|---|---|
| 1 | Clash | 3100000 | 100100 | student student | student student | 27.406 mm | 0.182 mm | Clash + Contact |
| 2 | Clash | 3100000 | 100100 | student student | student student | 27.534 mm | 0.182 mm | Clash + Contact |
| 3 | Clash | 3100000 | 100100 | student student | student student | 27.406 mm | 0.182 mm | Clash + Contact |
| 4 | Clash | 3100000 | 100100 | student student | student student | 27.405 mm | 0.182 mm | Clash + Contact |
| 5 | Clash | 3100000 | 100100 | student student | student student | 27.53 mm | 0.182 mm | Clash + Contact |
| 6 | Clash | 3100000 | 100100 | student student | student student | 27.4 mm | 0.182 mm | Clash + Contact |

**Figure 23–26**

5. Note the detected clash conditions listed in the *System Status* column.

6. Select the first row where clash is indicated. The model zooms in to display the location of the clash on the model. The clash is between the **T-Support** and the **Bolt** as shown in Figure 23–27.

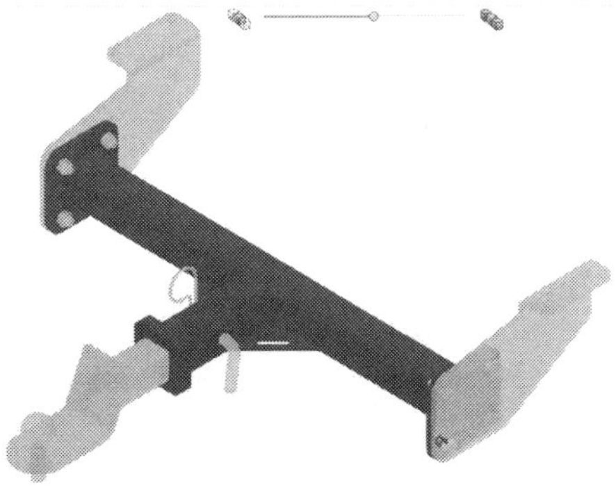

Figure 23–27

7. Continue to review the other clashes in the model. There is a problem with the placement of some of the bolts, and possibly the retaining pin, and the **Ball_Mount** product.

8. Click  in the upper right of the table to close the panel and exit the analysis.

**Task 3 - Investigate the cause of the clash with measurements and sectioning.**

1. In the *Tools* section of the Action Bar, click  (Clipping Tool) to investigate the location of the first clash.

*If you accidentally select in the background, the Clipping Tool will finish. To get back into editing the Clipping Tool, select  (Edit Clipping) from the Action Bar.*

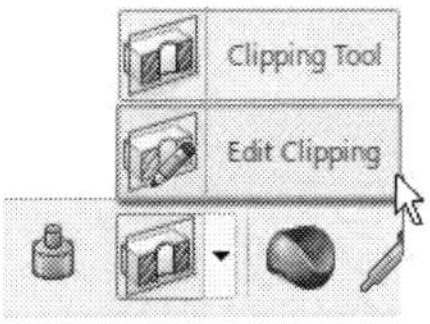


2. Once the Clipping Tool has been activated, a gray rectangle indicating a clipping plane will display. Select on the clipping plane to display the context menu.

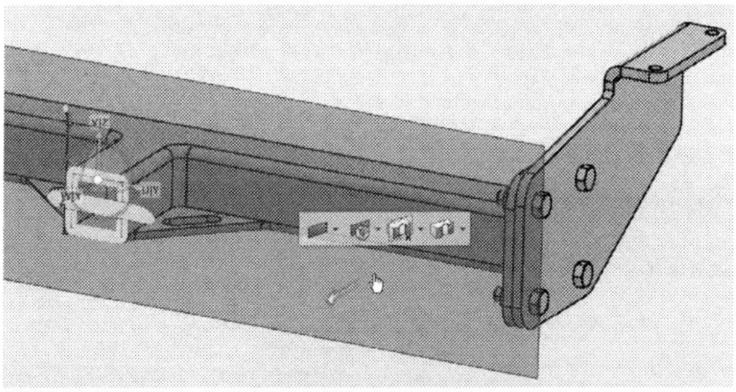

Figure 23–28

3. In the context toolbar, click (Specify Position) Select the center axis of each bolt as shown in Figure 23–29. Turn the model as needed to be able to easily select those references.

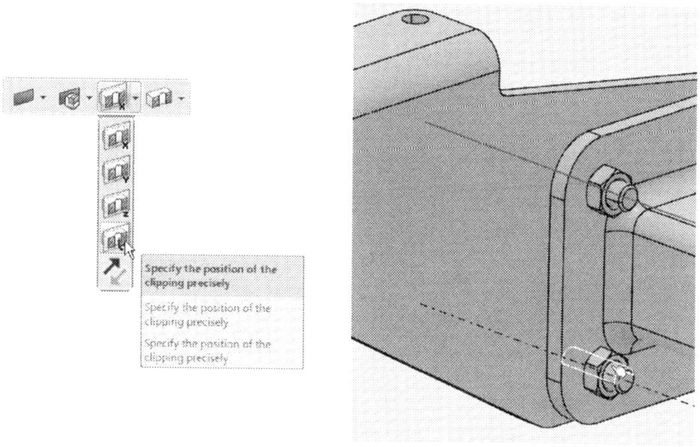


**Figure 23–29**

4. Zoom in and rotate if necessary on the bottom bolt clash location to examine the reason for the clash, as shown in Figure 23–30. Selecting (Back) from the *View* section will help with this as well.

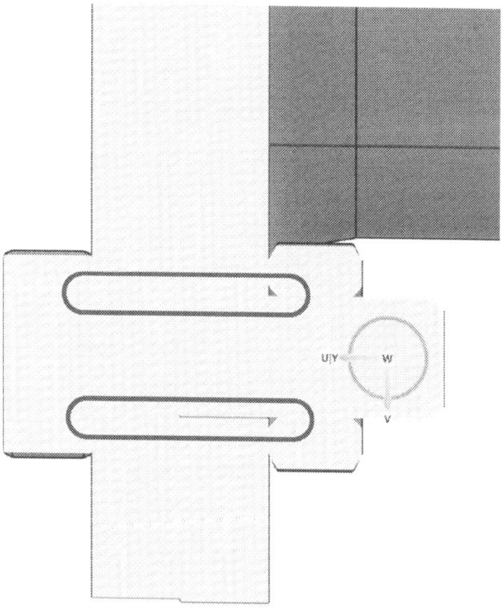

**Figure 23–30**

5. It maybe difficult to see the interference with half of the model still showing and all the parts the same color. Select on the Clipping Plane to get the context menu to appear and select (Only Contour), as shown in Figure 23–31. The upper portion of the intersection should display interference and the lower portion of the intersection should display clearance zoom in as needed.

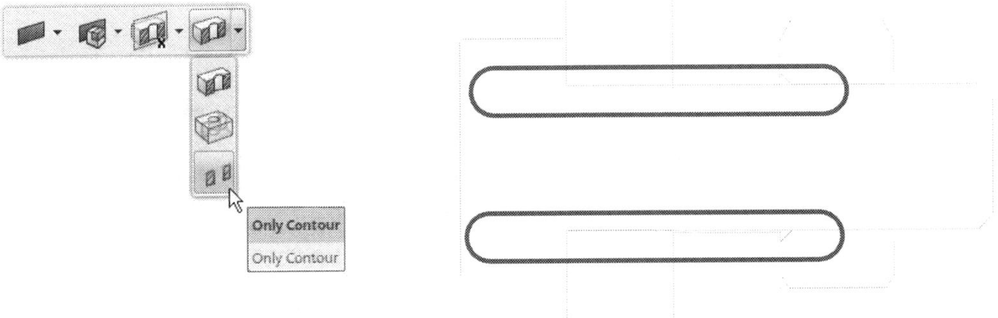


**Figure 23–31**

6. Select in the white background to complete the **Clipping Tool** command.

7. The assembly will remain sectioned to deactivate the section select (Clipping Tool) in the *Tools* section of the Action Bar again to toggle it off.

8. Click (Measure Item) from the *Tools* section to investigate further.

9. Select the edge of the support as shown in Figure 23–32. Its value is **89.2mm**.

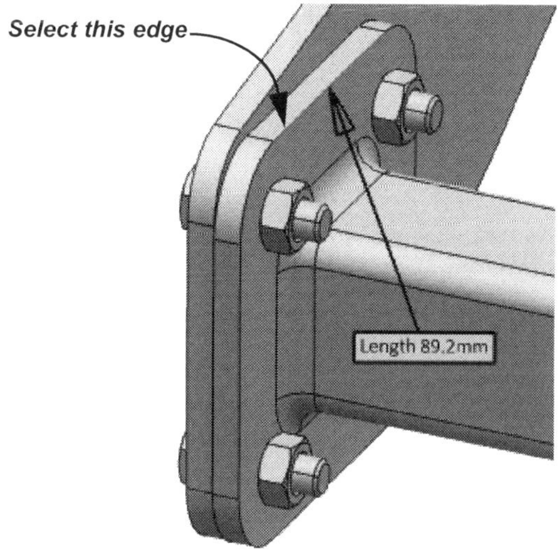


**Figure 23–32**

10. Select the edge shown in Figure 23–33. Its value is also **89.2mm**. These dimensions are used for the increment of the hole pattern.

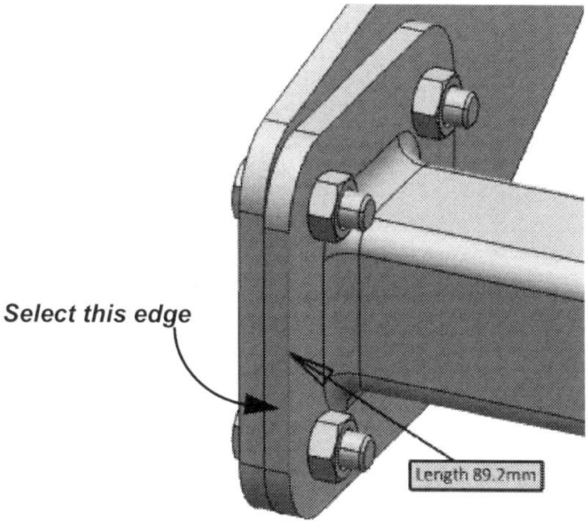


**Figure 23–33**

11. Click **OK** in the Measure Items window to close the window.

12. Verify that the dimensional increment of RectPattern.1 and RectPattern.2 for part **3100000** is **89.2mm** in both directions.You can do this by double-clicking on part **3100000**, then double-clicking on the patterns.

13. When done, make sure that Product 65100011 is active by double-clicking on it at the top of the tree. It should turn blue.

14. Click (Measure Between) in the *Tools* section of the Action Bar.

15. Measure between the spacing of the holes in the brace, as shown in Figure 23–34. Here, you can select the axis of the bolts because they are aligned with the holes.

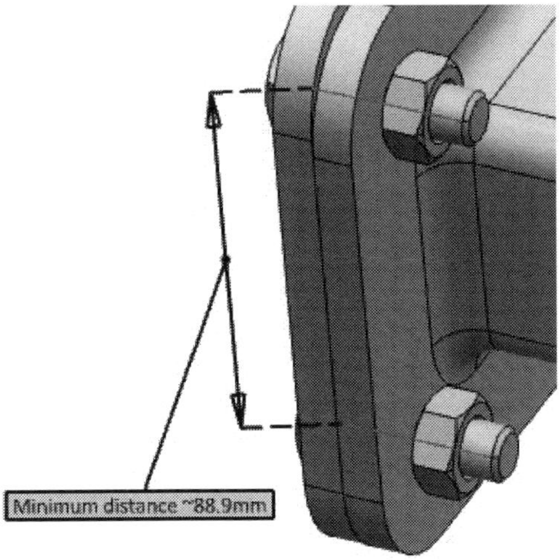


**Figure 23–34**

16. Note that the hole spacing for this pattern is **88.9** and not **89.2**, which is the dimension used by the pattern.

17. Modify the spacing of RectPattern.1 in both the **3100001** and **3100002** parts to [**89.2**]. And select (Exit Assembly Feature Specification app) after each part modification.

18. Update the assembly. Verify that the top-level assembly is active by double-clicking on **65100011** in the specification tree.

19. Check for clash again. There should not be any clash involving the bolts.

20. Click (Measure Inertia) and investigate the mass properties.

21. Save the assembly and close the tab.

# Practice 23b Weight Calculations

## Practice Objectives

- Assign material.
- Calculate weight.
- Assign weight.
- Analyze the weight distribution.

In this practice, you will assign material to a model to calculate its weight. You will also assign weight using the B.I Essentials tool, and will analyze the overall weight distribution.

### Task 1 - Import the part called Support_Info and review how it is modeled.

1. Import **Ball_Mount_Weight.3dxml**.
2. Right-click Ball Mount and select **Open**.
3. Set the view orientation to (* iso), and if necessary, click (Fit All In). The part displays as shown in Figure 23–35.

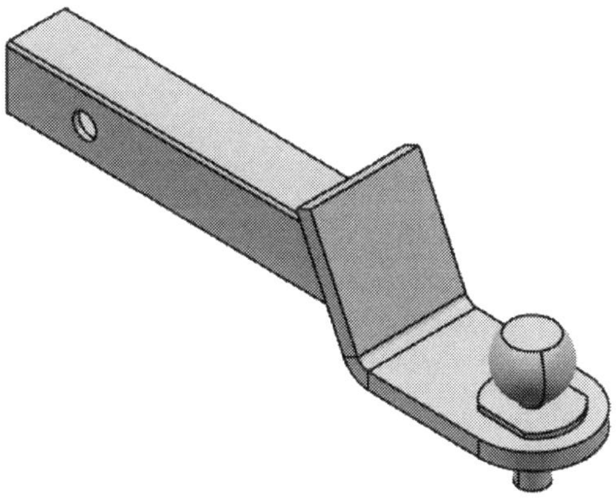

**Figure 23–35**

### Task 2 - Review the weight of the assembly components.

1. In the *Tools* section of the Action Bar, click (B.I. Essentials).

2. In the Choose information to reveal drop-down list, select **Weight Definition**, as shown in Figure 23–36.

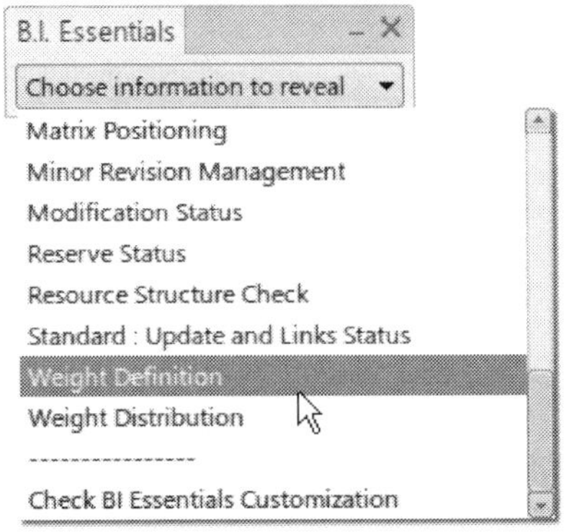


**Figure 23–36**

3. The model, B.I. Essentials dialog box, and specification tree, all update to show the components with weight assigned, calculated, and so on, as shown in Figure 23–37.

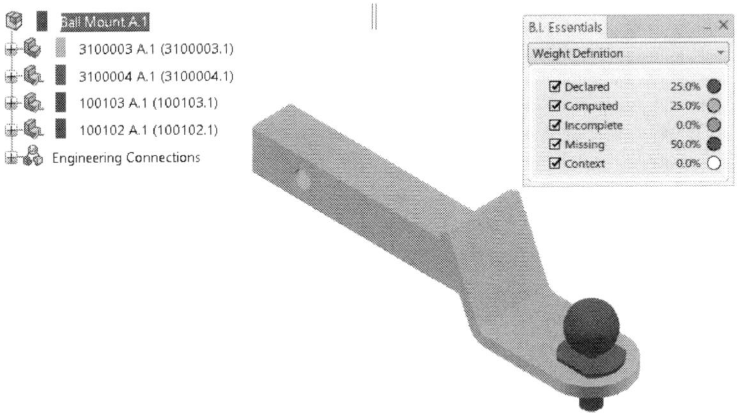


**Figure 23–37**

4. Select the ball part and note it has an assigned weight of 0.5kg, as shown in Figure 23–38.

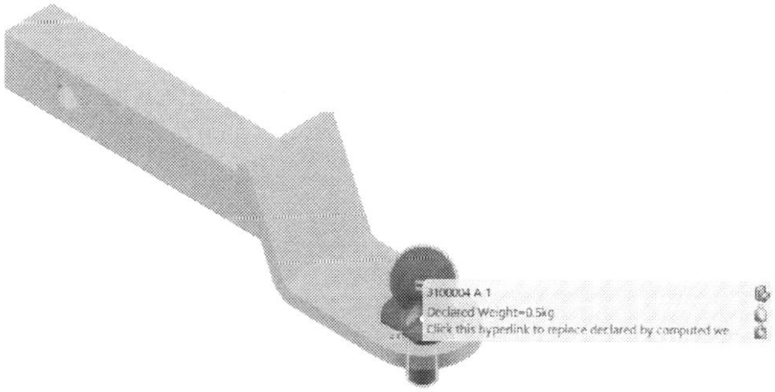


**Figure 23–38**

**Task 3 - Assign a material to the ball part, then calculate the weight.**

1. In the *Tools* section of the Action Bar, click  (Material Browser) to open the material library.
2. Select **MaterialSteel** in the Material Browser window.
3. Right-click and select **Apply**.
4. Select **3100004** in the specification tree.
5. Click  (Close Context Toolbar).
6. With the ball part still selected and the BI box open, click **Click this link to replace declared weight with computed**.

7. In the Weight Table, click (Update) as shown in Figure 23–39.

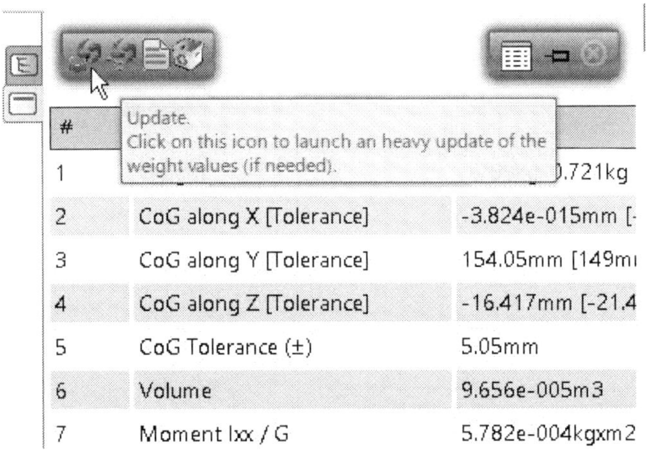


Figure 23–39

8. Close the Weight Table and click on the screen.

9. Note that there are now only two Missing weights, as shown in Figure 23–40.

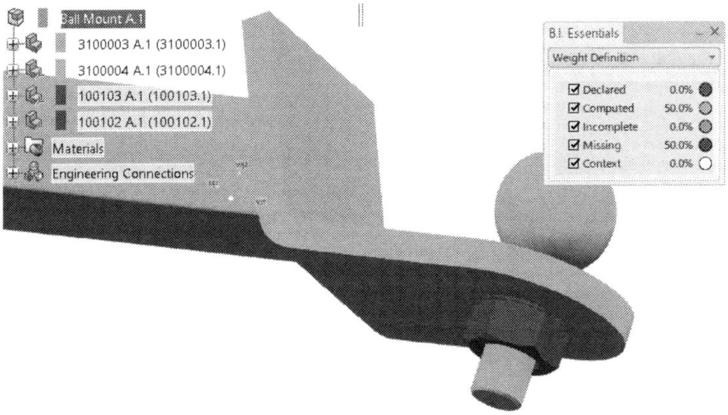


Figure 23–40

## Task 4 - Assign weight for the nut and washer.

1. Select the washer on the screen.
2. Click the link shown in Figure 23–41.

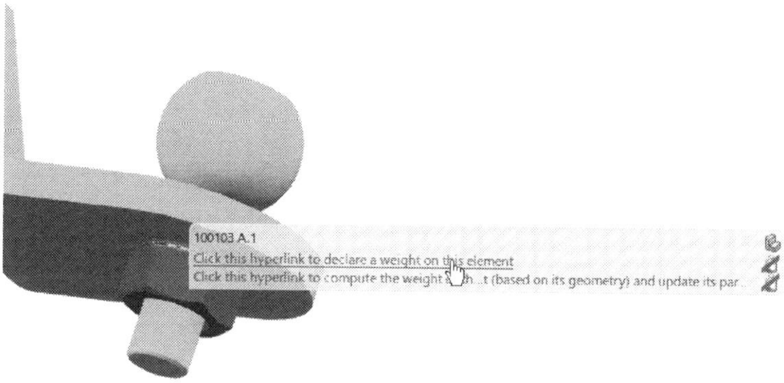


Figure 23–41

3. In the Weight Table, enter **.0075kg** for the weight, and in the *Comments* field, enter **Weight entered from supplier catalog**.
4. Close the Weight Table.
5. Select the nut and use the same process followed for the washer, but enter a weight of **0.1kg**.
6. Close the Weight Table and click on the screen. Note that there are no longer any Missing weights, as shown in Figure 23–42.

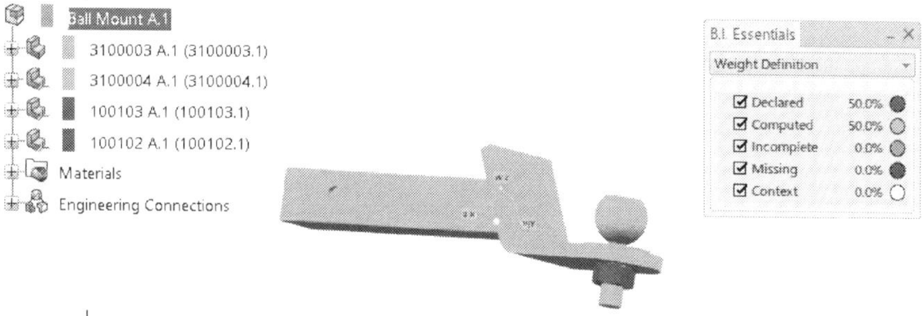


Figure 23–42

## Task 5 - Review the Weight Distribution.

1. In the B.I. Essentials dialog box, select Weight Distribution from the drop-down list, as shown in Figure 23–43.

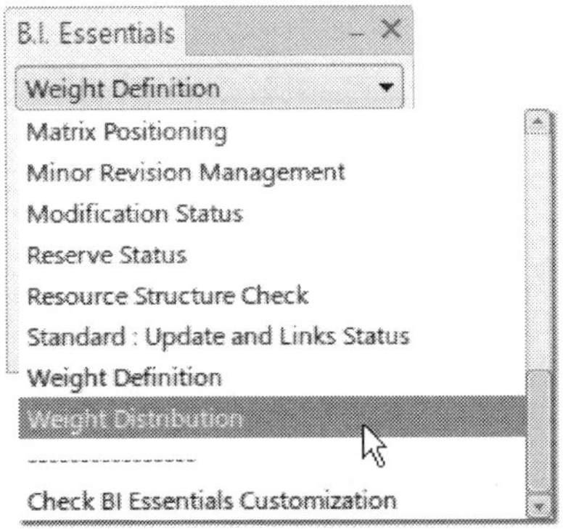


**Figure 23–43**

2. The model and B.I. Essentials dialog box display as shown in Figure 23–44.

*As you would expect, the majority of the weight of this product (88.8%) comes from the sider component.*

**Figure 23–44**

3. Save the assembly and close all tabs.

# Chapter Review Questions

1. You must be in the Part Design to apply material to a component.
   a. True
   b. False
2. Material can be applied to the entire assembly or individual components, if required.
   a. True
   b. False
3. In the Check Clash dialog box, clicking **OK** runs the analysis and closes the dialog box while clicking **Apply** keeps the dialog box open, enabling you to review the results of the analysis.
   a. True
   b. False
4. What types of analysis can be reviewed in the Check Clash dialog box? (Select all that apply.)
   a. Clash
   b. Contact
   c. Clearance
5. A Bill of Material report can be exported out of CATIA to either an HTML or an Excel file.
   a. True
   b. False
6. In the Check Clash dialog box, a negative number in the *Value* column indicates ______________________.
   a. Contact
   b. Clearance
   c. Clash.
   d. None of the above.

**Answers:** 1a, 2a, 3a, 4abc, 5a, 6c

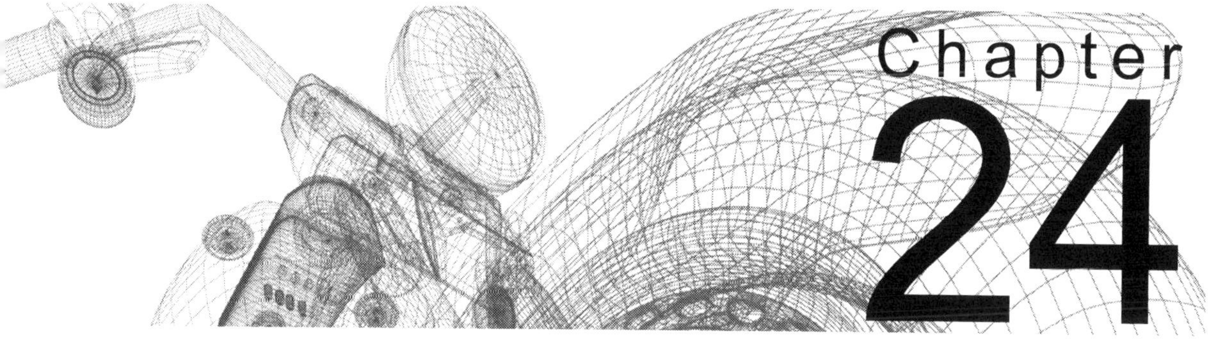


# Lifecycle Management

This chapter teaches you how to use lifecycle management tools within the 3DEXPERIENCE platform interface. Lifecycle management tools enable you to track modifications and lifecycle status changes and to generate design alternatives made to a component.

## Learning Objective in This Chapter

- Using Lifecycle Management

# 24.1 Using Lifecycle Management

Lifecycle Management encompasses management of the phases of design data from concept to release through obsolescence. Lifecycle Management functionality in the 3DEXPERIENCE platform enables you to control:

- File access
- Ability to add design modifications
- Engineering change versioning

Lifecycle Management tools also enable you to generate 3D Part and Product files with a different name to enable exploration of design variants.

## Lifecycle Management Tools

Lifecycle management tools can be accessed by clicking 3D in the Compass and clicking  (Collaborative Lifecycle). The Action Bar updates to provide access to the Lifecycle and Collboration tools, as shown in Figure 24–1.

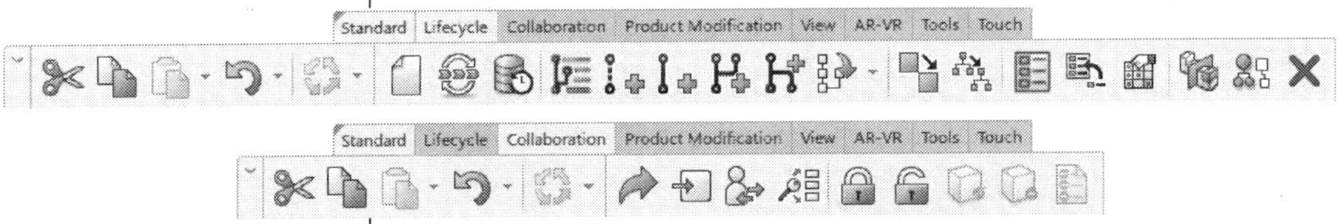


**Figure 24–1**

Some of the key tools are listed in the following table.

| Icon | Option | Description |
|---|---|---|
|  | **Change Maturity** | Controls the data lifecycle status. Five maturity states are available: **IN_WORK**, **RELEASED**, **FROZEN**, **REMOVED**, and **OBSOLETE**. |
| 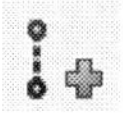 | **New Minor Revision** | Creates a new minor revision of an object (e.g A.1 becomes A.2). |
|  | **New Revision** | Creates a new revision of an object (e.g. A.1 becomes B.1) |

 

| Icon | Option | Description |
|---|---|---|
|  | **New Revision From** | Creates a new revision of an assembly by integrating changes from another assembly. |
|  | **New Branch** | Creates new content from existing content while maintaining a link to the original (e.g. P1.A1 becomes P2.A1). |
|  | **Iterations** | Replaces objects with previous iterations, if enabled by administrator. |
|  | **Delete** | Enables deletion of part references and representations from the database. Requires sufficient security access and should be used with caution as it results in a permanent deletion and cannot be undone. |
|  | **Revisions** | Explore Revisions, Duplicates and Evolutions of the selected object. |
|  | **Lock** | Locks files and prevents other users from propagating (save) modifications to locked items in the database. |
|  | **Unlock** | Unlocks files and enables other users to propagate (save) modifications to previously locked items in the database. |
|  | **Change Owner** | Enables object ownership to be transferred to another user working on the same project in the same company. Object ownership rights are required for transferring to another user. |

## Maturity

Maturity sets the state of the part at its current revision level. There are five options: Private, In Work, Frozen, Released, and Obsolete, as shown in Figure 24–2.

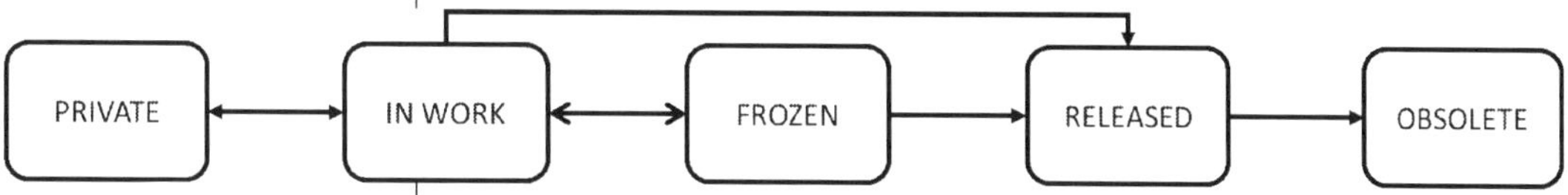


**Figure 24–2**

A private part may be transferred to In Work. An In Work part can be demoted to Private, promoted to Frozen, or directly promoted to Released. A Frozen part may be demoted back to In Work or promoted to Released. A Released part can no longer be demoted.

 

When a part is marked Released, it can no longer be modified. A new version will have to made in order to change the part.

### Change Maturity

Use the following steps to change the maturity of an in-session object:

1. Select the component(s) in the Product specification tree.
2. Click (Change Maturity) in the *Lifecycle* tab of the Action Bar.
3. Select the required Maturity level in the **Choose Transition** drop-down menu.
4. Click **OK** to finalize the Maturity modification and close the dialog box.

## Minor Revisions

A minor revision is a change that does not affect the form, function, or fit of a part. Therefore, the part is interoperable with other minor revisions. For example, the thickness of a wall of a part may be thinned for cost savings, but the part is otherwise functionally the same.

By default, minor revisions are not allowed unless enabled by an administrator.

Minor revisions will show as a number at the end of a part name, as shown in Figure 24–3.

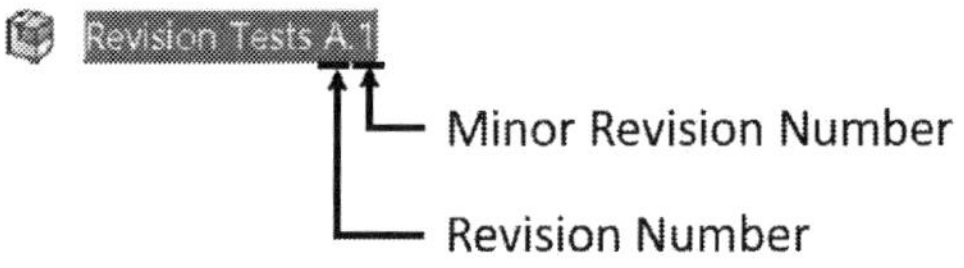


**Figure 24–3**

### Creating Minor Revisions

Use the following steps to create a New Revision of an object:

1. Select the component(s) in the Product specification tree.
2. Click (New Minor Revision) in the *Lifecycle* section of the Action Bar.
3. Click **OK** to finalize the creation of the new Revision and close the dialog box.

## New Revisions

A New Revision usually involves a change to the form, fit, or function of a part. For example, a hole for a bolt may be moved to a more structurally-sound location on the part. Because the hole has now moved, this part is no longer interchangeable with other revisions. This is still considered the same part and will still have the same identifiers, such as the same part number, name, or title.

### Creating a New Revision

Use the following steps to create a New Revision of an object:

1. Select the component(s) in the Product specification tree.
2. Click (New Revision) in the *Lifecycle* section of the Action Bar.
3. Click **OK** to finalize the creation of the New Revision and close the dialog box.

## New Revision From

This command is used for a separate group to make a change, then later reintegrate it. For example, a supplier company may need to create their own revision of the data, work on it, then reapply their changes to the OEM's data.

## New Branch

A New Branch is very similar to a Revision, but with one major difference: The identifier of the part is changed. For example, a new part may need to be built from an old one, but the new part will have a different part name and number. However, the history of the model will still show its ties to the original part.

### Creating a New Evolution

Use the following steps to create a New Branch of an object:

1. Select the component(s) in the Product specification tree.
2. Click (New Evolution) in the *Lifecycle* section of the Action Bar.
3. Click **OK** to finalize the creation of the New Revision and close the dialog box.

## Iterations

If enabled by administration, an iteration of the file is stored every time the file is saved. This command allows you to compare and revert to previous iterations of a part.

## Delete

This command will remove the selected data from the database. Caution is needed as this is permanent.

## Revisions

Press 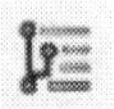 (Revisions) to display a chart, as shown in Figure 24–4, that shows previous revisions of the current model and to show how the current revision is related to other revisions.

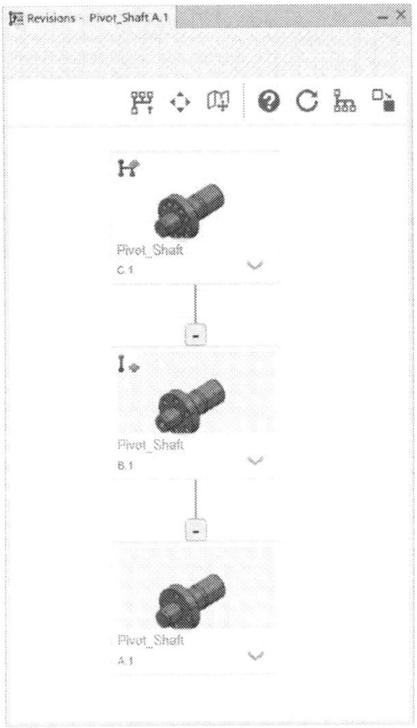


**Figure 24–4**

## Replacing Parts

Once variations of a particular component have been created and saved, **Replace** can be used to quickly explore various design alternatives.

Use the following steps to replace an assembled component with a similar component:

1. Select the component to be replaced.
2. Right-click on the component to replace. Select **Replace > Replace by Existing** (or Replace **by Latest Revision** or **Replace by Revision**) in the context menu.

 

3. If using **Replace by Existing**, use **Search** to identify the component and select the replacement component from the results listing. If using **Replace by Revision**, select the replacing version from the Select a version dialog box. **Replace by Latest Revision** uses the newest revision. The system updates the assembly once a component has been replaced.

Assembly constraints do not have to be redefined when replacing a component that has been created using **New Revision**. Any child components of the replaced component automatically reference the replacement components.

**New Revision** combined with **Replace Component** enables efficient design changes and exploration of the *what if* scenarios typical of an early prototype environment.

# 24.2 Managing Rights and Ownerships

## Lock

To help collaborate with other users, you may want to reserve the access to a certain file so that others will not be able to save over your data. Locking a file is similar to “checking out” from a database. When you have locked a file, other users are prevented from making changes to the shape and writing over it. Some actions, such as creating revisions, are still permitted.

When a file is locked, a green key will appear in the icon, as shown in Figure 24–5, indicating that currently you are the user with save access to this file.

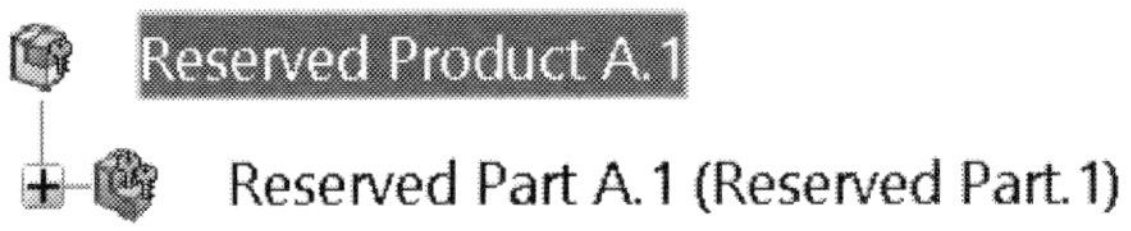


**Figure 24–5**

For parts in an assembly, there are two potential keys. The upper one is the “Instance” which controls the position of the item in the assembly. The lower key is the “Reference” and refers to the shape data of the part.

Data locked by other users will display red locks instead of green keys, as shown in Figure 24–6.

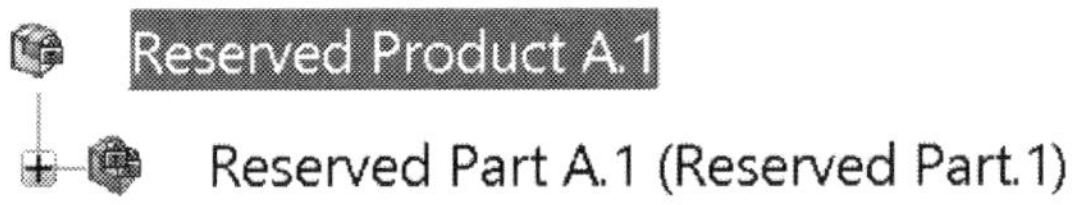


**Figure 24–6**

## Unlock

If you have reserved a file and wish to make it available for others to modify, (Unlock) it. This is a “check in” process.

## Change Ownership

Certain user roles may be placed into groups that have access to specific sets of data. For example, the design group may be allowed to modify the product, while the test group is not. Instead, the test group creates and modifies the jigs and fixtures they use to help with testing.

If a user from a different group needs access to modify an item that they typically cannot, the ownership must be changed to them. It could be that a designer wants to allow the test group to make changes to a specific part. They could change the ownership to the test group.

### To Change Ownership

1. Select the items to be transferred.
2. Click  (Change Ownership).
3. Find the user that this data will be transferred to by using the search located in the top bar, shown in Figure 24–7.

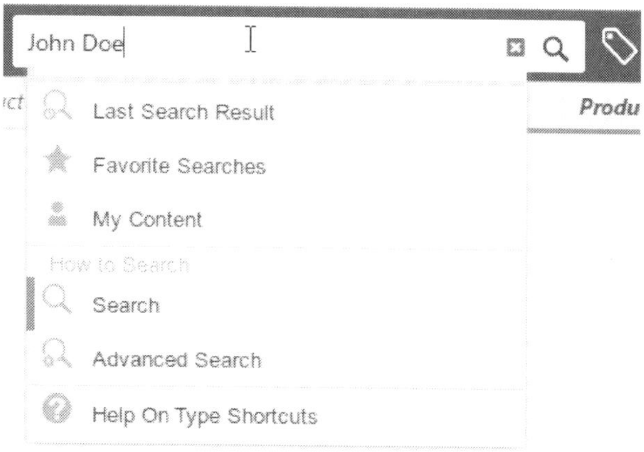


**Figure 24–7**

4. Select on the user to complete the operation.

# Practice 24a Lifecycle Management

## Practice Objectives

- Change product maturity.
- Create a new Major Version.
- Replace a component.

In this exercise, you will modify an assembly so that it displays as shown in Figure 24–8. You will change file maturity, create a new major version of a 3D Part, and modify it. You will then replace the original component with the modified component.

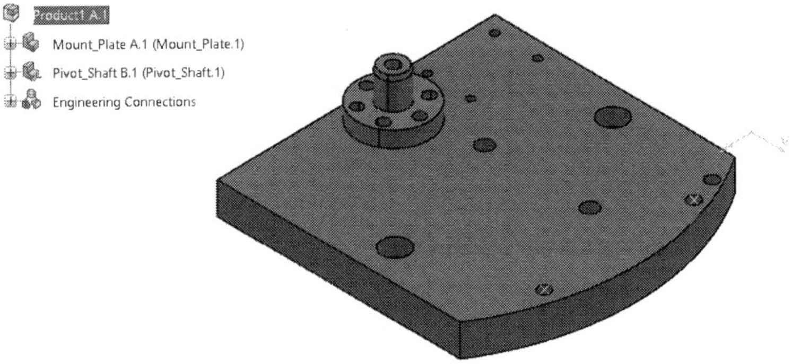


**Figure 24–8**

## Task 1 - Import the Fixture assembly.

1. Import **Fixture.3dxml**.
2. Right-click on **Product1** in the specification tree and select **Open**.
3. Set the view to  (* iso). If necessary, click  (Fit All In). The assembly displays as shown in Figure 24–9.

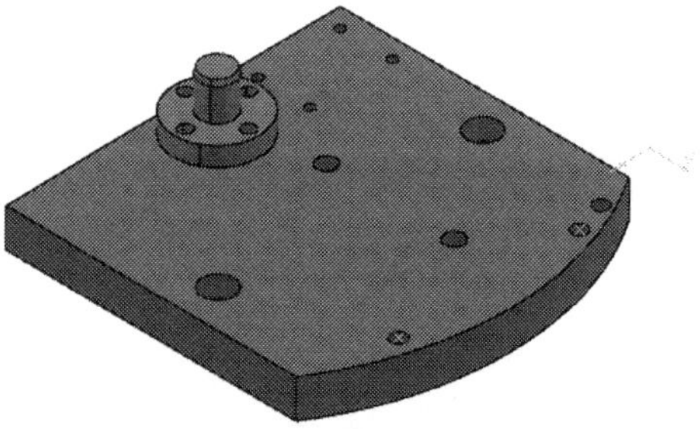

**Figure 24–9**

## Task 2 - Identify the Maturity Level of the Product and Components.

1. In the Compass, select outer circle called **Roles, Apps & Solutions portfolio**.

2. In the apps area, click (Collaborative Lifecycle).

**Hint:**

Do not click (Collaborative Lifecycle), as this will open a browser window for your 3DDashboard. Note that the small arrow in the upper right of the icon differentiates it from the Collaborative Lifecycle app icon.

3. Press and hold down <Ctrl>. Select the **Product1**, **Mount_Plate**, and **Pivot_Shaft** from the specification tree.

4. In the *Lifecycle* section of the Action Bar, click (Change Maturity) to open the Change Maturity dialog box, as shown in Figure 24–10.

*Note that the Current Status is* ***In Work****.*

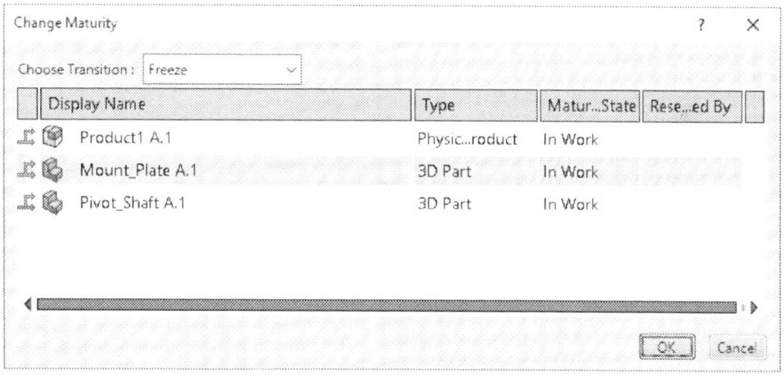


**Figure 24–10**

5. Click **Cancel** to close the dialog box without changing the maturity status for any of the selected items.

6. Click on the screen to clear any selected items.

7. Click (Change Maturity) and select **Mount_Plate** from the specification tree.

8. In the Change Maturity dialog box, expand the Choose Transition drop-down menu and select **Release** as shown in Figure 24–11.

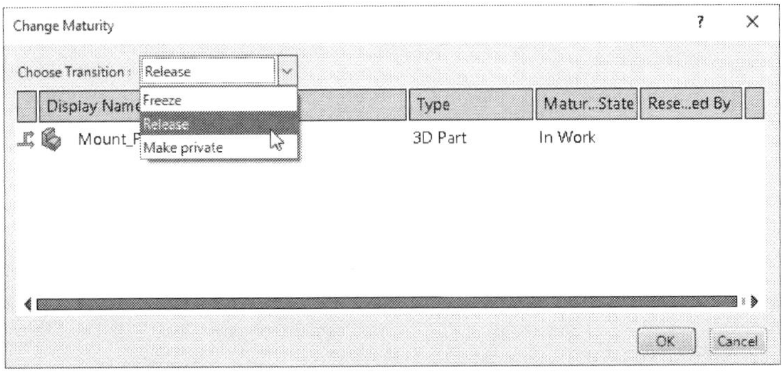


**Figure 24–11**

*Changing the Maturity to **RELEASED** makes the data visible in the database for project members with Viewer level access. See Appendix A for more information on User Roles and Security Context.*

9. Click **OK**, the message *Change Maturity Status Successful* should display in the main window.

## Task 3 - Reserve a component.

1. Click on the screen to clear any selected items.
2. In the *Collaboration* section of the Action Bar, click  (Lock) and select **Pivot_Shaft** from the specification tree.
3. Select the **Instance** and **Reference** options as shown in Figure 24–12. Reserving both options prevents modification of either of the 3D Part or 3D Shape (geometry) levels by another user.

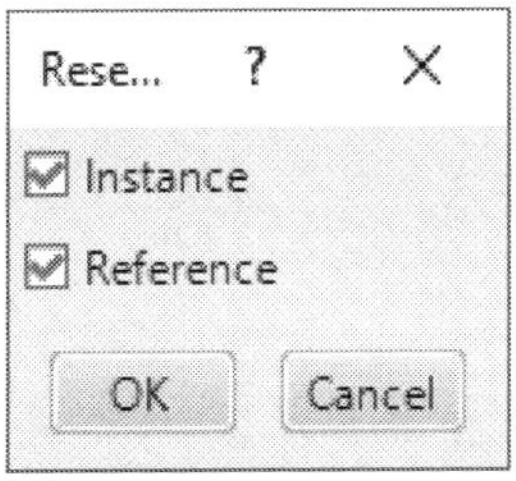


**Figure 24–12**

4. Click **OK**. The specification tree icon for **Pivot_Shaft** updates to reflect the locked status .

## Task 4 - Create a new Version of Pivot_Shaft.

1. In the *Lifecycle* section of the Action Bar, click  (New Revision).
2. The New Revision dialog box displays as shown in Figure 24–13. If it doesn't display, ensure that the **Pivot_Shaft** was still selected from Task 3.

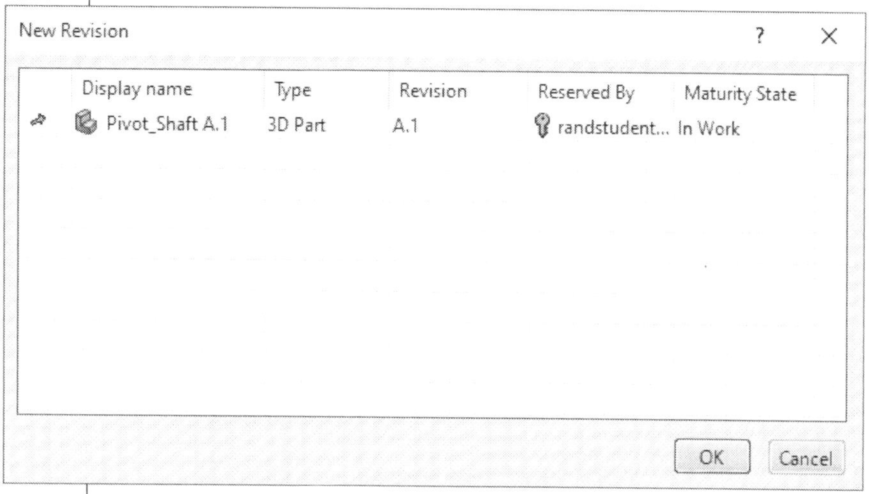


**Figure 24–13**

3. Click **OK**.
4. The **Pivot_Shaft B.1** model opens in a new tab.

## Task 5 - Develop an alternate design Pivot_Shaft.

1. Modify the number of instances in the Circular Pattern from *4* to [6].

2. Create an 8mm Hole feature through the entire part, concentric to the part axis, as shown in Figure 24–14.

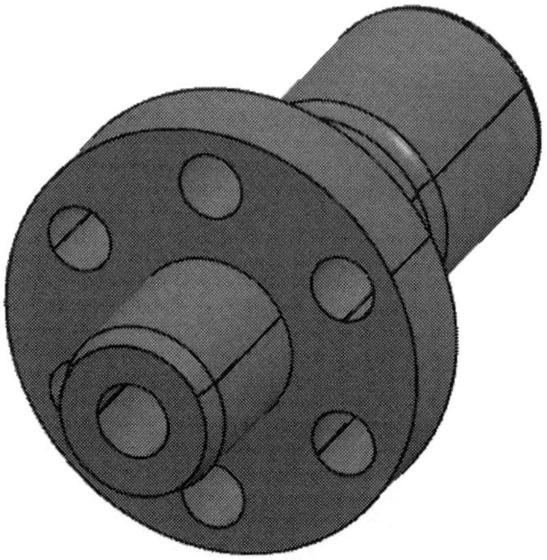

**Figure 24–14**

3. Save the changes and close the **Pivot_ShaftB.1** tab.

**Task 6 - Replace a component.**

1. Switch back to the Product1 tab, and right-click **Pivot_Shaft** in the specification tree and select **Replace>Replace by Revision** as shown in Figure 24–15.

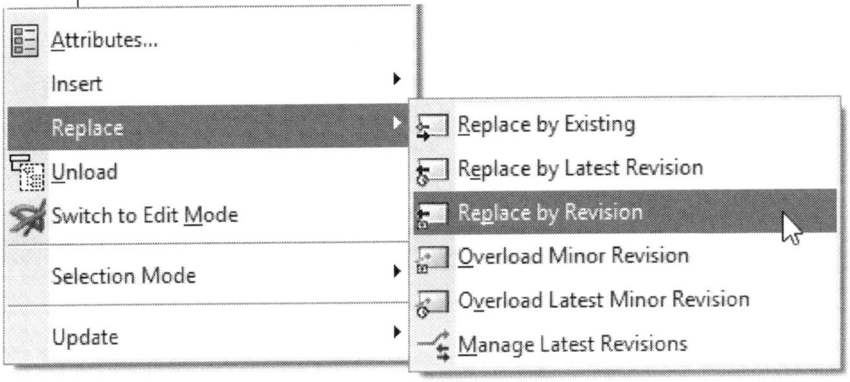


**Figure 24–15**

2. The Revision Selector dialog box lists all of the files created using the **New Revision** command, as shown in Figure 24–16.

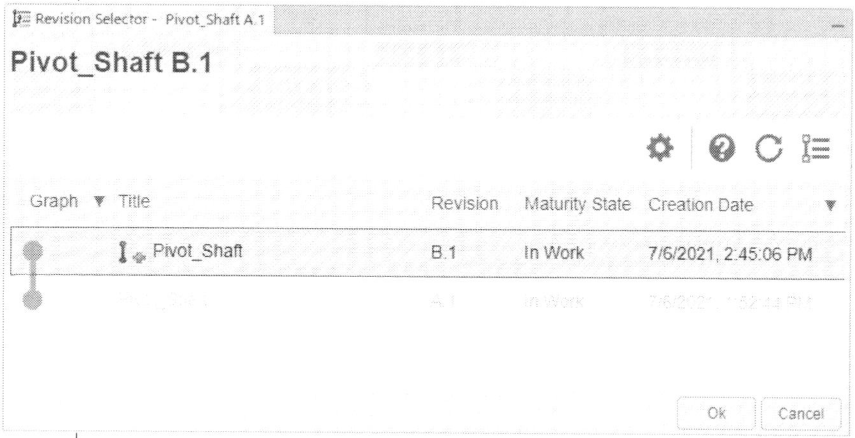


**Figure 24–16**

3. Select **Revision B.1** and click **OK**.

4. The product and specification tree should now display **Pivot_Shaft B.1** as shown in Figure 24–17.

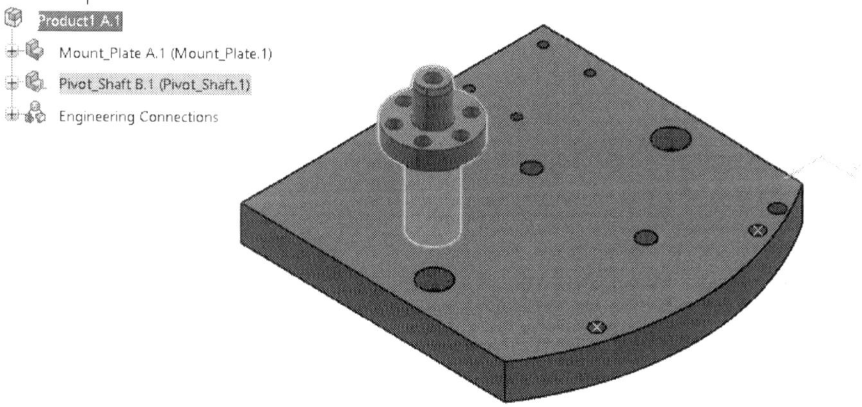


**Figure 24–17**

5. Save the product and close the tabs.

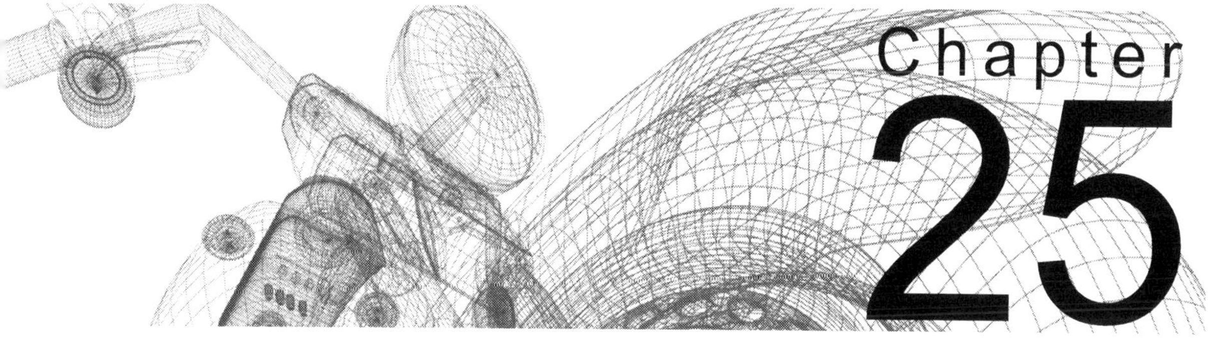

# Chapter 25

# Drafting App

This chapter introduces the Drafting app by outlining the drawing creation process. You learn how to create, modify, and manipulate drawing views. Once drawing views are placed on a drawing sheet, you must add dimensions and notes to communicate manufacturing information.

## Learning Objectives in This Chapter

- Understand the steps required to create a drawing.
- Review the Drafting app interface.
- Add views and create a drawing frame and title block.
- Understand the view orientation compass.
- Review the available view properties.
- Learn how to manipulate views.
- Manually create dimensions and move dimensions.
- Learn how to update a drawing when geometry changes.

# 25.1 Creating a New Drawing

All drafting view geometry and dimension information comes from the 3D model. The 3D model must be open to create a drawing.

Open the model that is to be included in the new drawing as shown in Figure 25–1.

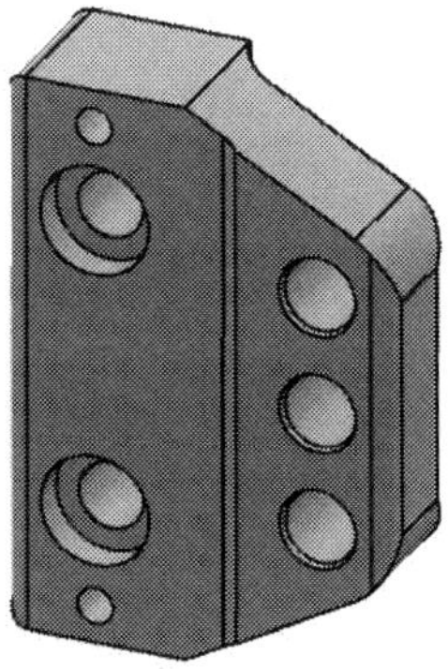

**Figure 25–1**

With the 3D Part or the Product Level active, right-click on the 3D Part level in the specification tree and select **Insert > Drawing** as shown in Figure 25–2.

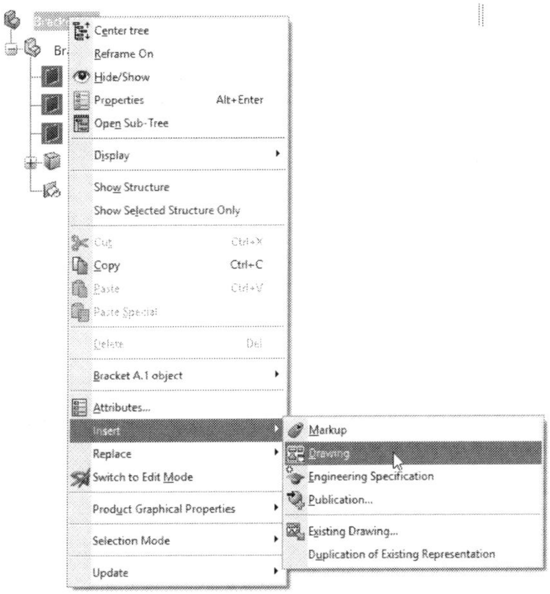


**Figure 25–2**

Enter the name for the new drawing in the *Drawing* tab in the Drawing/Physical Representation dialog box as shown in Figure 25–3.

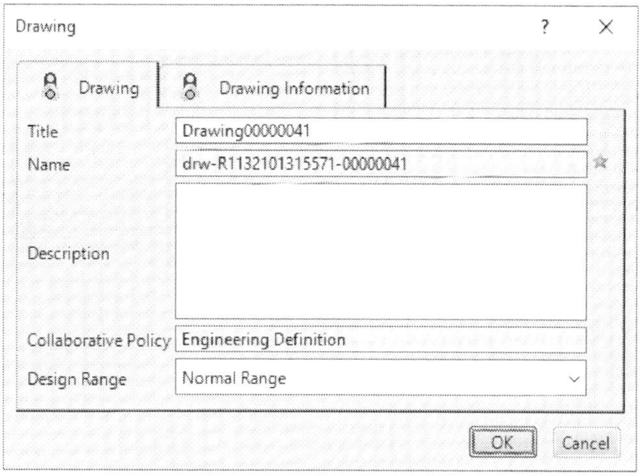


**Figure 25–3**

Select the *Drawing Information* tab and select the drafting **Standard** and **Sheet Style** options as shown in Figure 25–4.

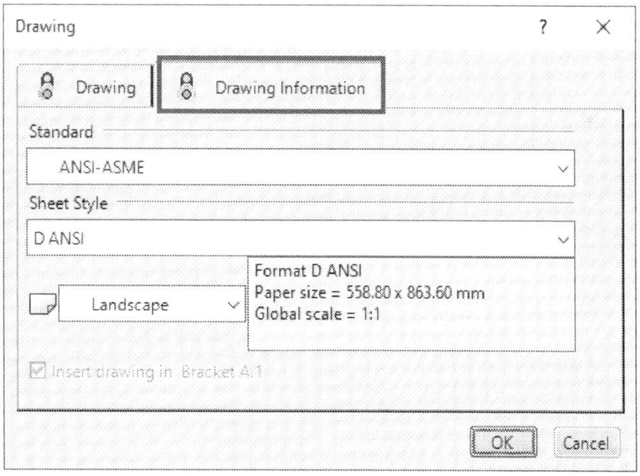


**Figure 25–4**

Click **OK** to begin with an empty drawing. The Drawing displays in the specification tree as shown in Figure 25–5. Double-click on the Drawing entity in the specification tree to open the drawing.

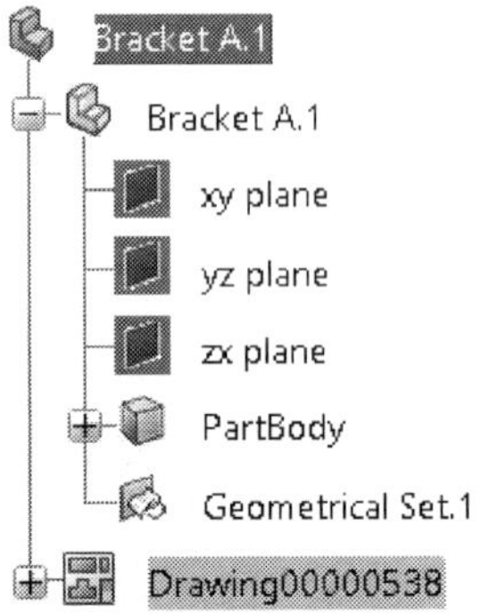


**Figure 25–5**

# 25.2 Drafting App Interface

The user interface of the Drafting app is shown in Figure 25–6.

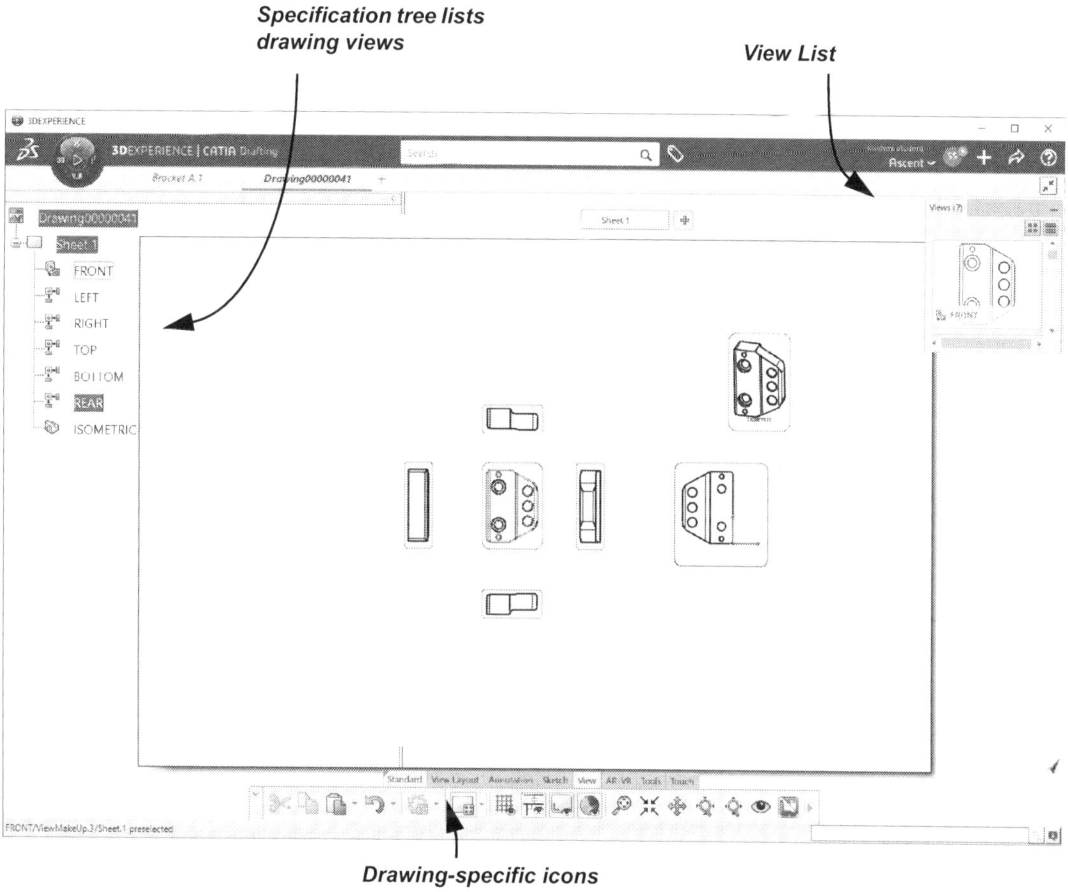


Figure 25–6

# 25.3 Creating Drawing Frame and Title Block

## Title Block

You can assign titles to identify the drawings. Use the following steps to insert a title block:

1. In the *View Layout* section of the Action Bar, click 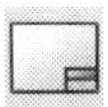 (Page Layout). The Page Layout dialog box opens as shown in Figure 25–7, where you can select the desired Frame, Title Block, and Revision Table.

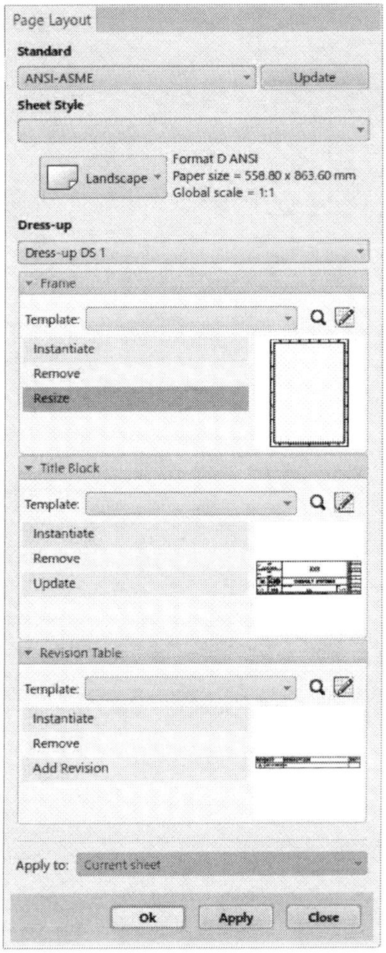


Figure 25–7

2. Click **OK** or **Apply**.

 

# 25.4 Adding Views

Views are added to the drawing using the icons in the *View Layout* section of the Action Bar, as shown in Figure 25–8.

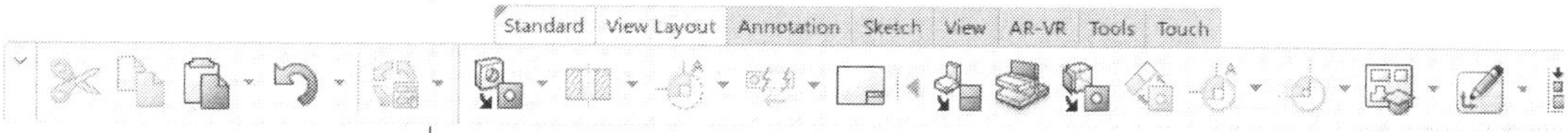


Figure 25–8

The placement and orientation of the first drawing view requires the selection of a reference from the 3D model. To facilitate this selection, you can click between tabs to move from the drawing to part and back, as shown in Figure 25–9.

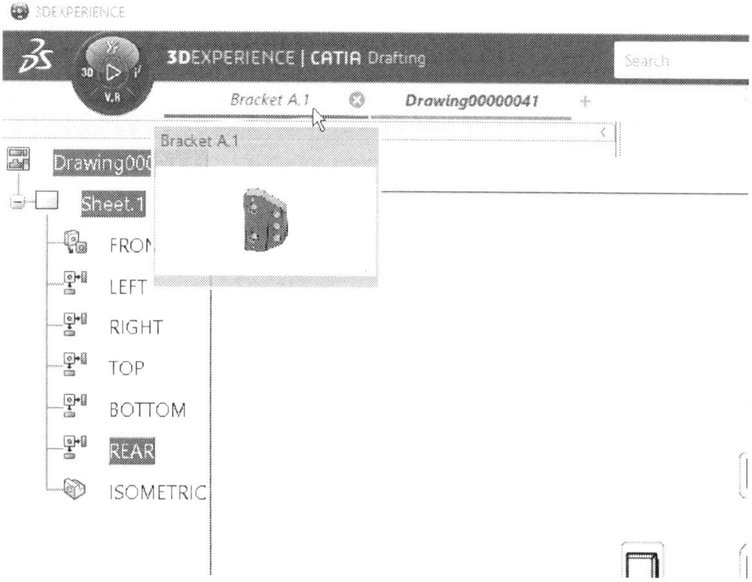


Figure 25–9

The first drawing view can be one of the view types listed in the table below. Select the appropriate icon in the Projections toolbar to initiate the creation of the first view.

| View Type | Description |
|---|---|
|  (Front View) | The front view is also known as the main view. You can use the view compass to orient it. 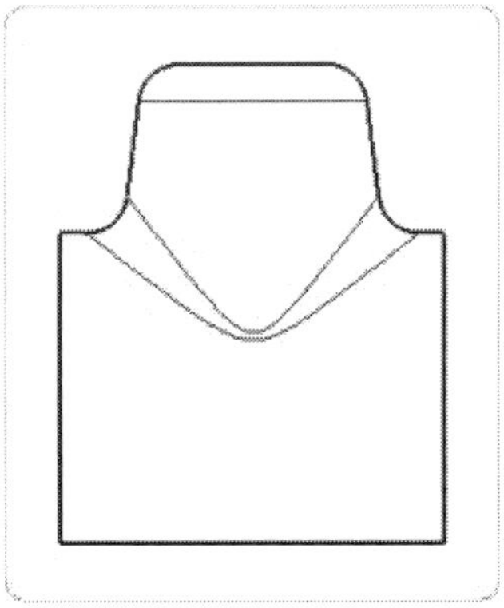 |
|  (Isometric) | An isometric view is used as a reference view, and is typically set at a smaller scale. A reference surface must be selected from the 3D model. You can use the view compass to orient this view. 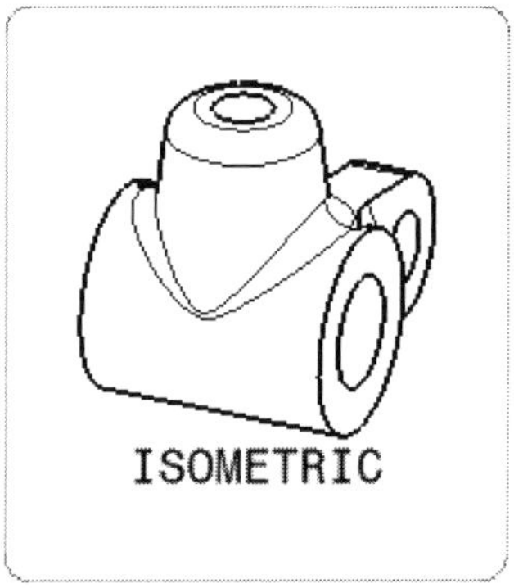  |

Once a view icon has been clicked, switch to the model window and select a planar surface, face, or reference plane. As you move your cursor over each surface, a preview displays to help you select the proper surface, as shown in Figure 25–10.

**Figure 25–10**

Once a reference surface is selected on the 3D model, the view orientation compass displays in the top right corner of the display, as shown in Figure 25–11.

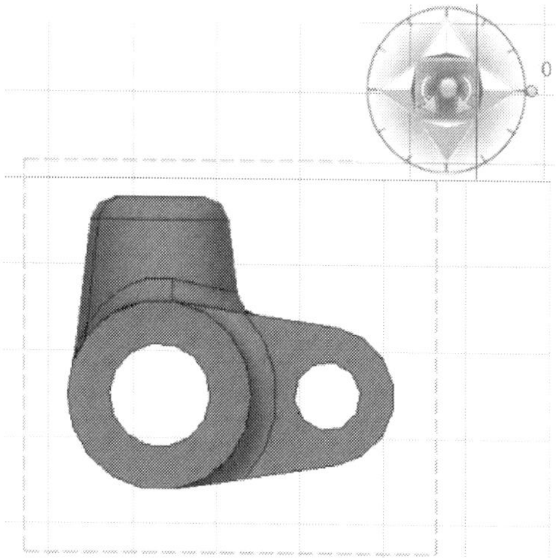

**Figure 25–11**

## View Orientation Compass

The view orientation compass enables you to rotate and flip the front view until the correct orientation displays. The view compass functionality is shown in Figure 25–12.

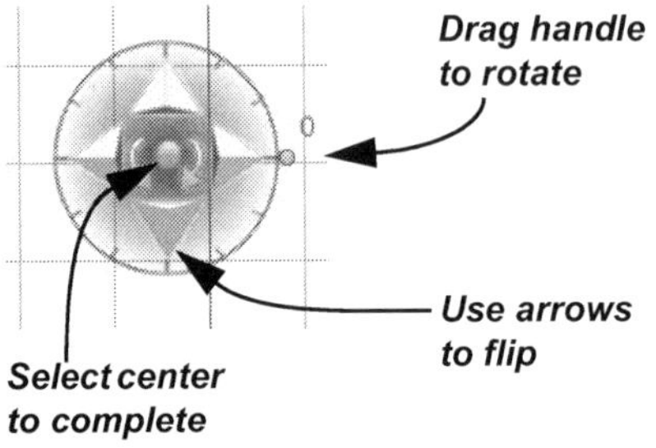


**Figure 25–12**

Use the right-click menu to change the compass properties, as shown in Figure 25–13 (right-click over the rotate handle).

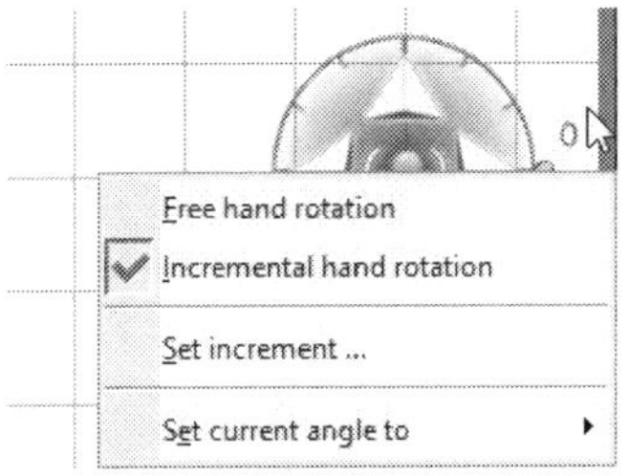


**Figure 25–13**

When you reach the required view orientation, select the center of the compass or select the active view to complete the view definition. The completed view definition is shown in Figure 25–14.

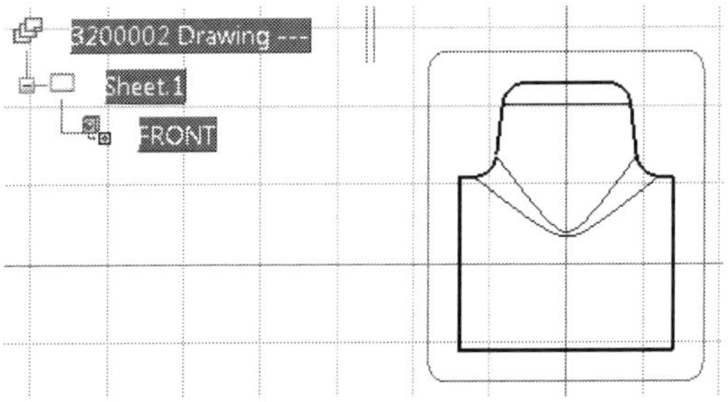


**Figure 25–14**

The view is added to the sheet in the drawing specification tree. The view displays on the drawing with a red border, indicating that it is the active view. When more than one view is present, a view can be activated by double-clicking on its border.

A variety of view types can be added to complete the drawing. Three of these view types are described in the table below.

| View Type | Description |
|---|---|
|  (Projection) | Projects a view perpendicular from the front view. It creates views, such as top, right, left, and bottom and is placed by selecting a location on the screen. The system applies the proper label (name) based on its position relative to the front view. It maintains the same scale value as its parent view.<br>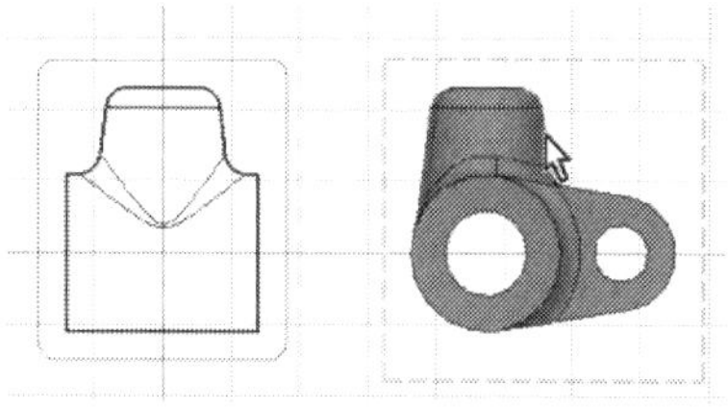 |
|  (Quick Detailed View) | Creates a scaled view focusing on a specific area of an existing view. It is created by sketching a circle on an existing, active view that encloses the geometry to be represented. To complete the view, assign a name, boundary type, and note location. The system automatically assigns a label identifying the scale value and view name of the detailed view. Orientation of this view corresponds to its parent view.<br>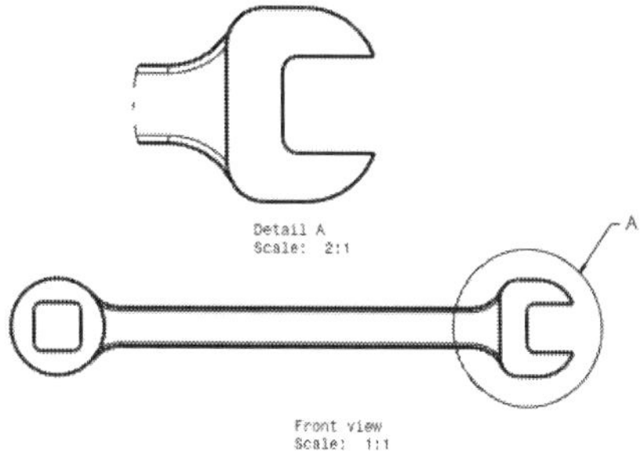 |

 

| View Type | Description |
|---|---|
|  (Offset Section View) | The offset section view creates a section that displays all of the edges that are behind the cutting plane. You can create this view as planar or as a sketched cutting plane. 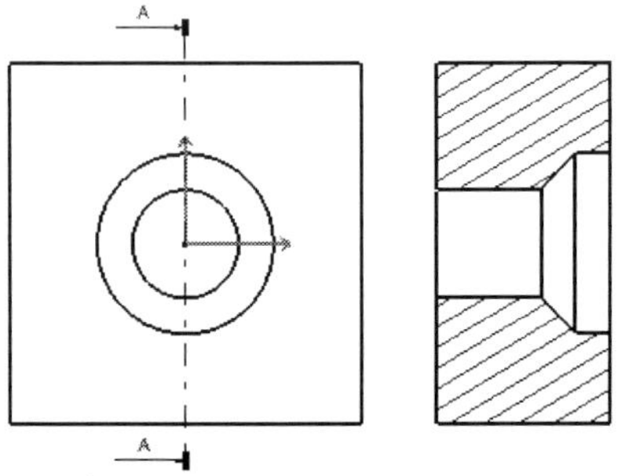  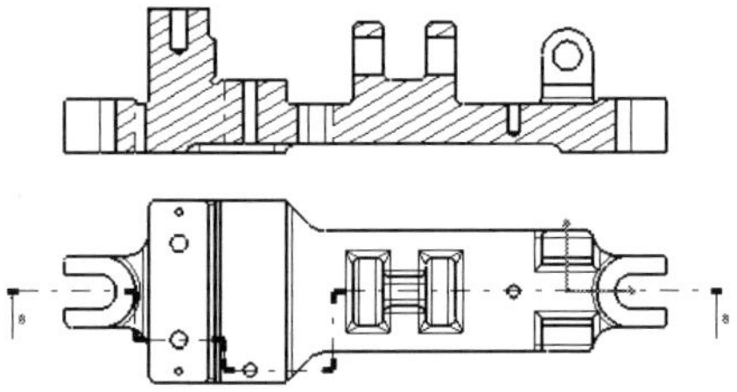 |

# 25.5 View Properties

View properties include scale and orientation, view name, frame display, hidden line display, and fillet display. The Properties dialog box is shown in Figure 25–15.

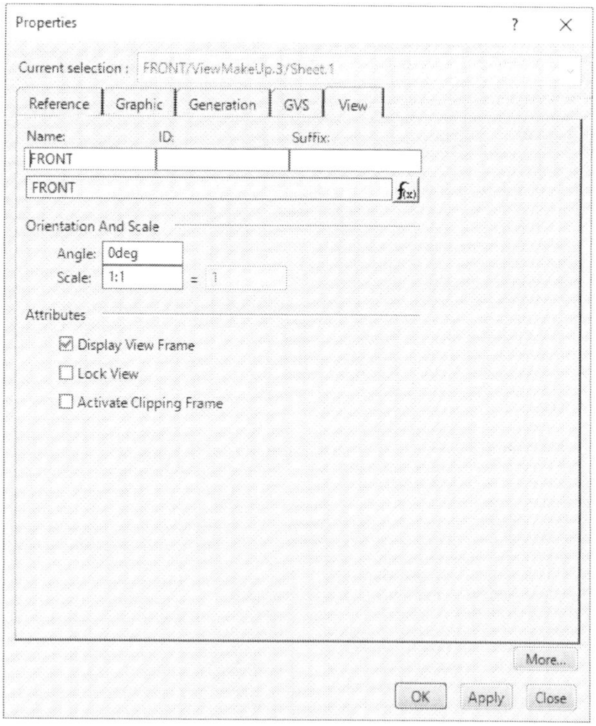


**Figure 25–15**

You can display your views in various ways, as shown in Figure 25–16.

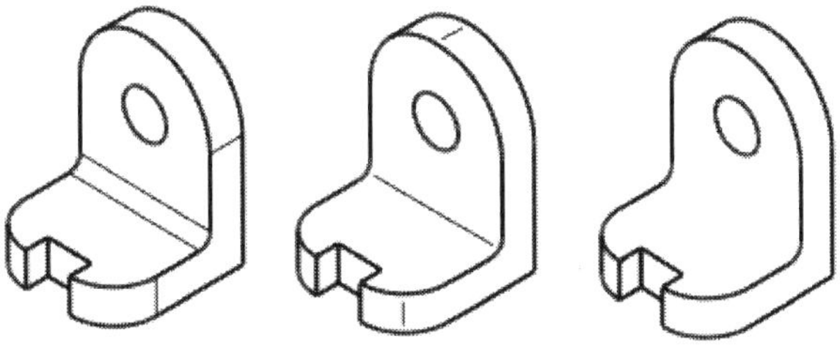

**Figure 25–16**

## Moving Views

You can move a view within the same sheet or to another sheet. To move a view within the same sheet, select the dashed line frame of the view and drag it to the required location.

*Standard windows shortcut keys, Cut (<Ctrl> + <X>) and Paste (<Ctrl> + <V>), can also be used.*

To move a view to another sheet, cut and paste it from the display or in the specification tree.

## Delete View

To delete a view, select the view from the display or in the specification tree, right-click and select **Delete**.

## Hide/Show

You can hide a view to simplify the sheet. To hide a view, select the view from the display or specification tree, right-click and select **Hide/Show**.

## Section Arrow Properties

To modify section arrows, select the arrows, right-click and select **Properties**.

## Hatching

To modify section hatching, select the section view from the display, right-click and select **Properties**.

# 25.6 Manually Creating Dimensions

Use the **Dimensions** flyout in the Annotations toolbar, as shown in Figure 25–17, to manually create dimensions.

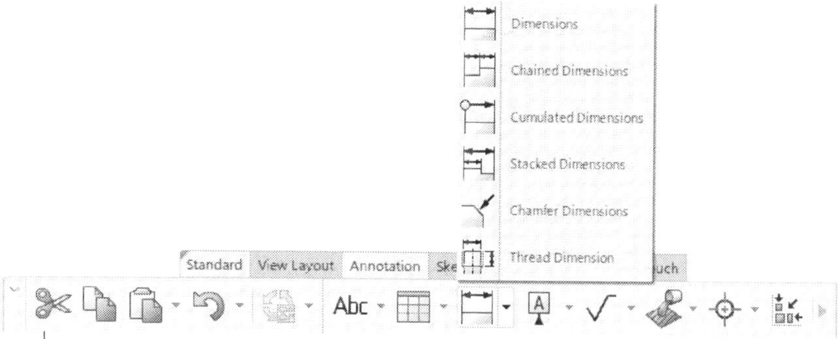


Figure 25–17

Use the following steps to manually create a dimension:

1. Click the icon that resembles the required dimension type.
2. Select entities as dimension references, as shown in Figure 25–18.

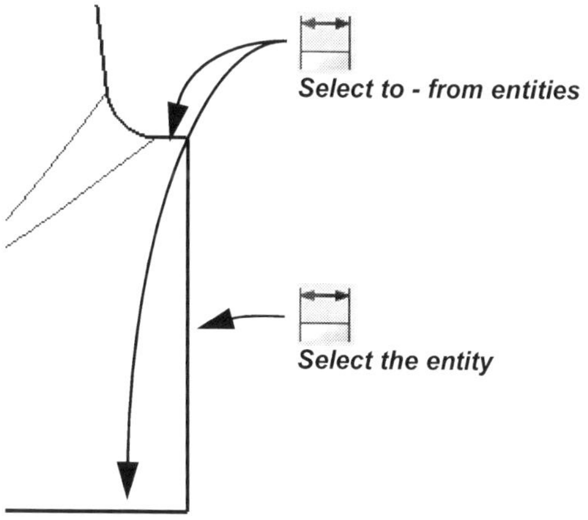


Figure 25–18

3. Place the dimension, as shown in Figure 25–19.

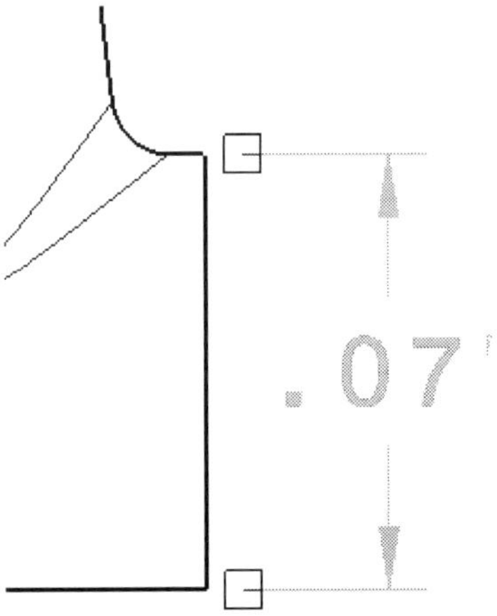


**Figure 25–19**

## Moving Dimensions

You can move dimensions to clean up the display. To move a dimension, use one of the following methods:

- Click and drag on a handle to move both extension lines independently.
- Click and drag on a dimension to move it left, right, up, or down.
- Click on an arrow head to *flip* it.

These methods are shown in Figure 25–20.

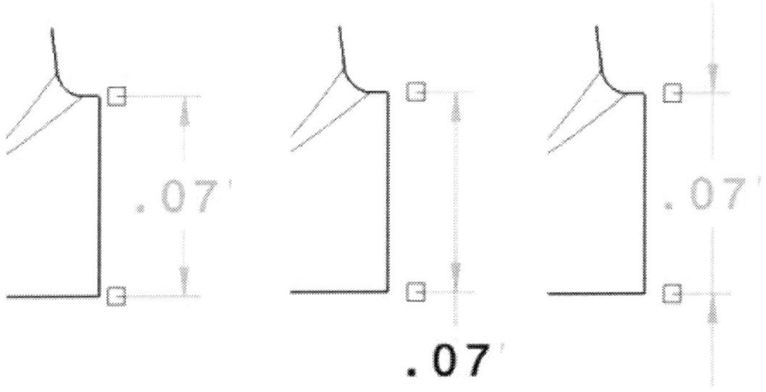


**Figure 25–20**

# 25.7 Changed Geometry

## Updating a Drawing

If a drawing has been created from a 3D model and the model geometry has changed, the drawing must be updated to reflect the changes.

To update the drawing, click  (Update Current Sheet) or press <Ctrl> + <U>.

A grayed out  indicates that the 3D model has not changed, and that the model does not need to be updated.

## Links to 3D Models

If a drawing is open and the 3D model it references is not open, the drawing cannot be updated. To open the referenced model, right-click on a drawing view and select Open 3D data. The 3D Part/Product opens in a new window.

# Practice 25a Create a Drawing

## Practice Objectives

- Create a new drawing.
- Place views using the View Wizard.
- Manipulate the views in various ways.

In this practice, you will use a part to create a new drawing. The drawing will consist of two sheets and multiple views. One of the sheets displays as shown in Figure 25–21.

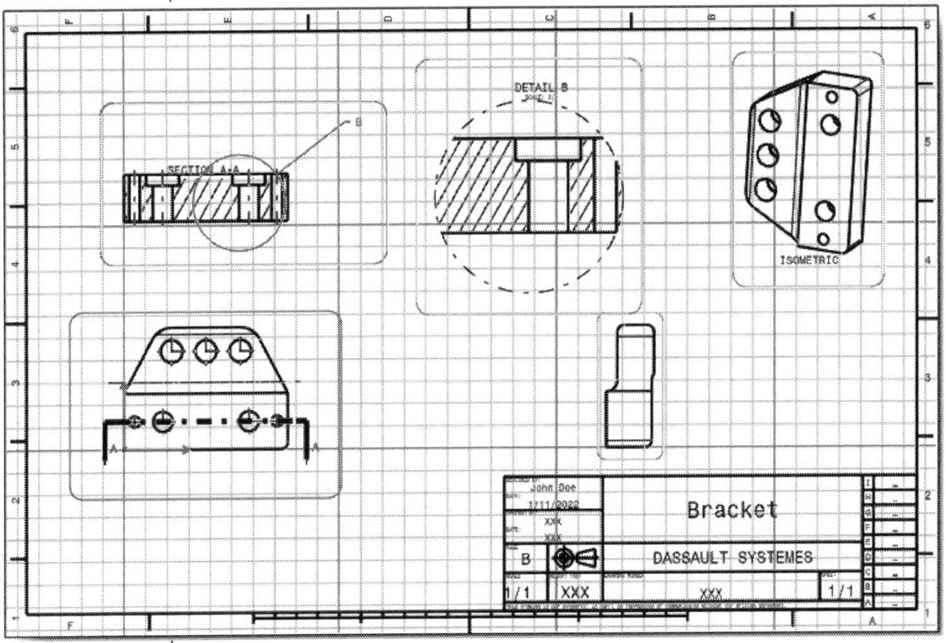


Figure 25–21

### Task 1 - Import the part Bracket.

1. Import **Bracket.3dxml**.
2. Right-click on Bracket in the specification tree and select **Open**. The model displays as shown in Figure 25–22.

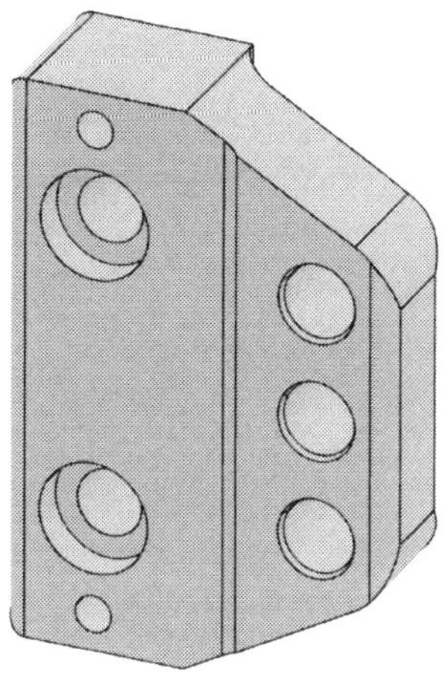

**Figure 25–22**

### Task 2 - Insert a Drawing in the 3D Part.

1. Double-click on the 3D Part level of the specification tree. The specification tree should display as shown in Figure 25–23.

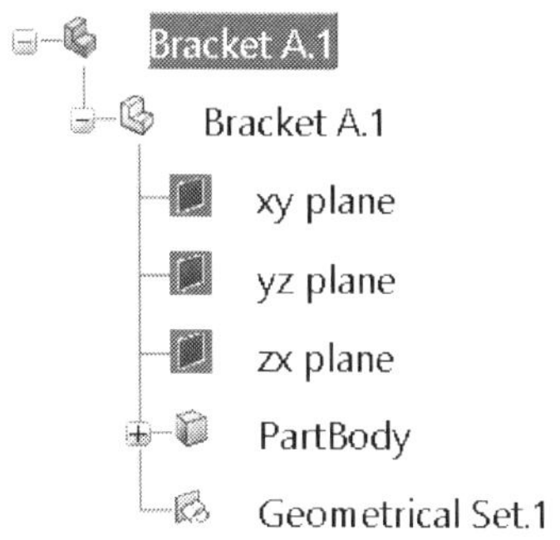


**Figure 25 23**

2. Right-click on the top line of the specification tree and browse to **Insert > Drawing** in the contextual menu as shown in Figure 25–24.

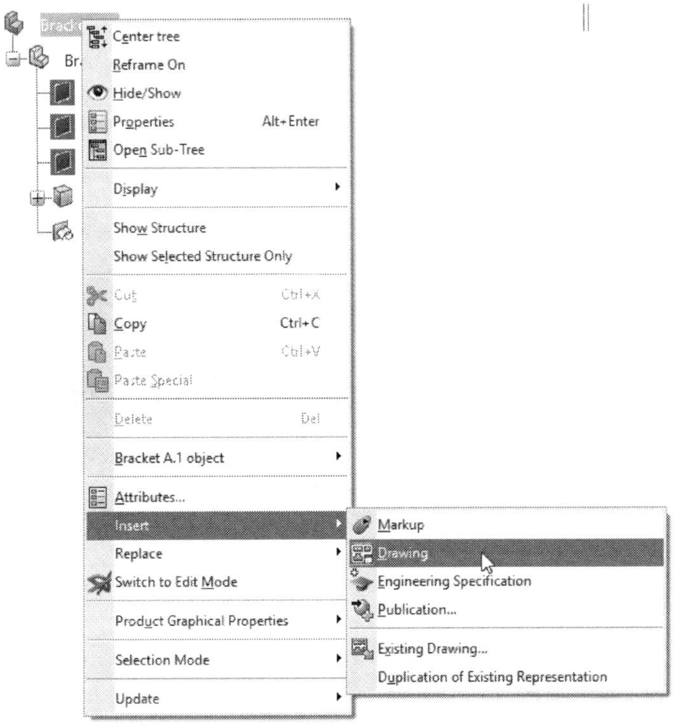


**Figure 25–24**

3. Enter the name ***Your_Initials*_Bracket** in the Drawing dialog box, as shown in Figure 25–25.

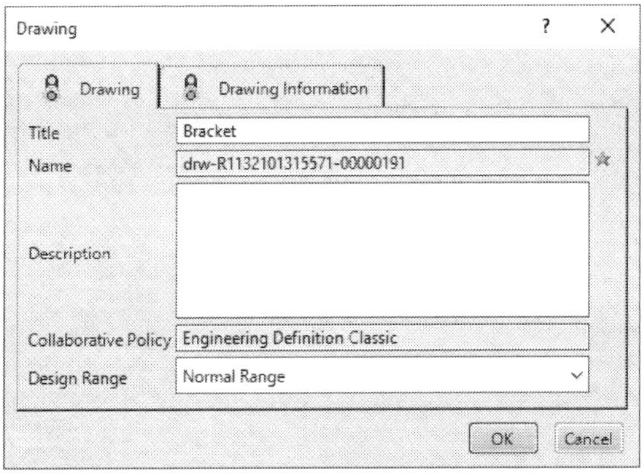


**Figure 25–25**

4. Select the *Drawing Information* tab.

5. Select the following options so the dialog box updates as shown in Figure 25–26:

   - Standard: **ANSI-ASME**
   - Format: **B ANSI**
   - Orientation: **Landscape**

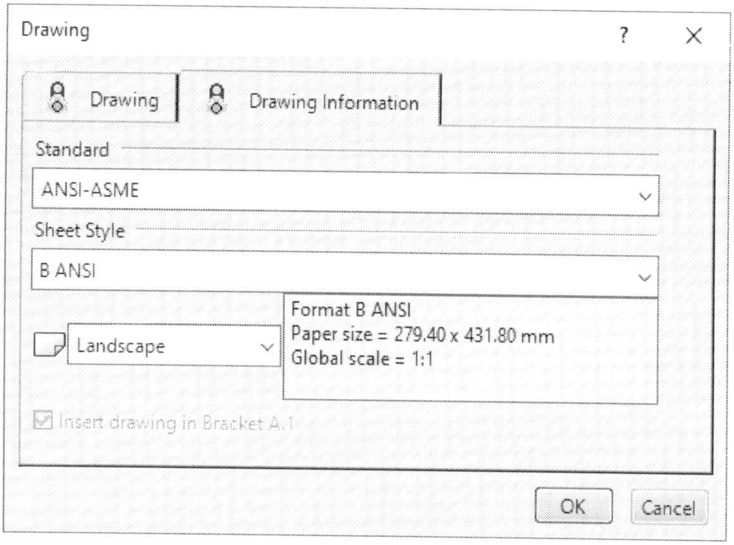


**Figure 25–26**

6. Click **OK** to finalize drawing creation.

**Task 3 - Create a front view.**

1. Double-click on the drawing name in the specification tree, to open the drawing.

2. In the *View Layout* section of the Action Bar, click  (Front View).

3. Select the *Bracket* part tab. You must now orient the view by selecting a face from the model. Select anywhere in the **Bracket** window and hover over the faces of the model. An Orientation Preview window displays the resulting view orientation.

4. Turn the model and select the face shown in Figure 25–27. This surface is selected to face the front of the screen in the front view.

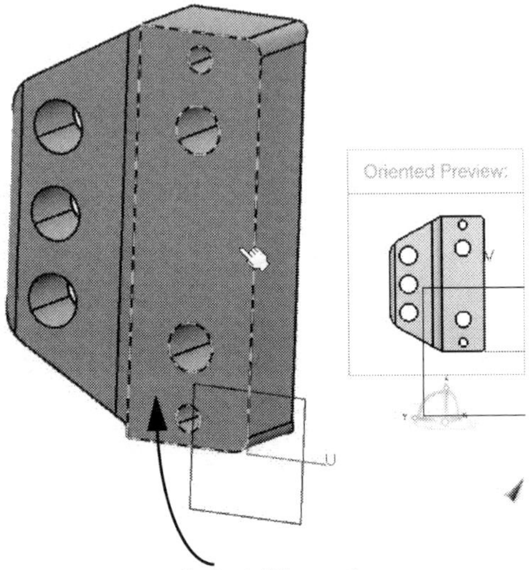


**Figure 25–27**

5. The display automatically toggles back to the drawing sheet. A compass displays in the top right corner of the display. Use the cursor to drag the green handle to the 270° location. The front view is oriented as shown in Figure 25–28.

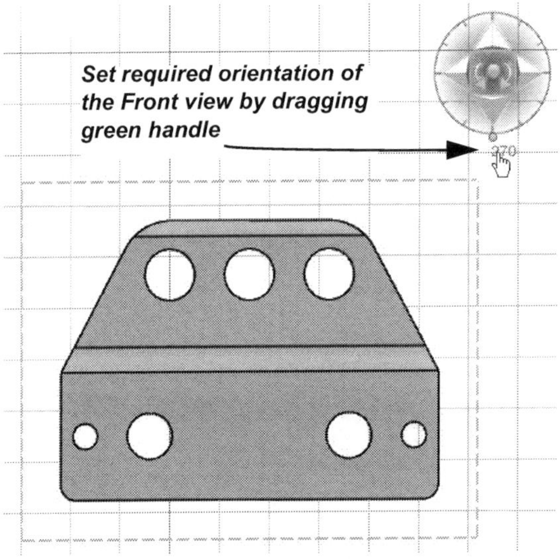


**Figure 25–28**

*At any time the grid can be toggled on/off by selecting*  *(Display Grid) icon in the View section of the Action Bar.*

6. Click anywhere in the drawing to complete the orientation. Maximize the drawing window. The drawing sheet is shown in Figure 25–29.

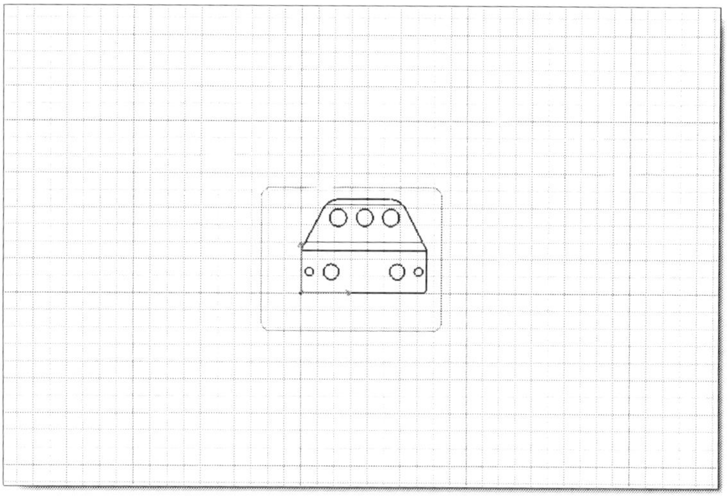

**Figure 25–29**

## Task 4 - Create an isometric view.

1. In the *View Layout* section of the Action Bar, click  (Isometric) in the **Front View** flyout.
2. Activate the *Bracket* tab and select a face on the model. The system orients the Isometric view using the current model orientation. Therefore, the face selected is not important. The system places the view on the drawing and the orientation compass displays.

 

3. Select the dashed green border of the view and drag it to the top right corner of the drawing, as shown in Figure 25–30.

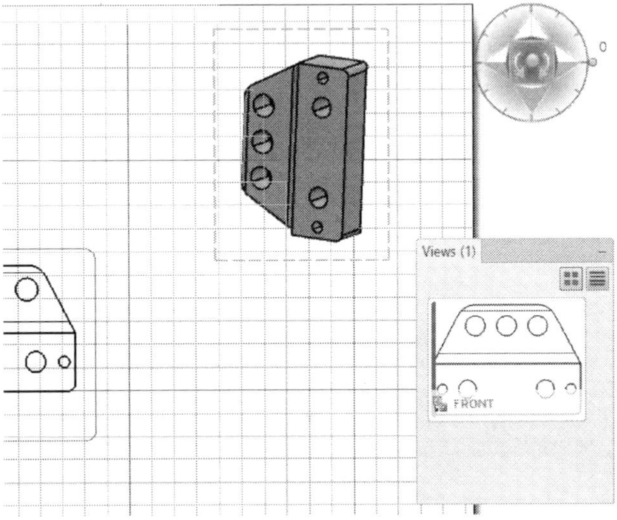


**Figure 25–30**

4. Select anywhere on the drawing to complete the creation of the view.

**Design Considerations**

The border of the front view is currently red, while the border of the isometric view is blue. The red border indicates that it is the active view. Any view operations are always performed on the active view. As well, the creation of a section or projection view will reference the active view. Double-click on the view border to activate a view.

## Task 5 - Create a projection view.

In this task, you will project a view from the front view. The front view must be active.

1. Ensure that the front view is active.

2. Click (Projection).

3. Position the cursor around the front view. Four possible projections can be created, as shown in Figure 25–31.

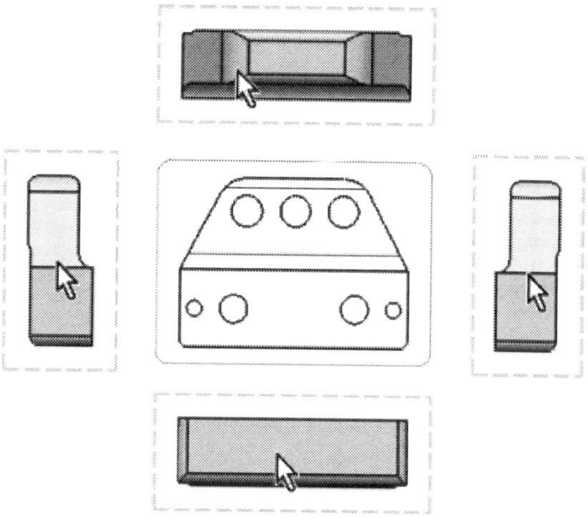

Figure 25–31

4. Create the projection to the right of the front view. The drawing view displays as shown in Figure 25–32.

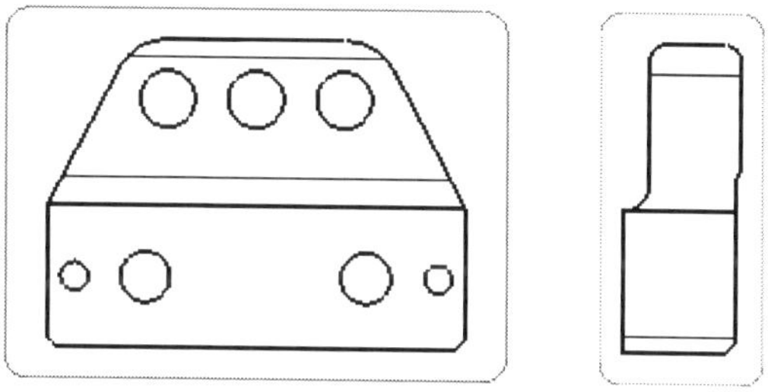

Figure 25–32

**Task 6 - Move the views.**

1. Select the view frame of the front view and drag it to the bottom left corner of the sheet.
2. Experiment by moving the right view. Move the Isometric view as well and note the differences between the linked and unlinked views.

**Design Considerations**

The projected right view is a child of the front view, so it maintains an aligned position with it. The isometric view can be moved independent of the front view.

## Task 7 - Change the properties of a view

1. Right-click on the FRONT view in the specification tree and select **Properties**.
2. Select **Center Line** and **Axis** in the *Dress-up* area in the *Generation* tab in the Properties dialog box, as shown in Figure 25–33.

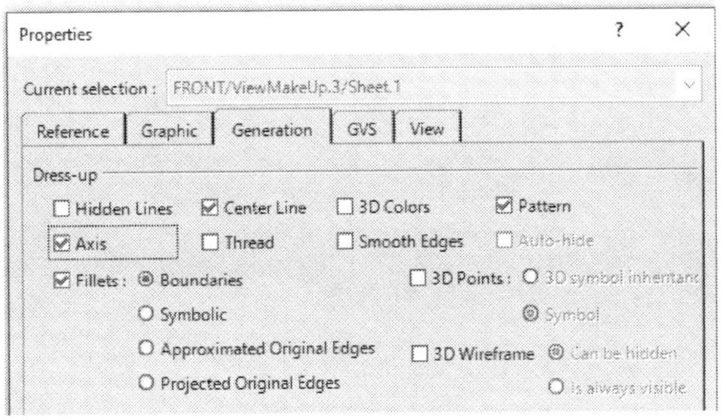


**Figure 25–33**

3. Click **OK**.

## Task 8 - Create a section view.

1. Zoom in on the front view.
2. Click  (Offset Section View) in the Views toolbar.
3. Sketch a line that starts to the left of the view, as shown in Figure 25–34. Enable the system to assume an alignment with the axis of the Hole feature.

*To align the start of the section line with the hole, try positioning the cursor over the hole to create a coincidence constraint before starting the creation of the line.*

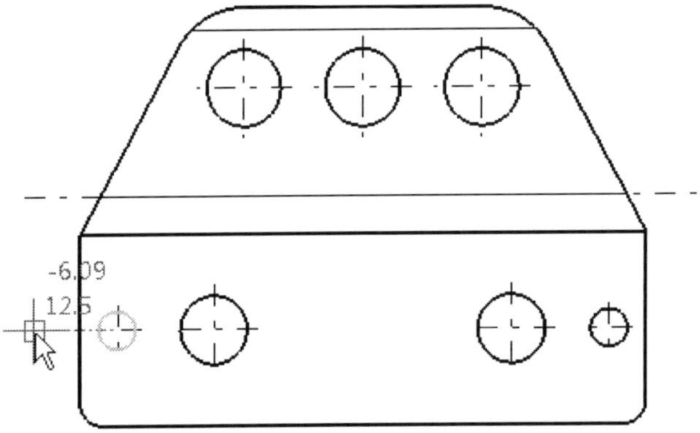


**Figure 25–34**

4. Move the cursor to the right of the front view and select a location approximately one grid square space to the right of the view, as shown in Figure 25–35.

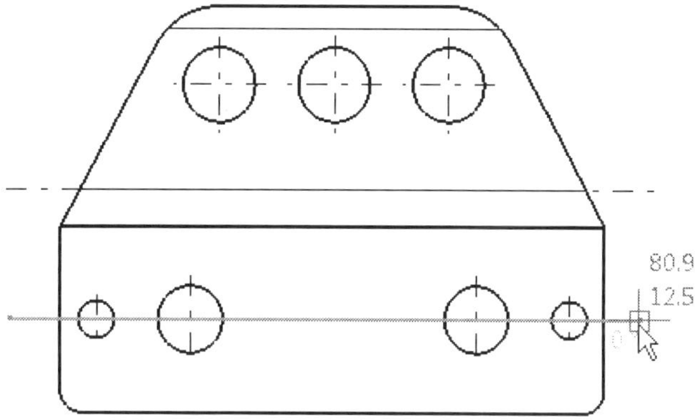


**Figure 25–35**

5. Double-click to complete the x-section definition.

6. Select a location above the front view. The view displays as shown in Figure 25–36.

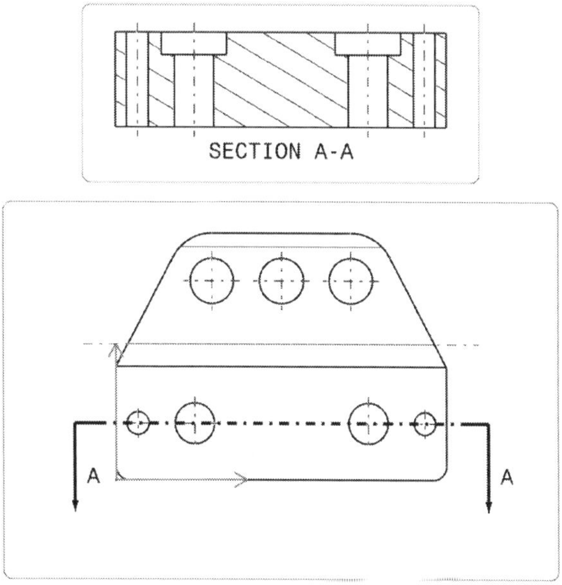


**Figure 25–36**

7. If the section view call out arrows are pointing in the wrong direction, right-click on the arrow and select **Callout (Section View).x object > Definition** as shown in Figure 25–37.

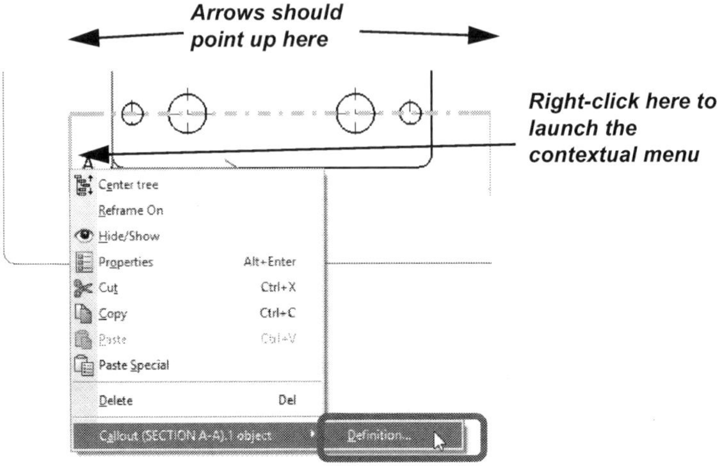


Figure 25–37

8. The Profile Edition mode is displayed. From the Edit/ Replace toolbar, click  (Reverse View Direction).
9. Click on the screen to complete the action.

## Task 9 - Add a detail view.

1. Zoom in on the section view.
2. Double-click on the frame of the section view to make it active. The border turns red and the name of the view in the view tree indicates that this view is the active view.
3. In the *View Layout* section of the Action Bar, click  to expand it, then click  (Quick Detail View).

4. Click a location on the right side of the counterbored hole feature and click again to create a circle callout, as shown in Figure 25–38.

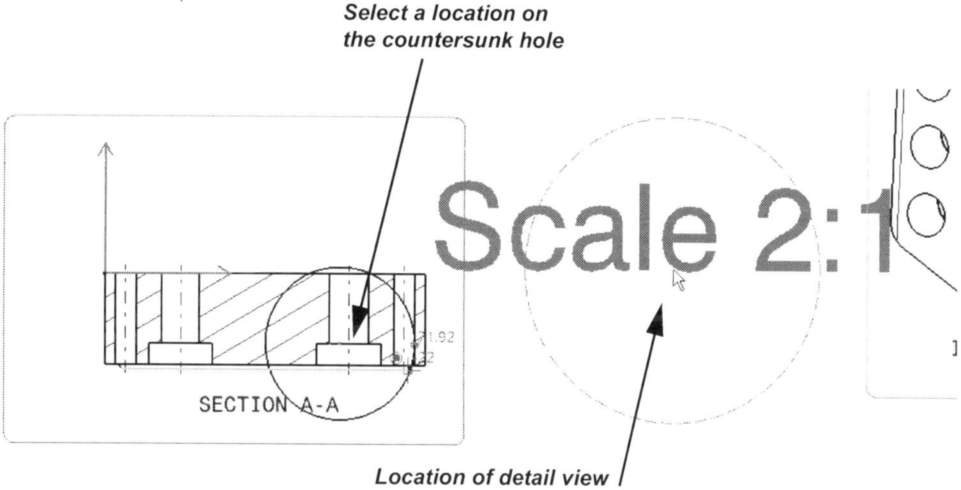


**Figure 25–38**

*If the axis is not visible, right-click and select **Properties** and then select the **Axis** option in the View tab in the Properties dialog box.*

5. Select a point to the right of the section view to define a location for the detail view. The complete detail view containing the callout is shown in Figure 25–39.

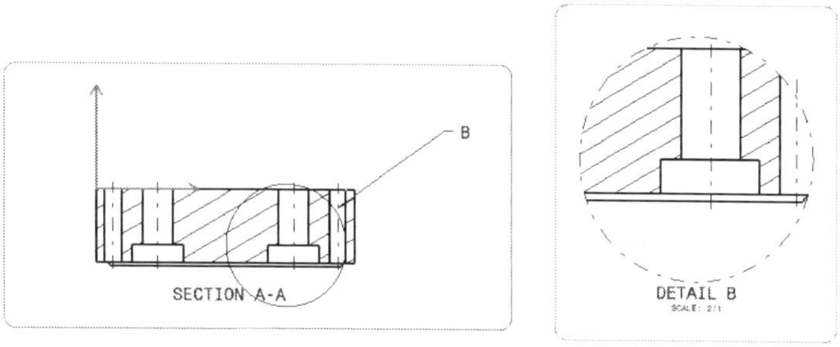


**Figure 25–39**

6. Right-click on the arrows in the front view, right-click and select **Callout (Section View).x object > Definition.**
7. Click  (Reverse View Direction) in the context toolbar.
8. Click on the screen and note that the circle defining the section view has moved.
9. Double-click the section circle to activate it.

10. Move and resize the section circle as shown in Figure 25–40.

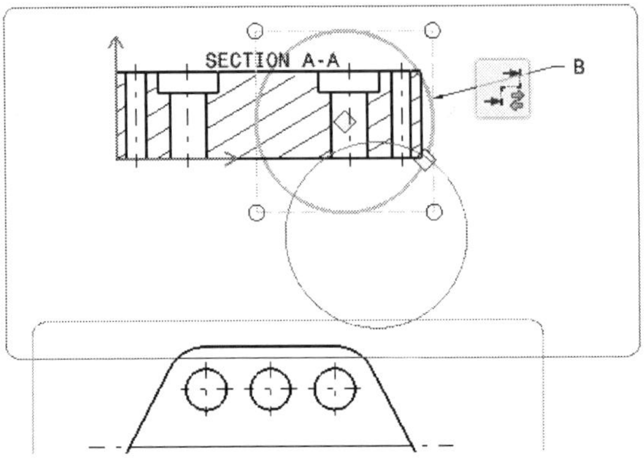


Figure 25–40

11. Click on the screen to complete the edit.

12. Move the section view to an appropriate location.

## Task 10 - Insert a frame and title block.

1. In the *View Layout* section of the Action Bar, click (Page Layout). In the Dress-up drop-down list, select **Drawing Titleblock Sample 1**, as shown in Figure 25–41.

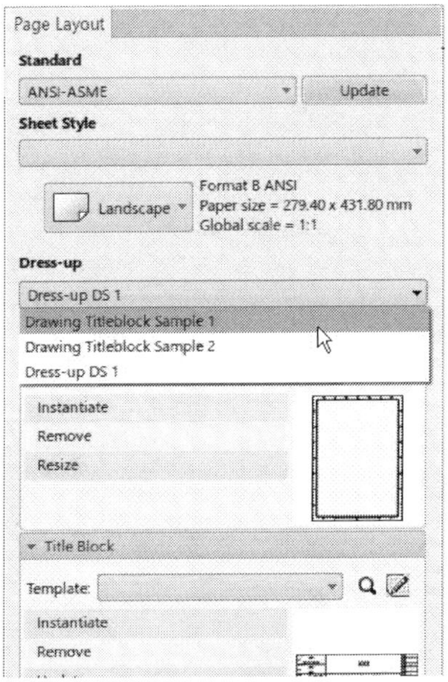


Figure 25–41

2. In the Frame and Title Block area, click **Create**.
3. Click **Apply**. The frame and title block are displayed. Close the Insert Frame and Title Block dialog box.
4. Save the drawing.
5. Do not close the tab. The drawing is used in the next exercise.

# Practice 25b Annotate a Drawing

## Practice Objective

- Create and manipulate dimensions.

In this practice, you will add dimensions to a drawing. You will modify these dimensions and explore their various properties. The end result is shown in Figure 25–42.

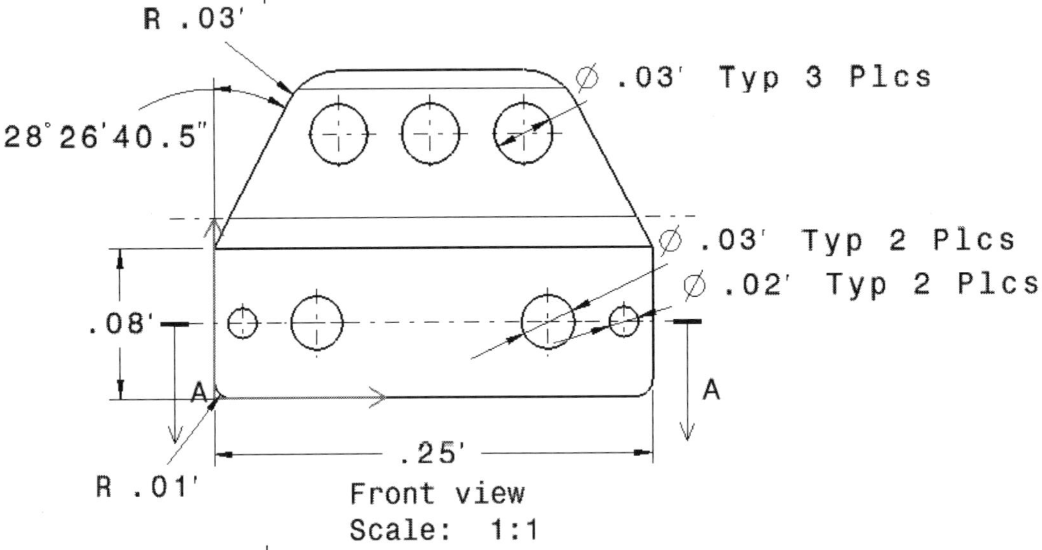


Figure 25–42

## Task 1 - Import the Bracket Drawing.

1. Either continue using the drawing from the previous exercise or import **Bracket_Views.3dxml** and open the drawing.
2. Activate the front view.
3. Hide all of the views except the front view.
4. If the grid is displayed and you want to toggle it off, select  (Display Grid) in the *View* section of the Action Bar.

## Task 2 - Generate manual dimensions.

1. Zoom in on the front view and, in the *Annotation* section of the Action Bar, click 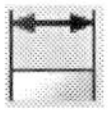 (Dimension).

2. Select the edge shown in Figure 25–43. The system creates a linear dimension for the edge.

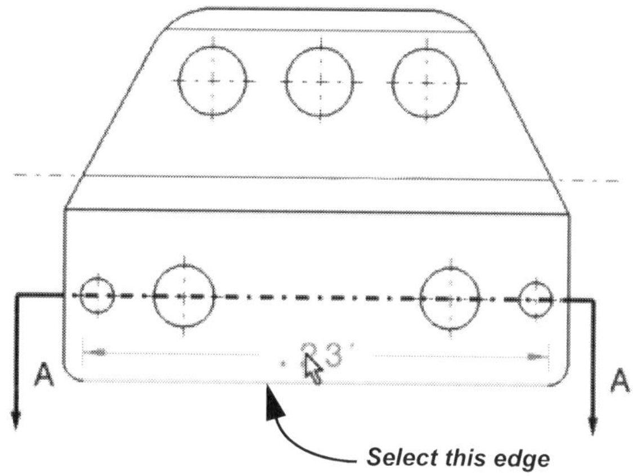


Figure 25–43

3. Select a second reference for the dimension, as shown in Figure 25–44. The system displays a length dimension between the two references.

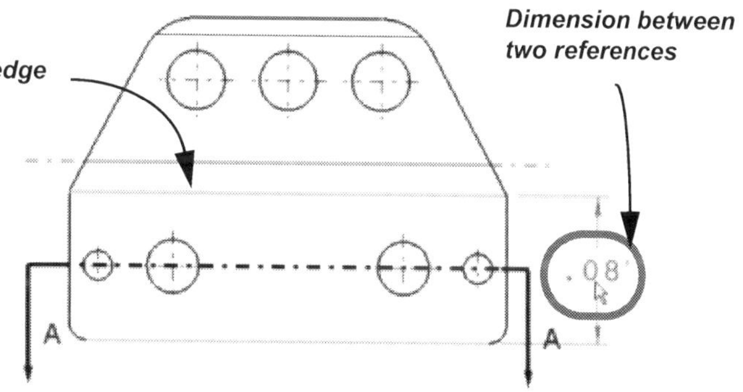


Figure 25–44

4. Press the left mouse button to complete the reference selection and place the dimension. The dimension highlights in blue and can now be moved.

5. Move the dimension to the side, as shown in Figure 25–45.

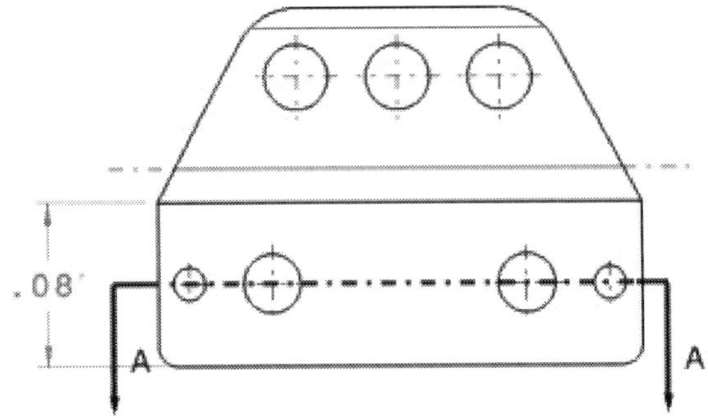


Figure 25–45

6. Create the horizontal dimension shown in Figure 25–46.

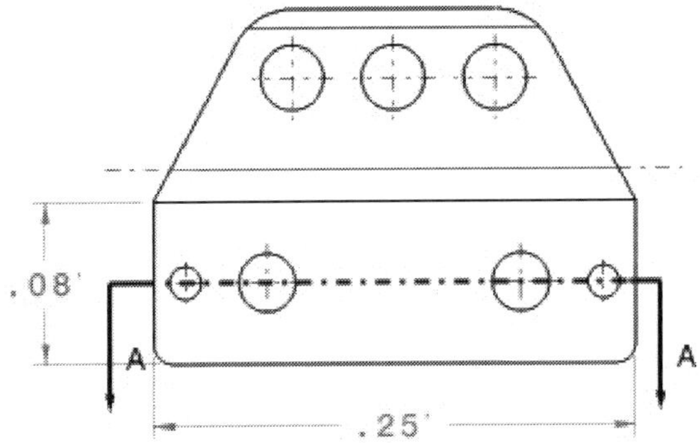


Figure 25–46

7. Select the circle as shown in Figure 25–47, and place the diameter dimension.

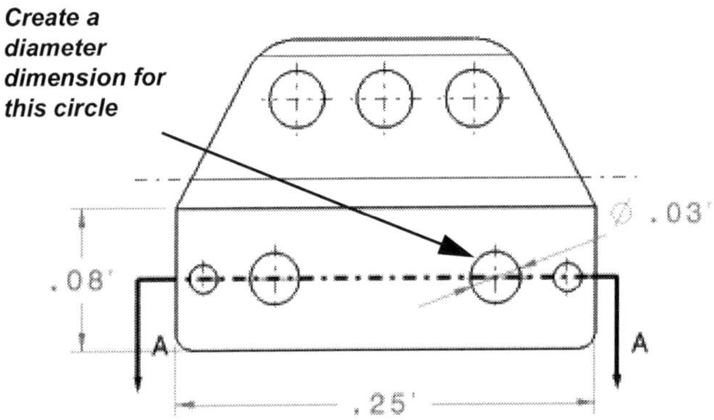


Figure 25–47

8. Create the other four dimensions as shown in Figure 25–48.

   Note: After selecting an arc/circle to place a dimension, it will give you either a Radius/Diameter. If what it gives you is incorrect, right-click immediately after selecting arc/circle and pick either **Diameter Center/Radius Center** to switch.

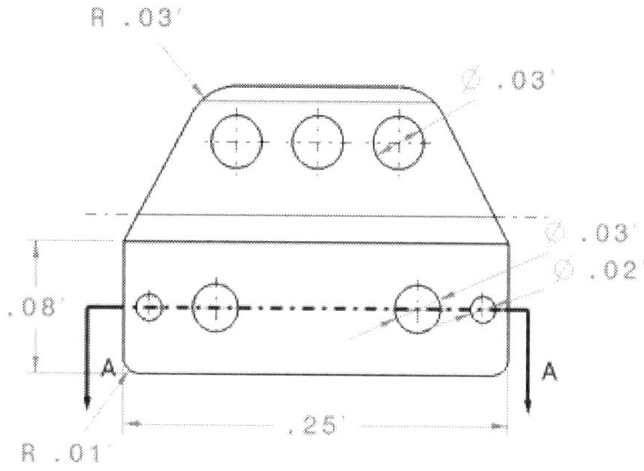


**Figure 25–48**

## Task 3 - Manipulate dimensions.

1. Select the **.03'** diameter dimension on the right Hole feature, as shown in Figure 25–49.

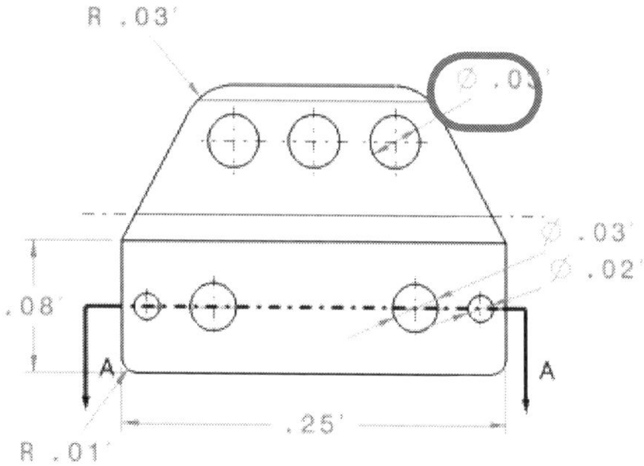


**Figure 25–49**

2. Right-click and select **Properties**.
3. Select the *Dimension Texts* tab in the Properties dialog box.

4. Enter **Typ 3 Plcs** in the suffix text field, as shown in Figure 25–50.

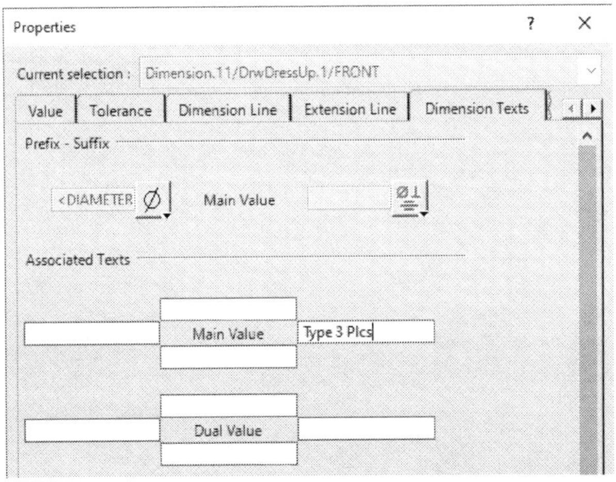


Figure 25–50

5. Click **Apply** and click **OK**. The dimension updates with the changes, as shown in Figure 25–51.

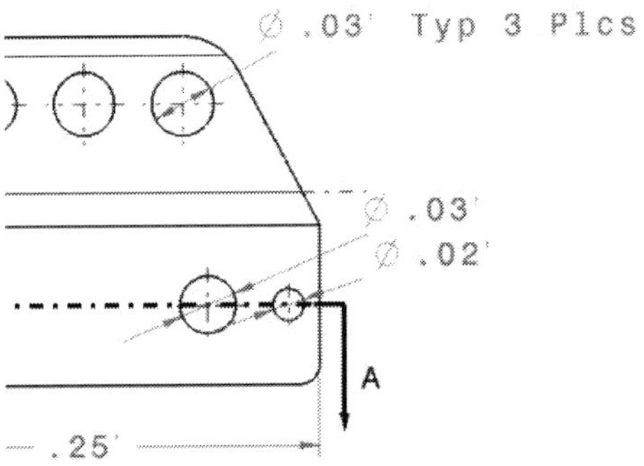


Figure 25–51

6. Select the **.03'** and **.02'** diameter dimensions (hold down <Ctrl> to select both) and add the suffix dimension text, as shown in Figure 25–52.

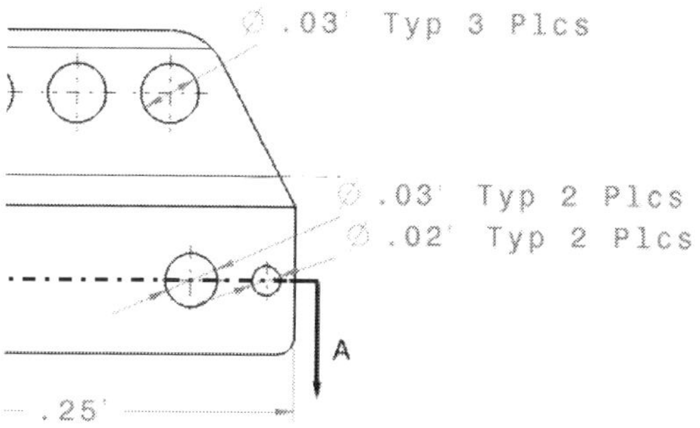


Figure 25–52

## Task 4 - Create an angle dimension on the Front view.

1. Click (Dimension) (click the flyout arrow if it is not visible) and select the two entities shown in Figure 25–53.

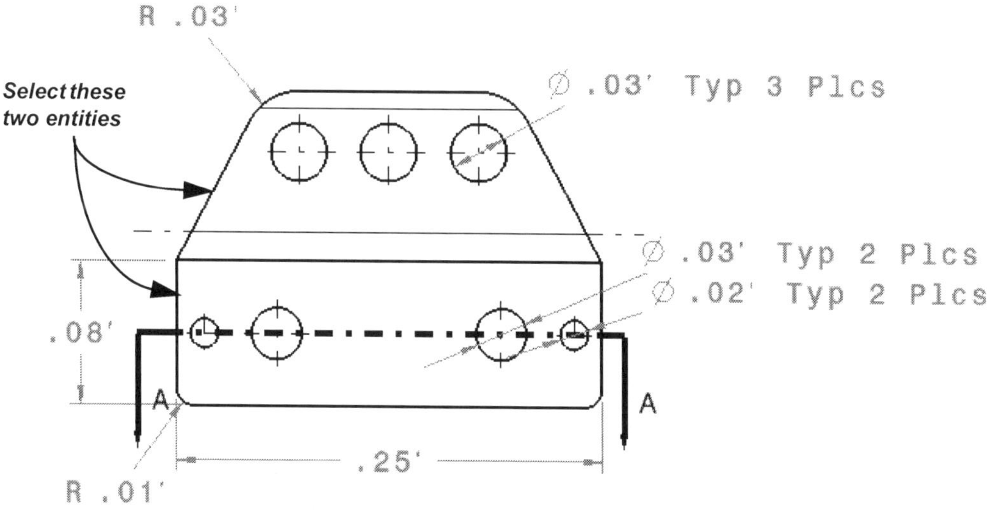


Figure 25–53

*Depending on where your cursor is located, you might need to select a different angle sector to get the result shown in Figure 25–55.*

2. Define how the angled dimension is generated. While moving the dimension into position, right-click and select **Angle Sector > Sector 2**, as shown in Figure 25–54.

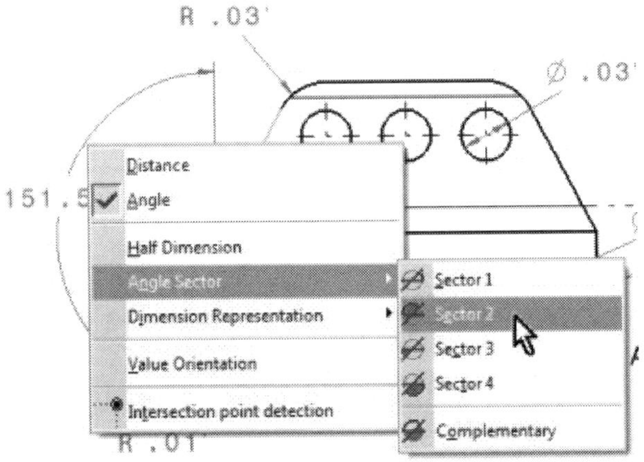


**Figure 25–54**

3. Click to place the dimension. It displays as shown in Figure 25–55.

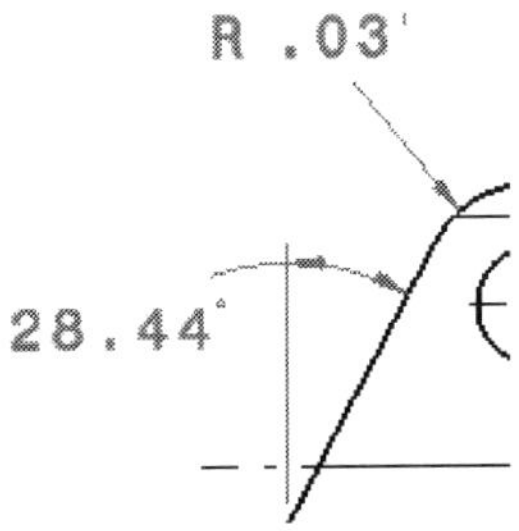


**Figure 25–55**

4. Modify the format of the angle dimension by right-clicking on it and selecting **Properties**.

5. Select the *Value* tab in the Properties dialog box. Modify the value in the *Display* field to **3 factors** and the value in the *Precision* field to **0.1** as shown in Figure 25–56.

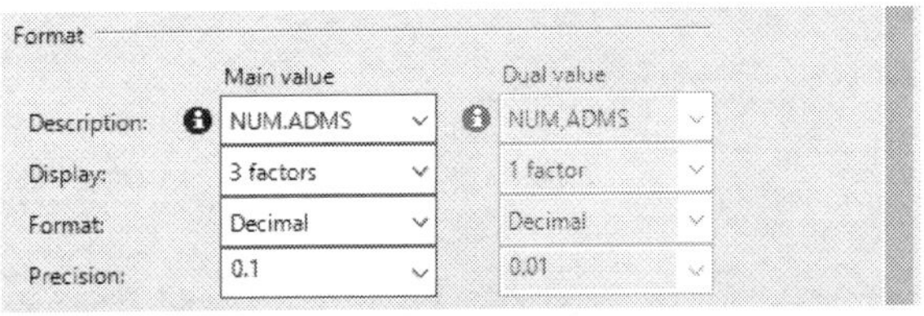


**Figure 25–56**

6. Apply the changes and close the Properties dialog box. The dimension displays as shown in Figure 25–57.

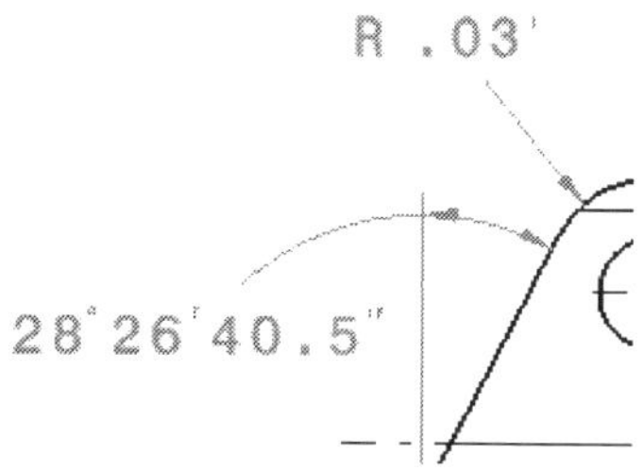


**Figure 25–57**

7. The completed drawing is shown in Figure 25–58. Save the drawing and close the window.

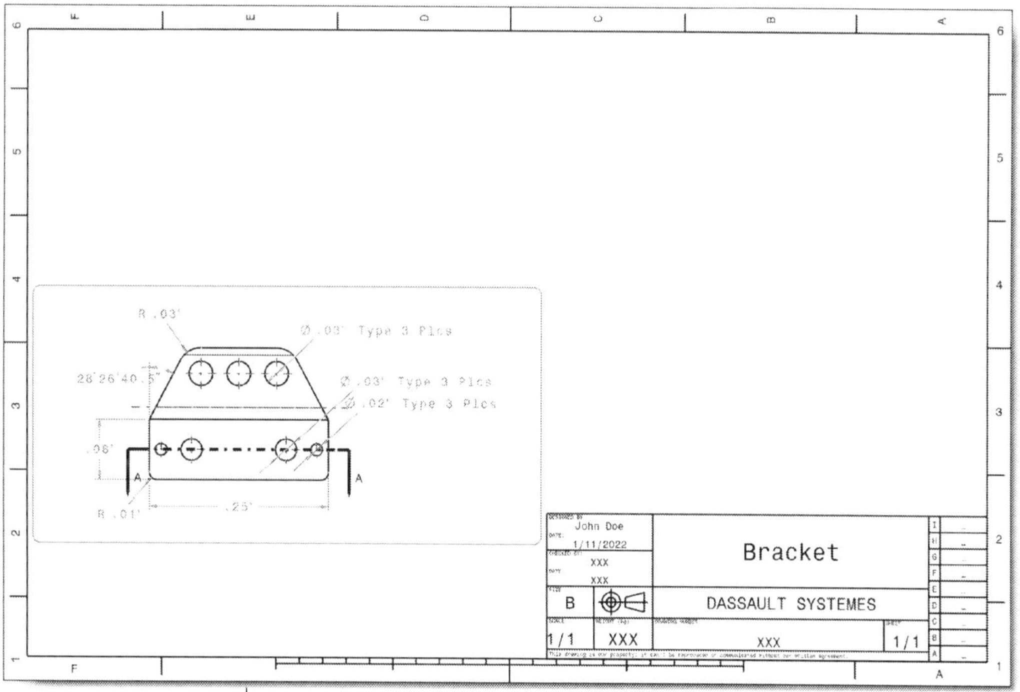


**Figure 25–58**

# Chapter Review Questions

1. Which of the following view types can be the first view in a drawing?
   a. Offset Section view
   b. Projection view
   c. Front view
   d. Detail view
2. When you delete a parent view, dependent views are automatically deleted.
   a. True
   b. False
3. An isometric view is placed in the drawing at the same orientation as in the model. This orientation can be changed inside the drawing using the compass before the view has been placed.
   a. True
   b. False
4. The only way to tell which view on a drawing is active is that is has a red border.
   a. True
   b. False
5. Dimensions created in a drawing update when changes are made to the model.
   a. True
   b. False
6. You cannot hide a drawing view.
   a. True
   b. False
7. Changes in the 3D model automatically display in the drawing.
   a. True
   b. False

**Answers:** 1c, 2b, 3a, 4b, 5b, 6a, 7b

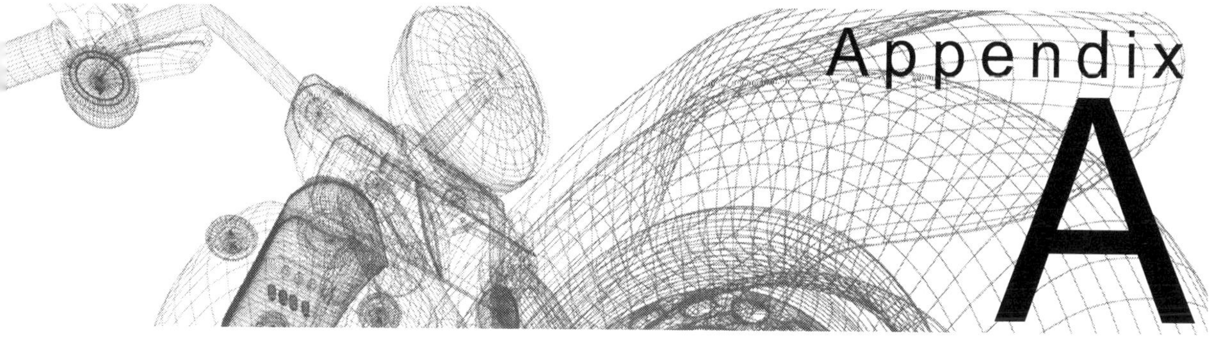


# Effective Modeling Review

This chapter reviews some important design considerations which ensures that your model captures the design intent more effectively. You also review some tips and techniques that improve the creation of your model.

## Learning Objectives in This Appendix

- Review the design considerations for creating models.
- Review various modeling best practices.
- Review various tools for investigating models.
- Create a model on your own that meets the defined design criteria.

# A.1 Design Considerations

A designer strives to create models that meet the following criteria:

- Communicates the design's intent.
- Can be prototyped to generate a model that meets design goals.
- Is flexible, so future design changes require minimal effort.
- Can be used to generate design documentation (drawings).

Before creating any model (part or assembly), consider its design intent. This helps to select the most appropriate options that maximize design flexibility. Considering *what if* scenarios that might be introduced into the model in the future helps to create a robust model that requires minimal effort when being modified.

## Part Design Considerations

Consider the following:

- What is the best choice for the base feature?
- Which parent/child relationships are required?
- Which parent/child relationships should be avoided?
- Which dimensions are required to drive the design?
- Which dimensions on the part might change?
- How should the part react to dimension changes?
- Should relations be added to capture design intent?
- What feature order best captures the design intent?

## Assembly Design Considerations

Consider the following:

- What is the best choice for the base component?
- Which assembly constraints capture the design intent?
- Which parent/child relationships are required?
- Which parent/child relationships should be avoided?
- Should the offset constraint be used, rather than contact? Will motion be simulated in the design?
- Should subassembly components be incorporated into the design?
- Should assembly relations be added to capture design intent?
- What component order best captures the design intent?
- What parts should display an assembly feature?

## External References

Ensure that the use of external references complies with company standards. Keep this functionality in the experience level of the users in your company.

# A.2 Modeling Tips and Techniques

Planning ahead helps you better understand the design intent that you want to achieve, resulting in a more robust model.

As you acquire new modeling tips and techniques, you should consider them all during the design stage. In addition, many companies have their own design requirements or best practice recommendations. A summary of some of the key items includes the following:

## Features

Features either add or remove material from the model to create the final design. Consider the following tips when adding features to the model:

- It is recommended to select a stable base feature that requires few changes. The base feature is used as a parent for additional features.
- Use feature types (dress-up or sketched) that best capture the design intent.
- Select references that correctly reflect the intent of the design. Any reference selected while creating a new feature establishes a dependency between the new feature and the reference.
- Carefully consider which sketching tools should be used to capture the design intent (3D projection).
- Use depth options (**Up to Next**, **Up to Last**, **Up To Surface**, etc.) to capture the design intent. Also, consider whether an **Offset** option is required.
- Create features in the order that best captures the design intent.
- Apply names to features so they can be easily identified in the specification tree.

## Drafts and Fillets

Review company standards when considering whether to add drafts to accurately represent your model. Some companies prefer not to add drafts to models, while others insist on it. Some considerations include the following:

- Does adding a draft increase model accuracy or does it adversely affect drawing creation?
- If a draft is not added to the model, how do you communicate this requirement to the manufacturer?
- Does the model need to undergo interference or analysis testing? If so, you might want to add the draft to ensure accurate results.

Fillets generally represent the finishing stages of the design. Similar to drafts, always consider company standards when deciding whether to add fillets to the model. Some considerations include the following:

- Is the model going to be used for FEA analysis? If so, fillets are generally removed before the analysis and are therefore not required.
- Depending on the type of fillets used in the model, the manufacturing department might remove fillets that are created at the end of the process. In this situation, you might want to add all fillets and only deactivate the ones that you do not need for generating the NC toolpaths.
- Variable fillets are difficult to manufacture. Consider the necessity of this feature as you create a model.
- Avoid using fillets as references, as they are often changed or completely removed in the design process. This could result in a major model failure.

The order of fillet and draft creation can affect the resulting geometry, and should be added as late as possible in the feature order. Always consider the order in which features are manufactured (for example, draft geometry should be added to the model before fillets). It is also recommended that you consider the order in which fillets are added to the model and how the order affects the geometry.

# A.3 Model Investigation

It is not practical to assume that you might always be creating new models. In many situations, you are required to continue someone else's design or make modifications to a previously completed model. It is recommended to investigate the model to review it. Some reviewing techniques that can be used include the following:

- Scan the model
- Specification tree
- Parent/child relationships

## Model Scan

The scan functionality reviews the construction history of a model, one feature at a time. This is especially useful when working with models that were created by others. The **Scan** tool can give you an idea of the modeler's design intent and modeling techniques by replaying and reviewing the design.

## Specification Tree

The specification tree displays all features in the model and can be used to review the model. Consider renaming features to enable others to easily search for features. Display relations and parameters.

## Parent/Child

The **Parent/Children** tool displays information on the parents and children of a selected feature. To activate the **Parent/Children** tool, select a feature in the specification tree or on the screen, right-click and select **Parent/Children**.

# A.4 Interactive Practice

The model shown in Figure A–1 must be designed so that the changes shown in Figure A–1 and Figure A–2 are possible. Consider the following issues:

- Types of features to be used
- Best feature order
- Dimension scheme

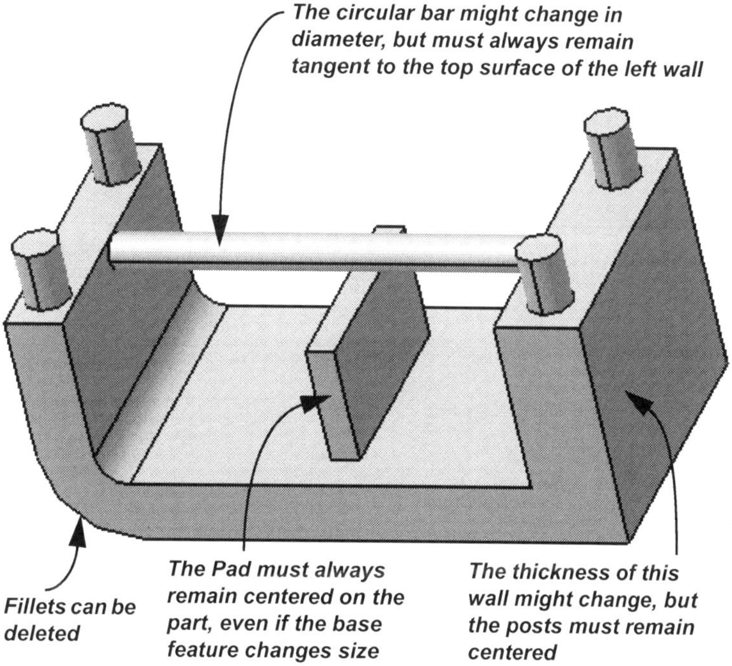


**Figure A–1**

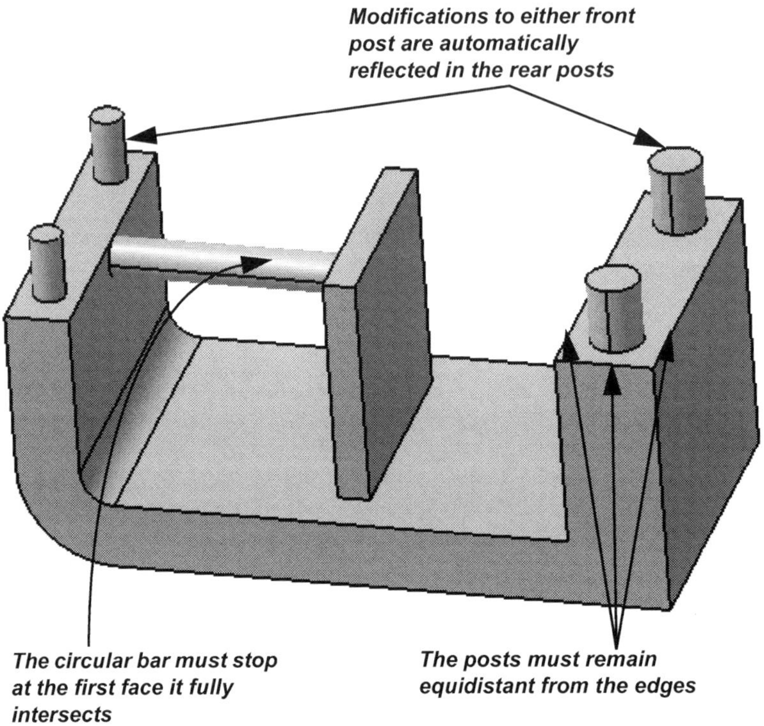
*Modifications to either front post are automatically reflected in the rear posts*
*The circular bar must stop at the first face it fully intersects*
*The posts must remain equidistant from the edges*

**Figure A–2**

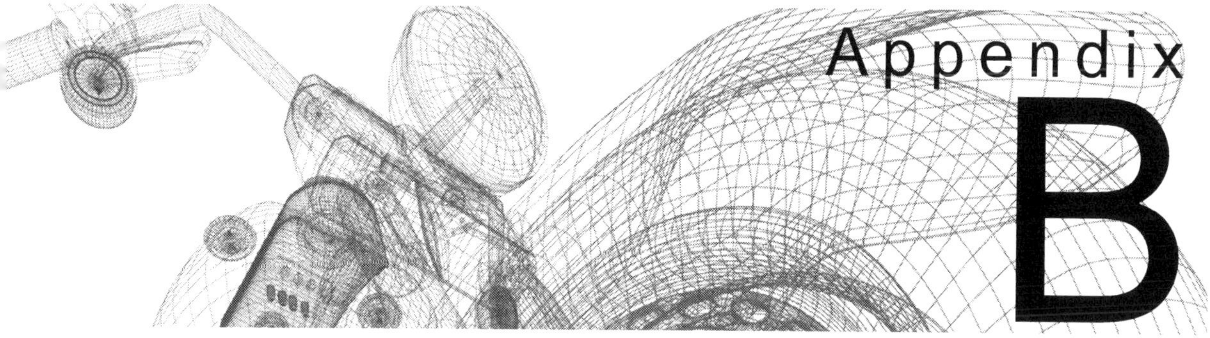

# Appendix B

# Additional Exercises

Draft features are used to angle the surfaces of the model to allow for the removal of molds in cast and plastic parts.

# Practice B1

# Sketcher Practice I

## Practice Objective

- Create a sketch without instructions.

Create a new part called **SketchProfile** and sketch the profile shown in Figure B–1. Use the YZ plane as the support for the sketch. Do not be concerned with the size of the profile; just ensure that the same shape is developed.

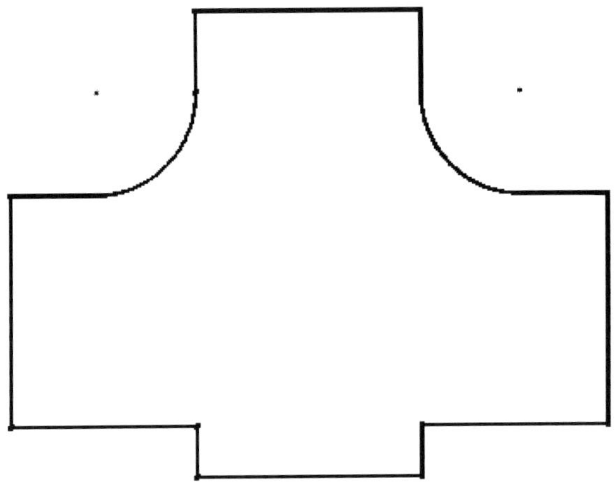

**Figure B–1**

# Practice B2

# Sketcher Practice II

## Practice Objective

- Create a sketch without instructions.

Create a new part called **OutletProfile** and sketch the profile shown in Figure B–1. Use the YZ plane as the support for the sketch. Do not be concerned with the size of the profile; just ensure that the same shape is developed.

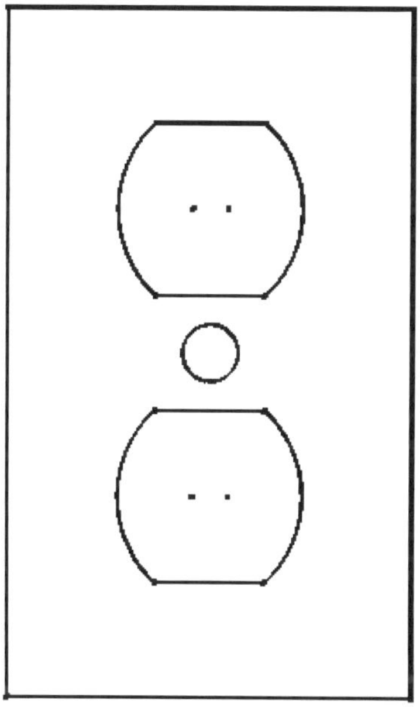

**Figure B–2**

# Practice B3 Additional Pockets

## Practice Objective

- Create a Pocket feature.

In this practice, you will create the part shown in Figure B–3. You will open an existing part and add two Pocket features.

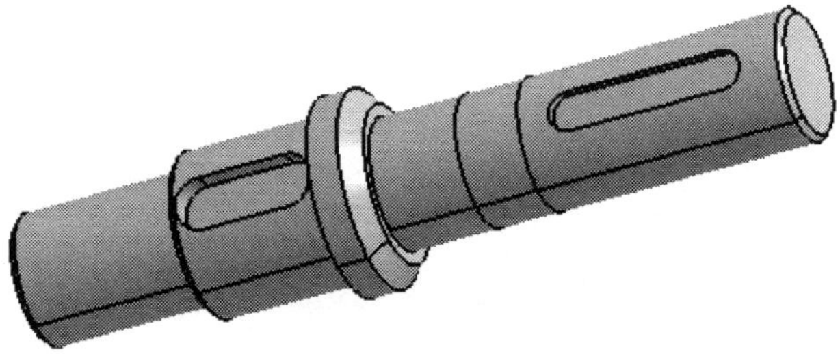

Figure B–3

1. Import **Shaft.3dxml**.
2. Create the two Pocket features as shown in Figure B–4. Place them in the approximate locations as shown with appropriate dimensioning schemes.

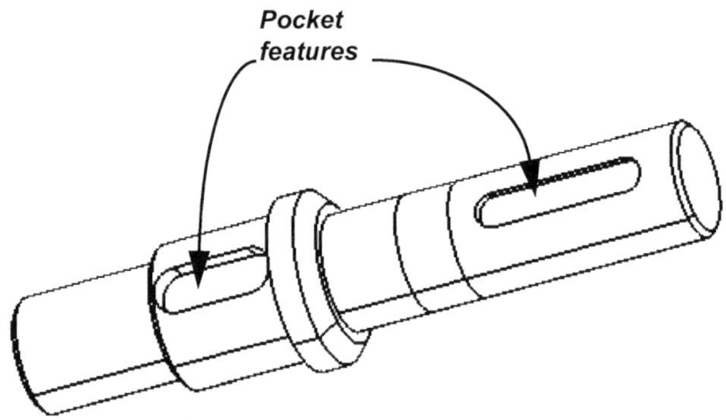


Figure B–4

3. In the Top Bar, click (Share)>**Save** to save the part.
4. Close the ***Shaft** A.1* tab.

# Practice B4

# Crank

## Practice Objective

- Create a part using pads without any instructions.

Create the **Crank.** part shown in Figure B–5.

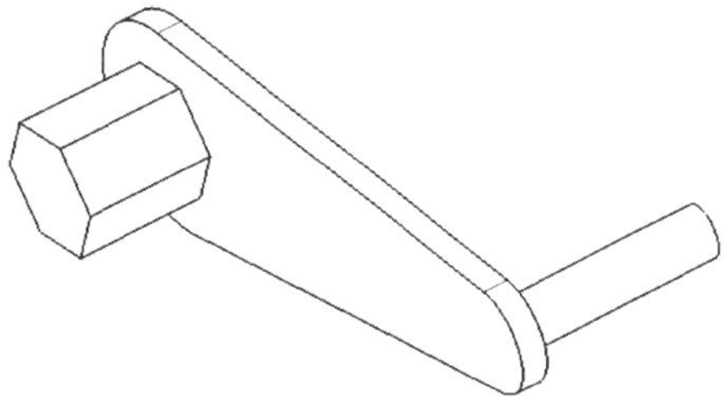


**Figure B–5**

Drawing views are shown in Figure B–5 and Figure B–6.

- 10 (0.394 in)
- 20 (0.787 in)
- 25 (0.984 in)
- 40 (1.575 in)
- 50 (1.969 in)
- 80 (3.150 in)
- 200 (7.874 in)

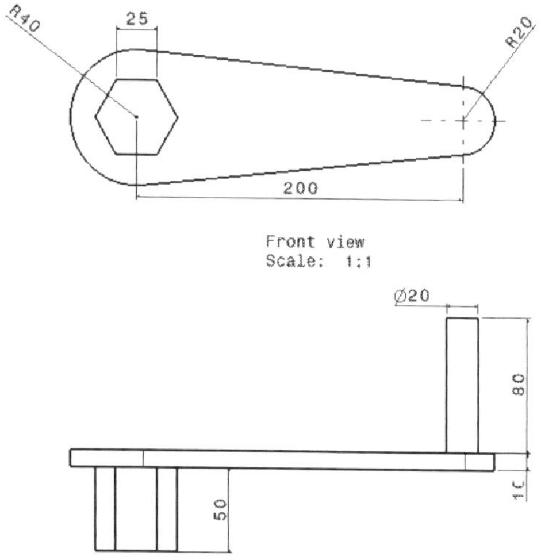


**Figure B–6**

# Practice B5 Cylinder Block

## Practice Objective

- Create a base feature and Pocket features without instruction.

Create the **CylinderBlock** part model shown in Figure B–7.

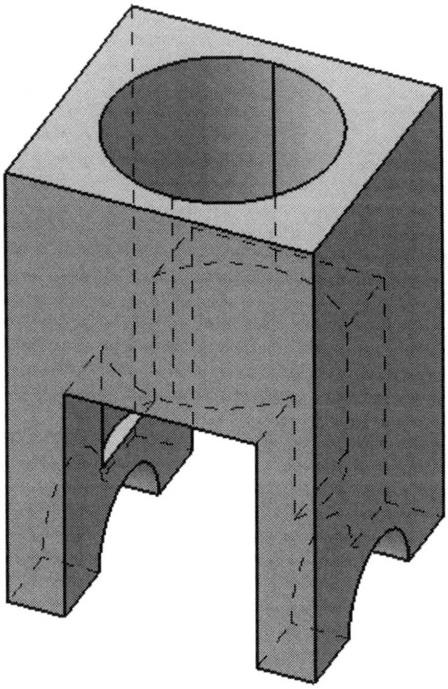

Figure B–7

# Practice B6 Using Reference Elements

## Practice Objectives

- Create reference elements.
- Create solid features using reference elements.

In this practice, you will complete the features of a coat stand by creating and using reference elements.

## Task 1 - Create arms for the coat hanger.

1. Import **CoatStand.3dxml**. You must complete the model by adding arms to the main shaft.
2. Create an arm with the following dimensions, as shown in Figure B–8 and Figure B–9:
    - *length:* **300 (11.811 in)**
    - *radius:* **50 (1.969 in)**
    - *height:* **1500 (59.055 in)** (above the XY plane)
    - *angle:* **45** degrees (pointing upwards)
    - *rotation:* **45** degrees (from the YZ plane)

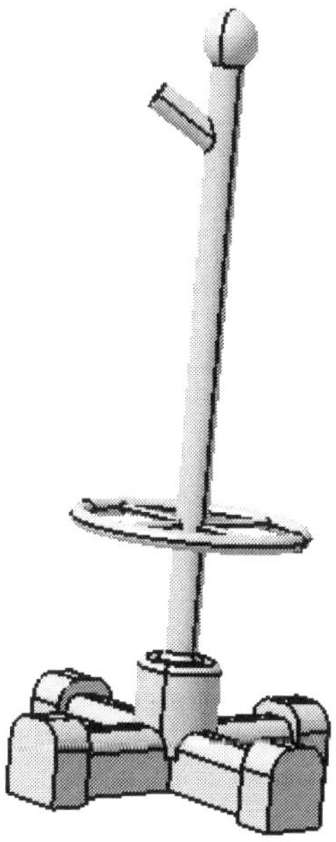

Figure B–8

Figure B–9

3. Then, create an arm with the following settings, as shown in Figure B–10 and Figure B–11:
   - *length:* **600 (23.622 in)**
   - *radius:* **50 (1.969 in)**
   - *height:* **1200 (47.244 in)** (above the XY plane)
   - *angle:* **45** degrees (pointing upwards)
   - *rotation:* **45** degrees (from the YZ plane in the opposite direction as the other arm)

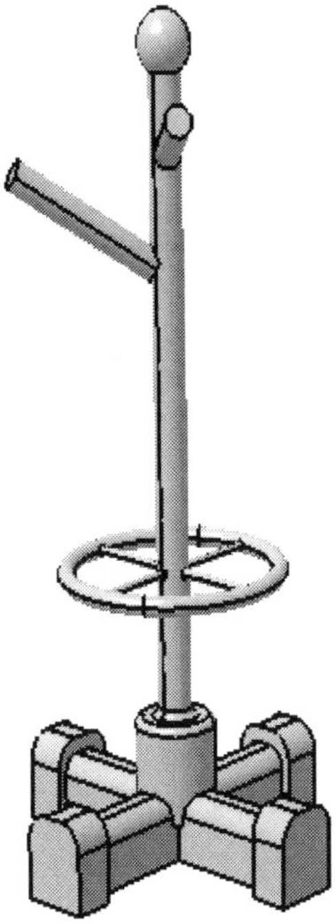

Figure B–10

Figure B–11

## Task 2 - Create pockets for the arms.

Create circular pockets with a *radius* of **30 (1.181 in)** halfway up each arm, as shown in Figure B–12. Ensure that the pockets are perpendicular to the XY plane.

The completed model displays as shown in Figure B–13.

**Figure B–12**

**Figure B–13**

# Practice B7 King Chess Piece

## Practice Objective

- Create Pad and Shaft features without instructions.

Create a new part titled **King_Piece**, as shown in Figure B–14. Exact dimensions are not required.

**Figure B–14**

# Practice B8 Creating Shafts and Grooves

## Practice Objective

- Create Shaft and Groove features with minimal instruction.

In this practice, you will create a model of a spinning top using Shaft and Groove features. The completed model is shown in Figure B–15. As a good practice, create an axis system in the drawing as a foundation for building features.

**Figure B–15**

## Task 1 - Create a new model.

1. Create a new part titled **SpinningTop**.
2. Use the dimensioned drawings in Figure B–16, Figure B–17, and Figure B–18, to create the required geometry.

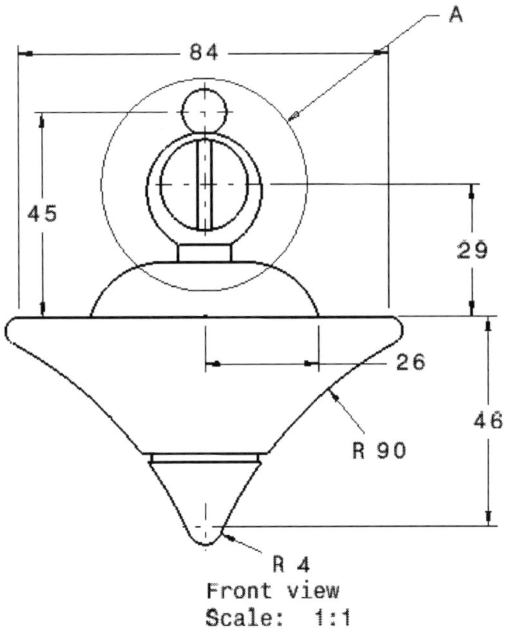


Figure B–16

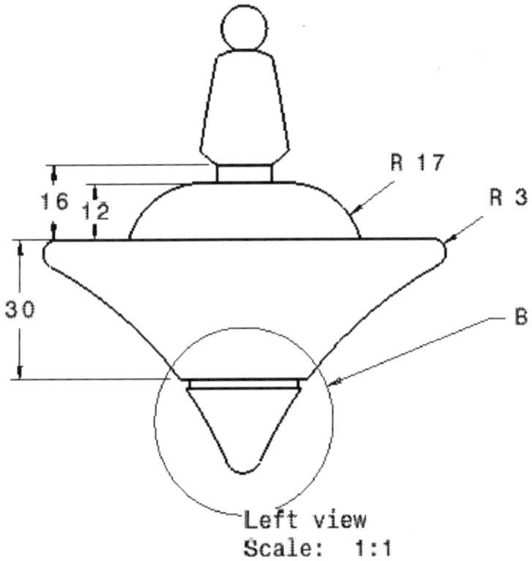


Figure B–17

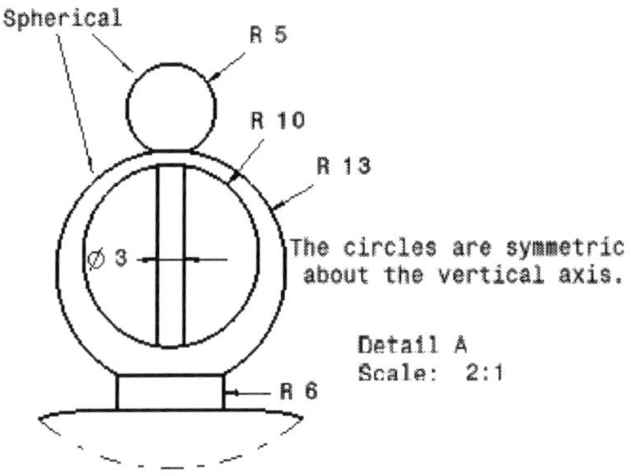


Figure B–18

# Practice B9 Crankshaft

## Practice Objective

- Create a part without instructional steps.

Create the **Crankshaft part** shown in Figure B–19.

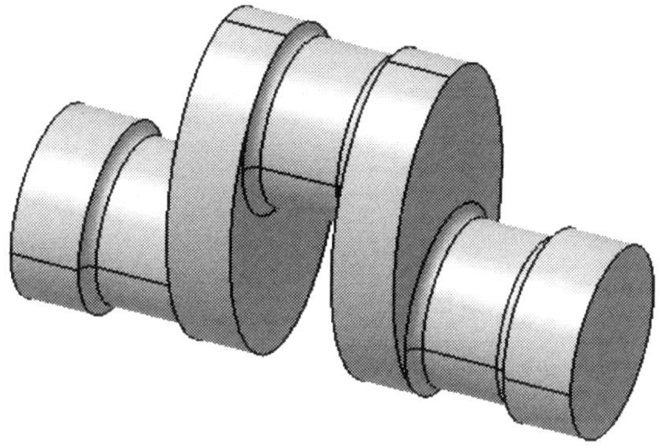

**Figure B–19**

Drawing views are shown in Figure B–20.

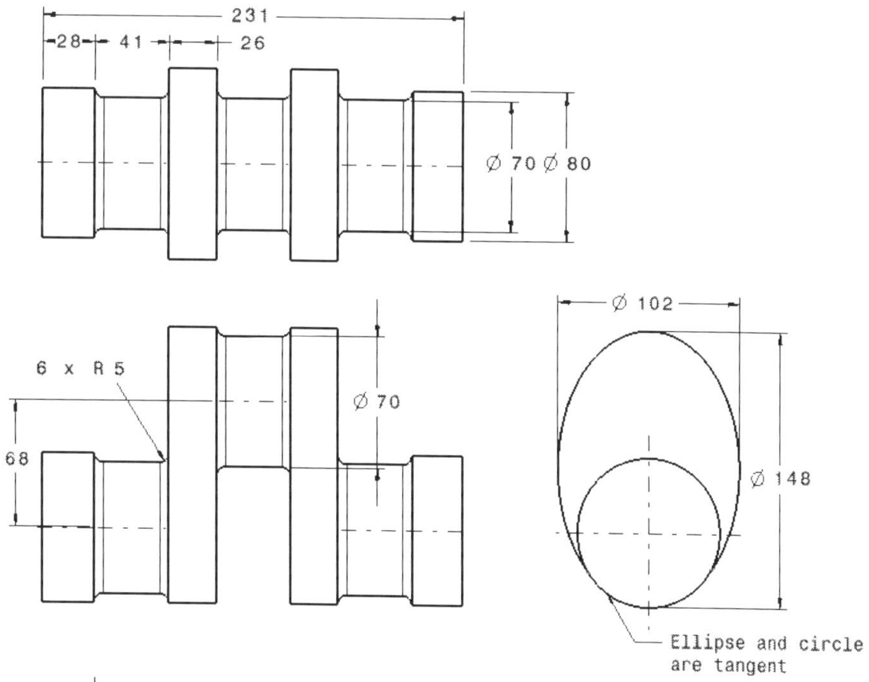


**Figure B–20**

# Practice B10 Link

## Practice Objective

- Create a part without instructional steps.

Create the **Link part** shown in Figure B–21.

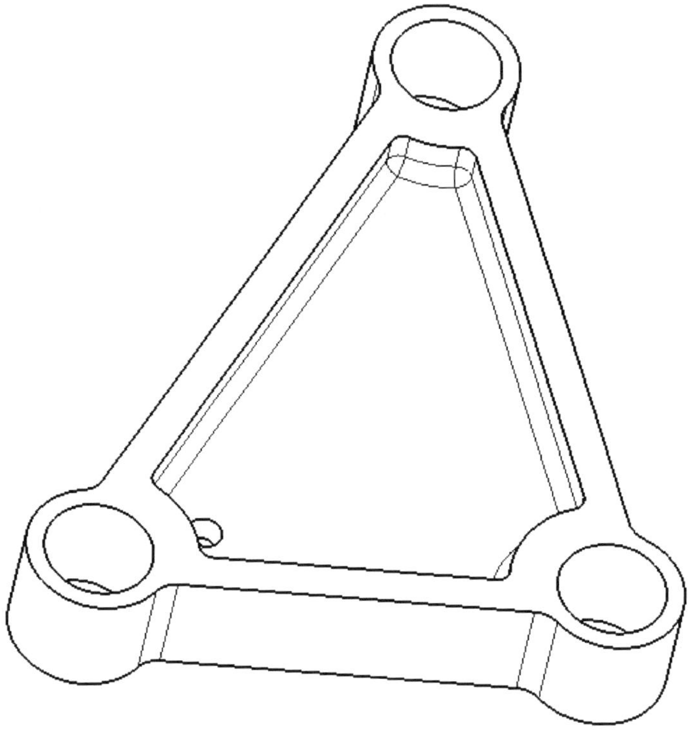

**Figure B–21**

Drawing views are shown in Figure B–22.

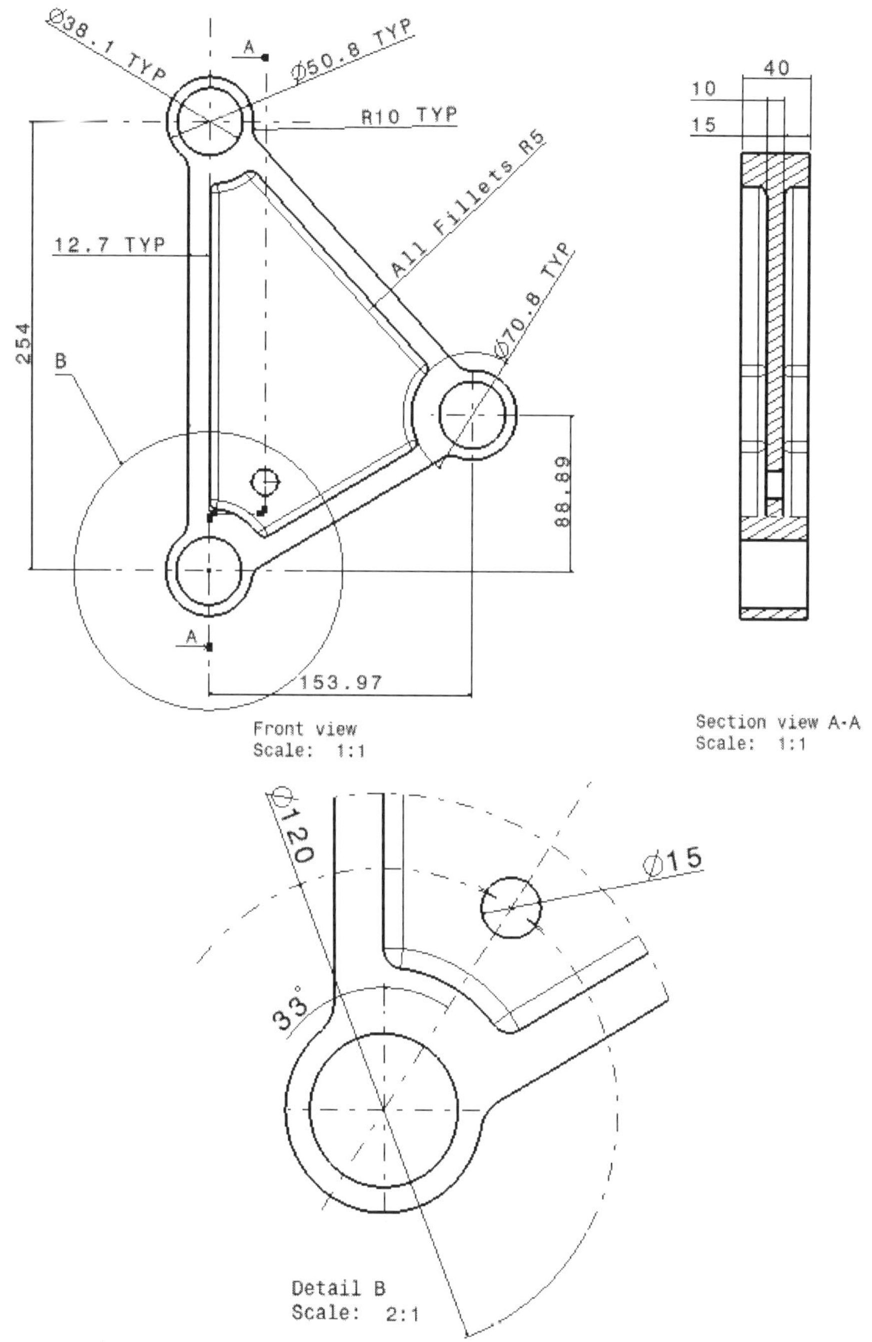
Ø38.1 TYP
A
Ø50.8 TYP
R10 TYP
All Fillets R5
12.7 TYP
Ø70.8 TYP
254
B
88.89
A
153.97
Front view
Scale: 1:1
40
10
15
Section view A-A
Scale: 1:1
Ø120
Ø15
33°
Detail B
Scale: 2:1

**Figure B–22**

# Practice B11 Tank

## Practice Objective

- Create a part without instructional steps.

Create the **Tank** part shown in Figure B–23.

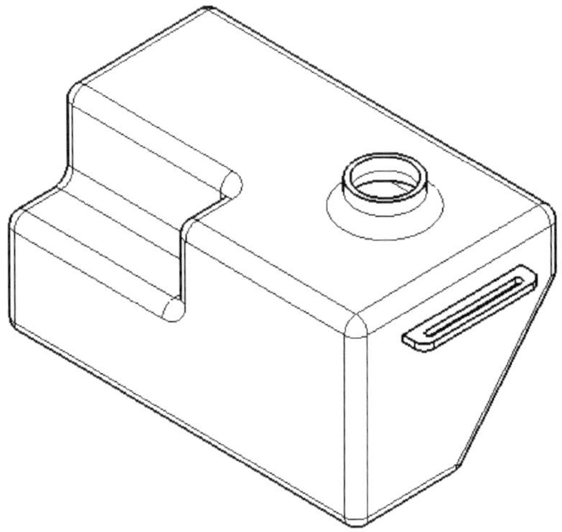

**Figure B–23**

Drawing views are shown in Figure B–24.

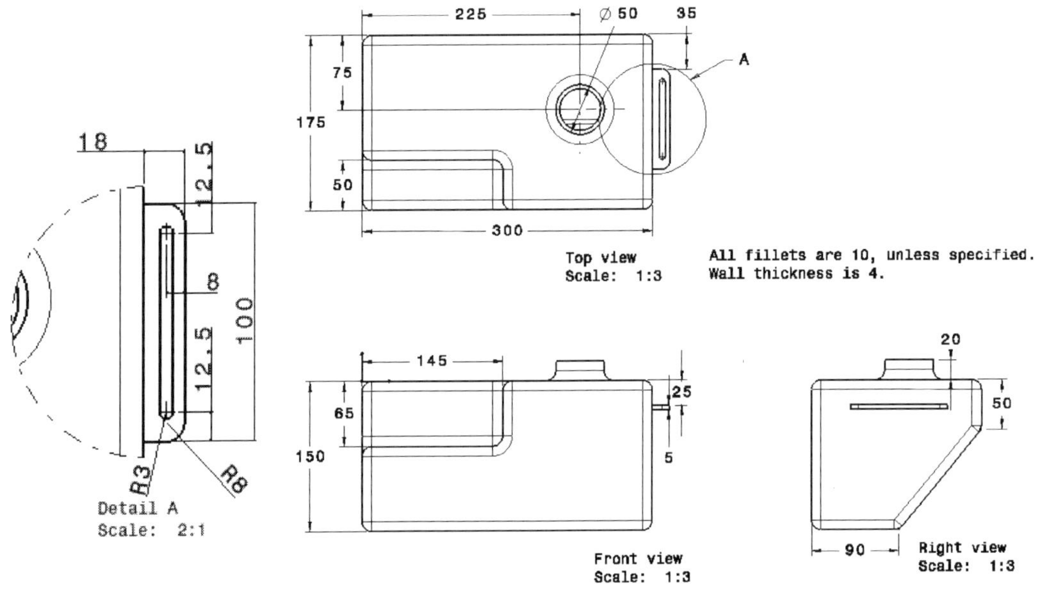


**Figure B–24**

# Practice B12 Connecting Rod

## Practice Objective

- Create a part without instructional steps.

Create the **ConnectingRod** part shown in Figure B–25.

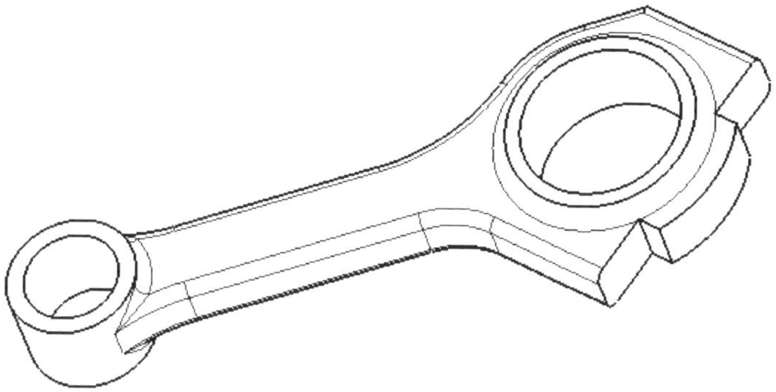

Figure B–25

Drawing views are shown in Figure B–26 and Figure B–27.

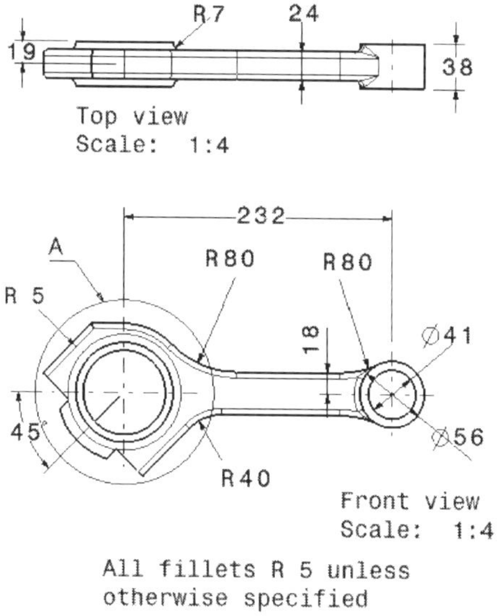


Figure B–26

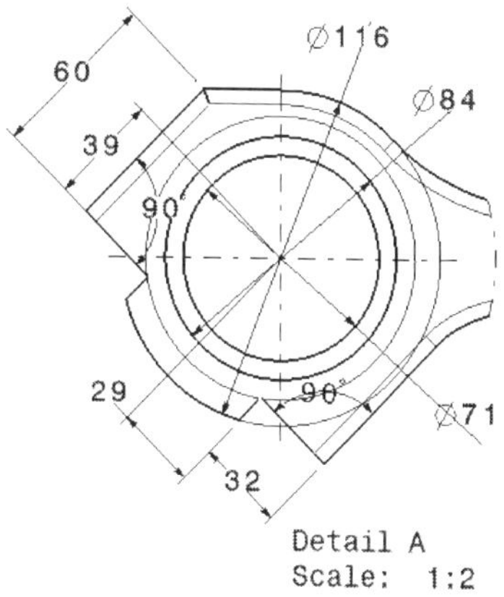


Figure B–27

# Practice B13 Piston

## Practice Objective

- Create more complex geometry without instructions

Create a new part titled **Piston**. Refer to the drawing shown in Figure B–28 for dimension values.

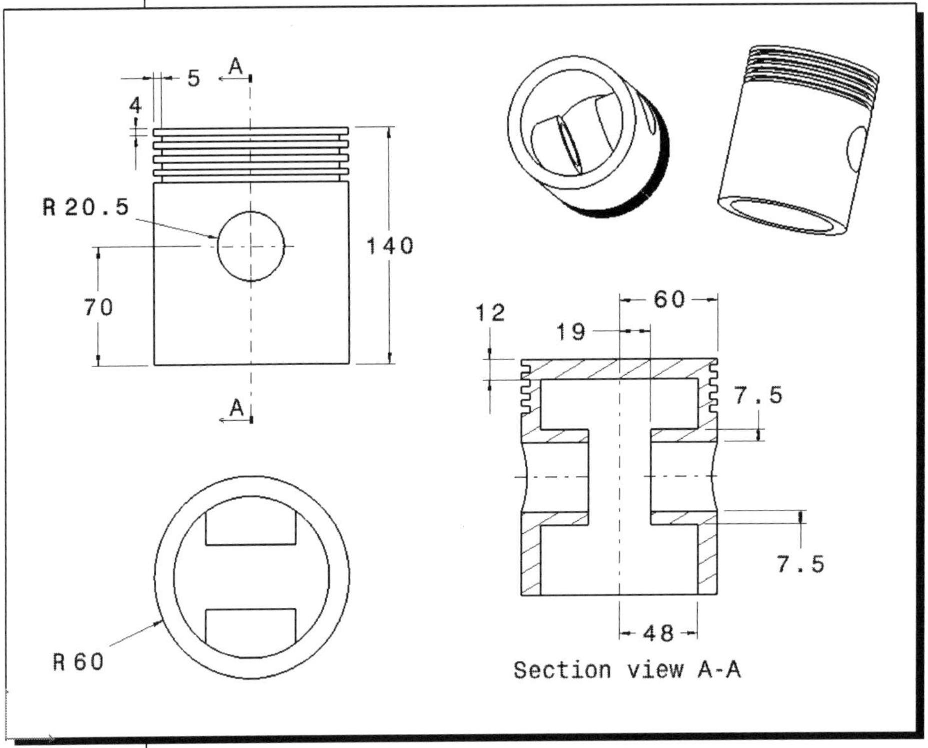


Figure B–28

# Practice B14 Flange

## Practice Objective

- Duplicate features without instructions

Create a new part titled **Flange**. Refer to the drawing shown in Figure B–29 for dimension values.

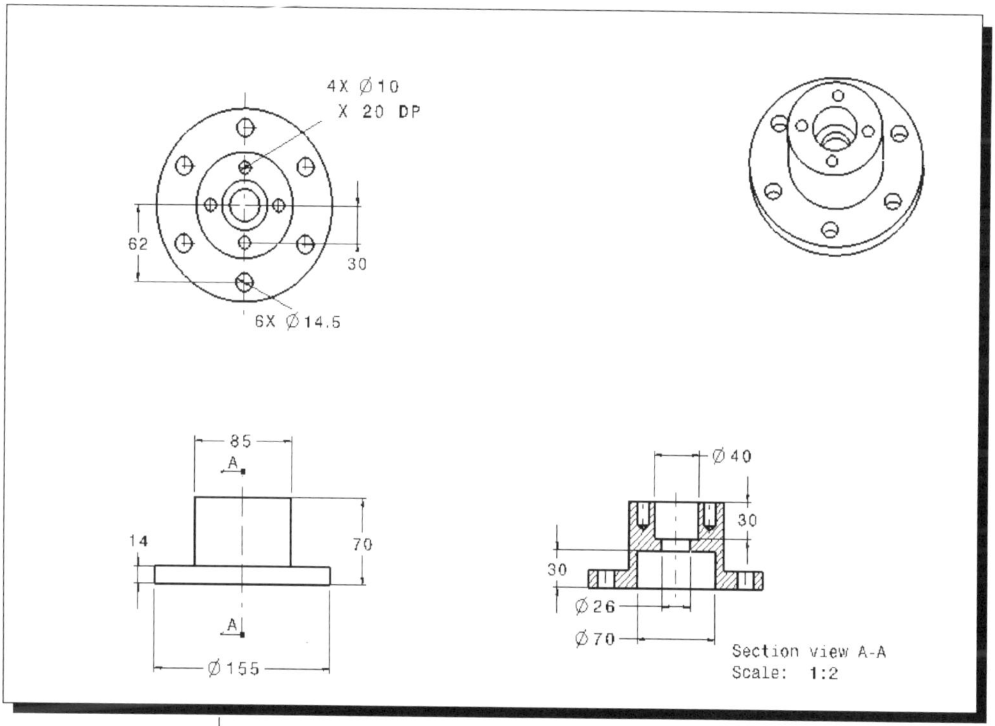


Figure B–29

# Practice B15 Axle Bracket

## Practice Objective

- Create a part without any instructions.

Create the **AxleBracket** part shown in Figure B–30.

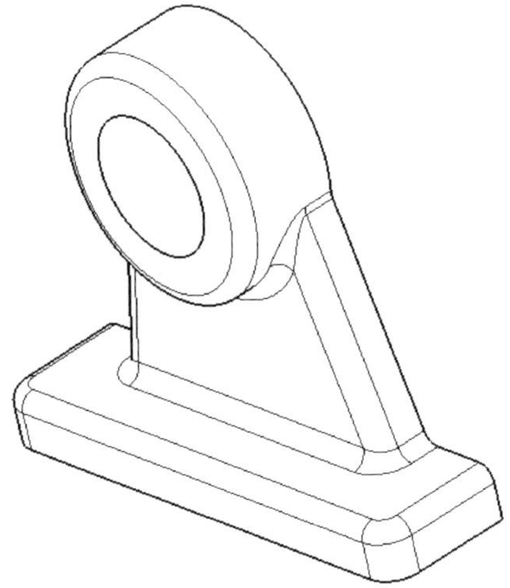

Figure B–30

Drawing views are shown in Figure B–31 and Figure B–32.

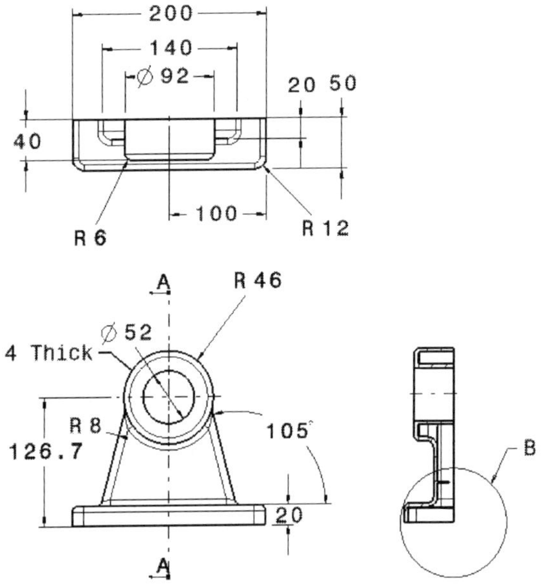


Figure B–31

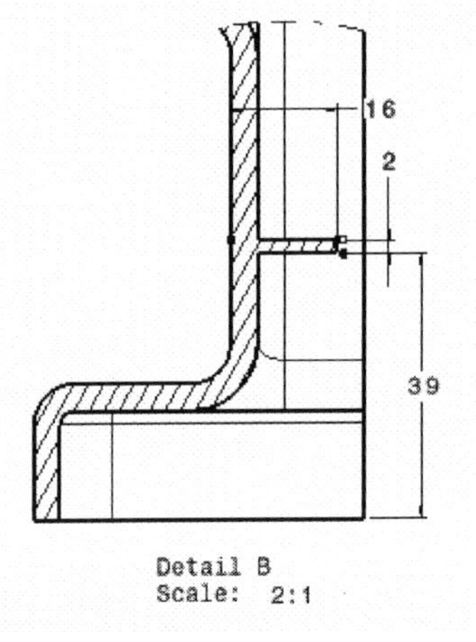


Figure B–32

# Practice B16 Dipstick

## Practice Objective

- Create a model with limited instructions.

In this practice, you will create two Rib features for a dipstick. One Rib feature will define the handle and the second will define the stick. The guide curves for each Rib have been created for you. The completed model is shown in Figure B–33.

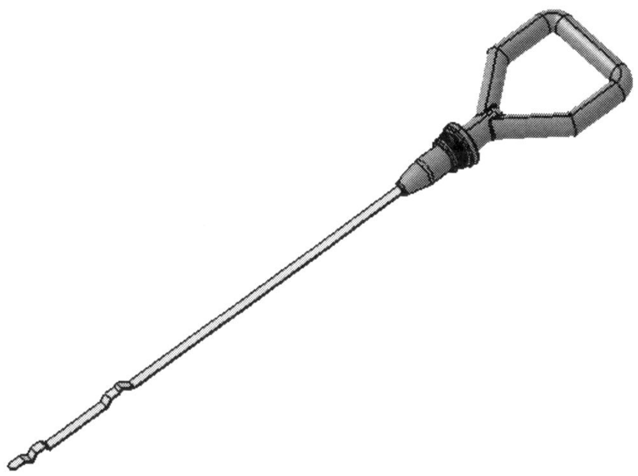

Figure B–33

1. Import **Dipstick.3dxml**.
2. Show the two reference planes from **Geometrical Set.2.**
3. To build the two Rib features, use positioned sketches to build the profiles for the ribs, and rename the features.

The drawing shown in Figure B–34 is provided for dimensional information.

- 1 (0.039 in)
- 5 (0.197 in)
- 11.8 (0.465 in)
- 14 (0.551 in)
- 72 (2.835 in)
- 315 (12.402 in)
- 416 (16.378 in)

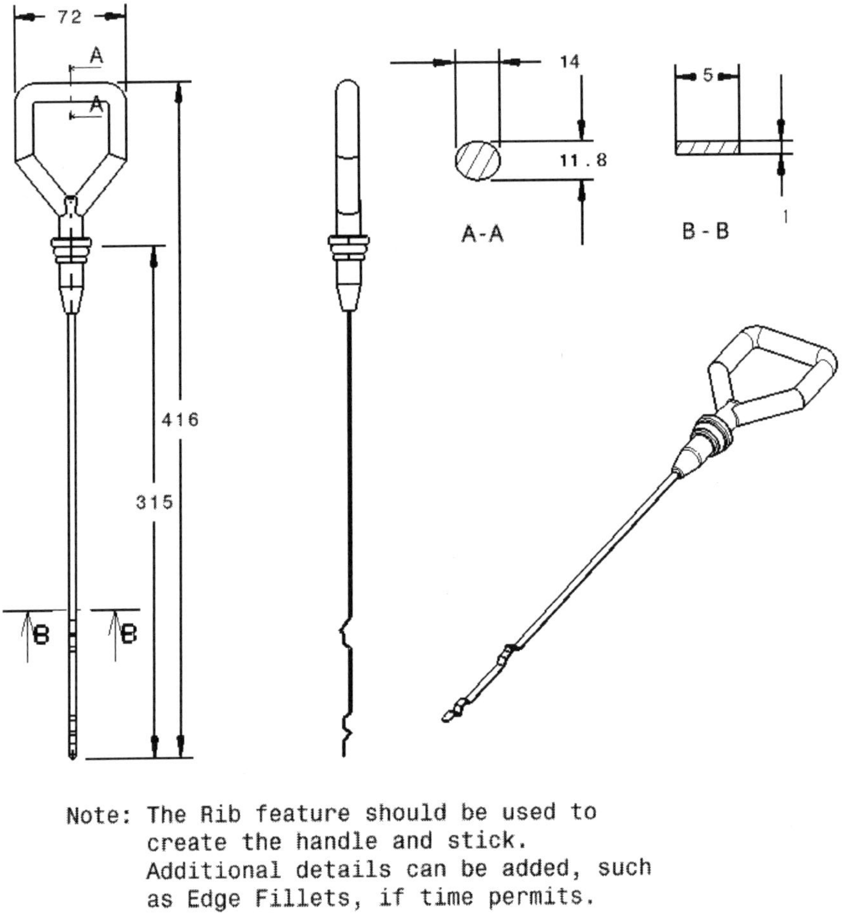


**Figure B–34**

# Practice B17 Screwdriver

## Practice Objective

- Create a Multi-sections Solid feature.

In this practice, you will finish modeling the screwdriver by creating a multi-section solid. Sketches and points have been provided for you. To successfully complete the feature, the multi-section solid will use a **Coupling** option. Coupling enables more control over how the multi-section solid blends from one section to the next. The completed model is shown in Figure B–35.

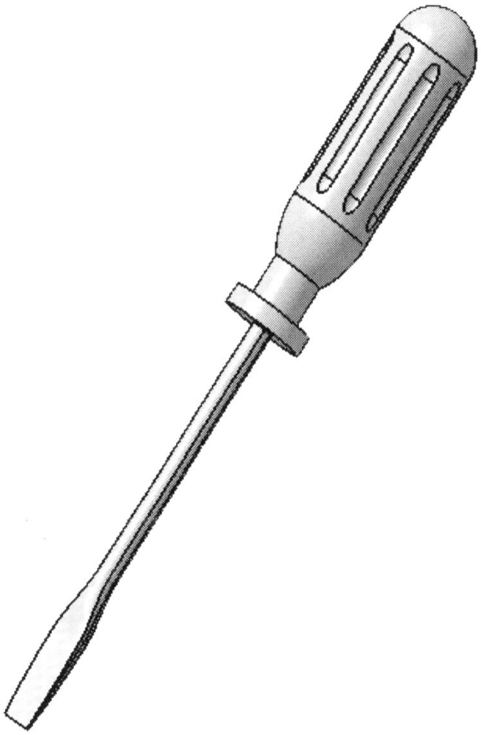

**Figure B–35**

## Task 1 - Create a multi-sections solid.

1. Import **Screwdriver.3dxml**.

2. Expand the specification tree to examine the provided elements.

3. Click  (Multi-sections Solid) to create a Multi-sections Solid feature.

*To change the location of a closing point, right-click on the point in the model and select* ***Replace****. Select a new location for the point by clicking directly in the model.*

4. Select **Sketch1** as the first section. Verify that the closing point is located on **Point.1**, as shown in Figure B–36. If required, select **Point.1** to set it as the Closing Point.

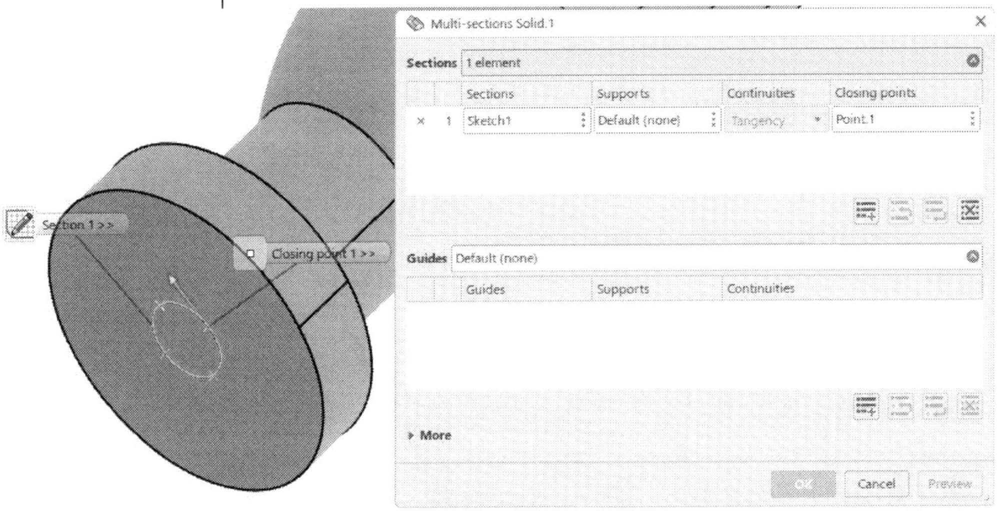


Figure B–36

5. Select  **(Add Line at End of Table)** in the Multi-Section Solid window.

6. Select **Sketch2** as the next section. Verify that the closing point is located on **Point.6** as shown in Figure B–37. Select **Point.6**, if required. If the closing point was changed in Step 4, you might not be able to select the next section. To select the section, select  **(Add Line at End of Table)** in the Multi-sections Solid Definition dialog box.

**Figure B–37**

*The two rectangular sections use their vertices as closing points.*

7. Select the rest of the sketches, as shown in Figure B–38. Verify that the closing points of the two rectangular sections are pointing in the required direction.

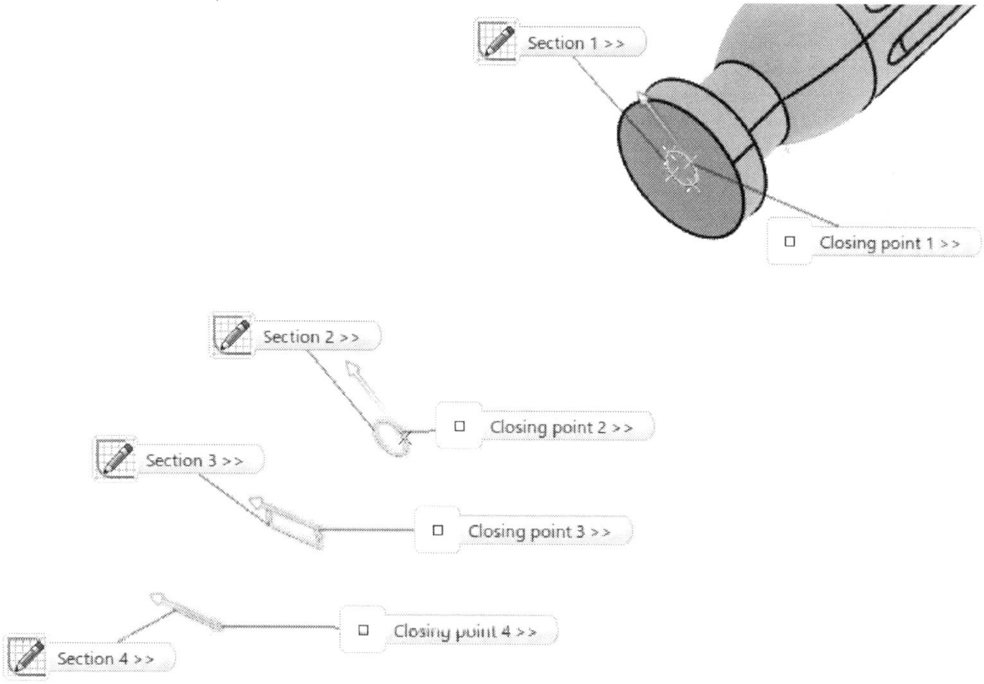


**Figure B–38**

8. Click **Preview**. An error message displays, as shown in Figure B–39. Click **OK**.

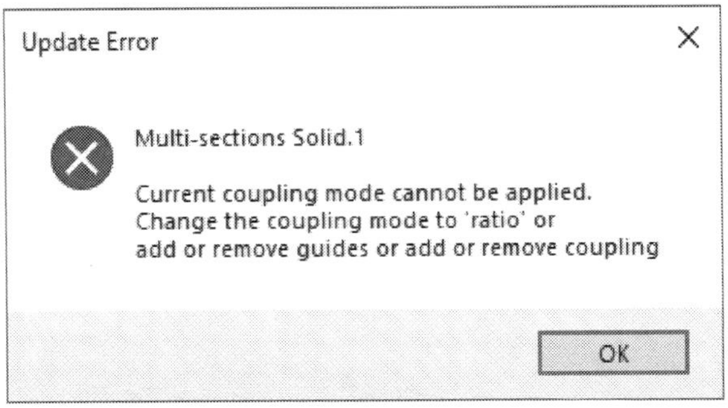


Figure B–39

9. In the Multi-sections Solid Definition dialog box, select **More** to expand the window as shown in Figure B–40. Set *Sections coupling* type to **Ratio**.

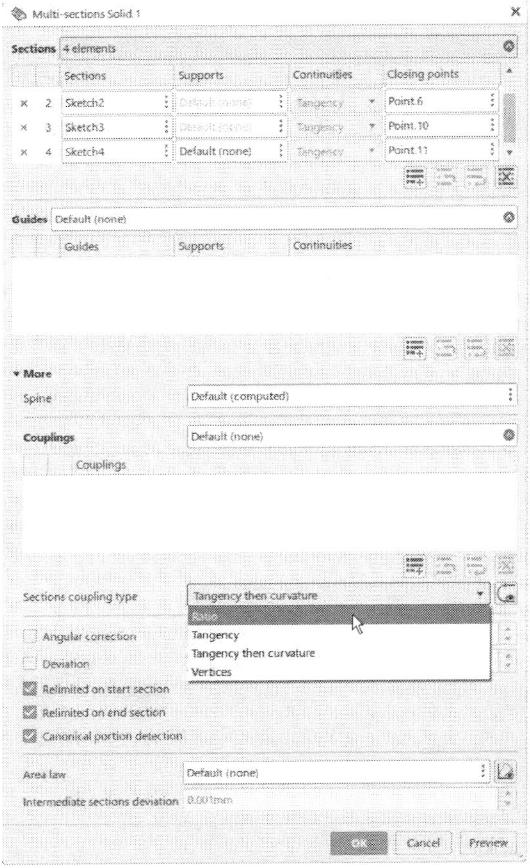


Figure B–40

10. Click **Preview** again. This time, no error messages display. However, the tip of the screwdriver is twisted, as shown in Figure B–41.

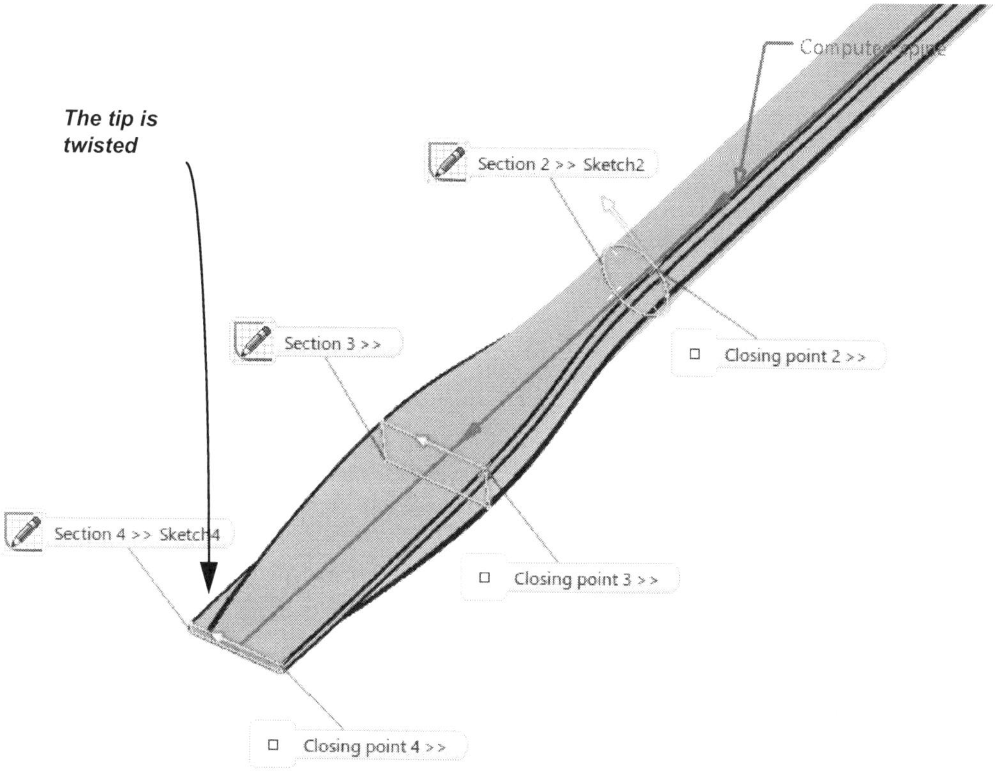


Figure B–41

11. Click **OK**.

## Task 2 - Create coupling curves.

1. Expand **Geometrical Set.2**, **Sketch.3**, and **Sketch.4**.
2. In the specification tree, double-click on multi-sections solid.

3. Select **(Add Line at End of Table)** under the *Couplings* section, as shown in Figure B–41.

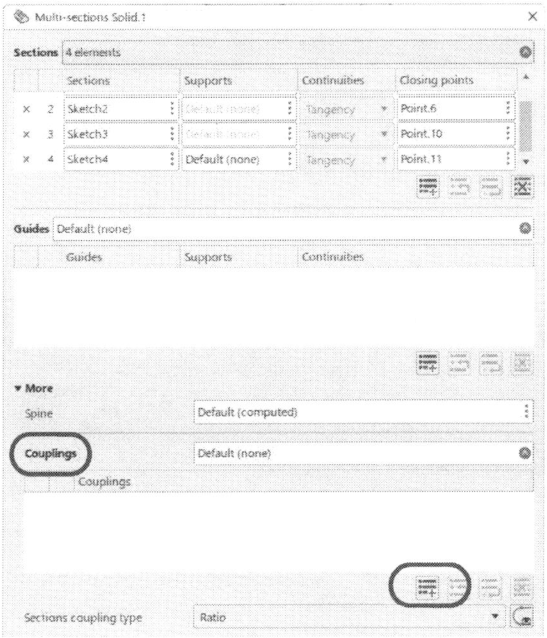


4. In the specification tree, select **Point.1**, **Point.6**, **Point.10**, and **Point.11**.

5. Click **Preview** to confirm the coupling curve is correct. The mode is shown in Figure B–42. The first coupling curve consists of four points that are located at the four closing points of the multi-section solid.

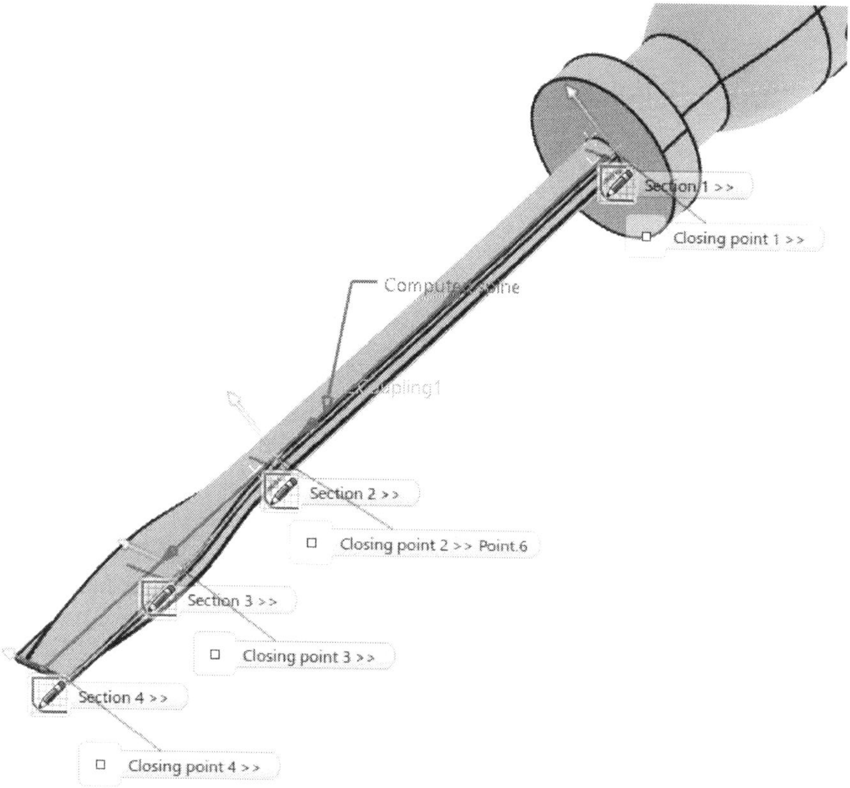


**Figure B–42**

6. For the second coupling curve, select the points in the order shown in Figure B–43.

*Display **Sketch3** and **Sketch4** located under the Multi-sections **Solid.1** branch in the specification tree.*

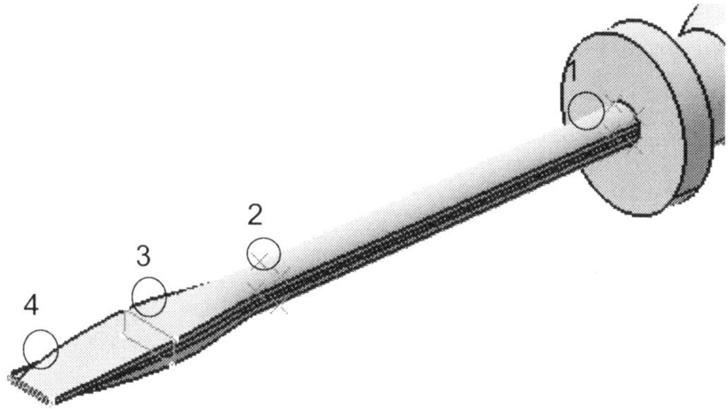


**Figure B–43**

7. Click **Preview** to confirm the coupling curve is correct.

8. Repeat the previous step to add two more coupling curves using the remaining points. Click **OK**. The twist in the tip is now repaired, as shown in Figure B–44.

**Figure B–44**

9. Save the file and close the tab.